Health Care in Malaysia

The health care system in Malaysia has undergone a fundamental transformation over the last two decades. For many years after Independence in 1957, Malaysia enjoyed widely available and accessible health care services. Funding was through central taxation, and hospital care almost totally provided by government. In the 1980s this began to change under the influence of growing health care demand and utilization fuelled by rising incomes, urbanization and the emergent middle classes. The hospital sector is now seeing the rapid rise of corporate, investor-owned services and specialist clinics, whilst the proposed National Health Security Fund will essentially transform Malaysian health care from a taxation-based system to a social insurance system.

This book examines this transformation in Malaysia's health care system, and explores the pressing issues it faces today. It describes the evolution of the system since Independence, from the colonial legacy of state provision to the impact of the global ideological shift against statism in the 1980s. It considers the exigencies for government policy as well as the consequences arising from it, and addresses important issues such as equity of provision, women's access to health care services, HIV/AIDS health care, care for the elderly and provision for indigenous peoples. Overall, this book provides a detailed examination of the changing face of health care in Malaysia, and its impact on Malaysian citizens, users and society.

Chee Heng Leng is a Senior Research Fellow at the Asia Research Institute at the National University of Singapore. Before that, she was attached to the Universiti Putra Malaysia, where she had been working since the late 1970s, in the area of community health and health care policy. Her publications include *Health and Health Care in Malaysia: Present Trends and Implications for the Future* (Institute of Advanced Studies, University of Malaya, 1990), and she was a member of the writing team for the World Health Organization report *Genomics and World Health* (WHO, 2002).

Simon Barraclough teaches health policy and international health relations in the School of Public Health, La Trobe University, Australia. His research interests include the political economy of health systems in developing countries, international investment in health services, health industry exports, international health relations and tobacco control policies in developing countries.

Routledge Malaysian Studies Series

Published in association with Malaysian Social Science Association (MSSA)

Series Editors
Mohammed Hazim Shah, University of Malaya
Shamsul A.B., University Kebangsaan Malaysia
Terence Gomez, University of Malaya

The Routledge Malaysian Studies Series publishes high quality scholarship that provides important new contributions to knowledge on Malaysia. It also signals research that spans comparative studies, involving the Malaysian experience with that of other nations.

This series, initiated by the Malaysian Social Science Association (MSSA) to promote study of contemporary and historical issues in Malaysia, and designed to respond to the growing need to publish important research, also serves as a forum for debate on key issues in Malaysian society. As an academic series, it will be used to generate new theoretical debates in the social sciences and on processes of change in this society.

The Routledge Malaysian Studies Series will cover a broad range of subjects including history, politics, economics, sociology, international relations, geography, business, education, religion, literature, culture and ethnicity. The series will encourage work adopting an interdisciplinary approach.

The State of Malaysia
Ethnicity, equity and reform
Edited by Edmund Terence Gomez

Feminism and the Women's Movement in Malaysia
An unsung (r)evolution
Cecilia Ng, Maznah Mohamad and tan beng hui

Governments and Markets in East Asia
The politics of economic crises
Jungug Choi

Health Care in Malaysia
The dynamics of provision, financing and access
Edited by Chee Heng Leng and Simon Barraclough

Health Care in Malaysia

The dynamics of provision, financing and access

**Edited by
Chee Heng Leng and
Simon Barraclough**

Routledge
Taylor & Francis Group

LONDON AND NEW YORK

First published 2009 by Routledge
2 Park Square, Milton Park, Abingdon, Oxon OX14 4RN

Simultaneously published in the USA and Canada
by Routledge
270 Madison Avenue, New York, NY 10016

*Routledge is an imprint of the Taylor & Francis Group,
an informa business*

Typeset in 10/12pt Times by Graphicraft Limited, Hong Kong
Printed and bound in Singapore by Markono Print Media Pte Ltd

British Library Cataloguing in Publication Data
A catalogue record for this book is available from the
British Library

Library of Congress Cataloging in Publication Data
A catalog record for this book has been requested

ISBN10: 0–415–41879–8 (hbk)
ISBN10: 0–415–48028–0 (pbk)
ISBN10: 0–203–96483–7 (ebk)

ISBN13: 978–0–415–41879–9 (hbk)
ISBN13: 978–0–415–48028–4 (pbk)
ISBN13: 978–0–203–96483–5 (ebk)

Contents

Tables

Figures

Contributors

Adela Baer is Adjunct Professor in the Department of Zoology, Oregon State University, USA.

Simon Barraclough is Senior Lecturer, in the School of Public Health, La Trobe University, Victoria, Australia.

Chan Chee Khoon is Professor in the School of Social Sciences, Universiti Sains Malaysia.

Chee Heng Leng is Senior Research Fellow in the Asia Research Institute, National University of Singapore.

Huang Mary S.L. is Associate Professor in the Department of Nutrition and Health Sciences, Faculty of Medicine and Health Sciences, Universiti Putra Malaysia.

Jomo K.S. is Assistant Secretary-General in the Department of Economic and Social Affairs of the United Nations.

Khoo Khay Jin is an independent researcher based in Kuching, Sarawak, Malaysia.

Mohd Nasir Mohd Taib is Senior Lecturer in the Department of Nutrition and Health Sciences, Faculty of Medicine and Health Sciences, Universiti Putra Malaysia.

Colin Nicholas is Coordinator for the Centre for Orang Asli Concerns, Selangor, Malaysia.

Nik Rosnah Wan Abdullah is Senior Lecturer in the Department of Administrative Studies and Politics, Faculty of Economics and Administration, University of Malaya.

Ong Fon Sim is Associate Professor in the Faculty of Business and Accountancy, University of Malaya.

Phua Kai Lit is Associate Professor in the School of Medicine and Health Sciences, Monash University Malaysia.

M. Ramesh is Associate Professor at the Lee Kuan Yew School of Public Policy, National University of Singapore.

Wee Chong Hui is Associate Professor, Economics in the Universiti Teknologi MARA, Kota Samarahan, Sarawak.

Wong Yut Lin is Associate Professor in the Health Research Development Unit, Faculty of Medicine, University of Malaya, Kuala Lumpur.

Preface

The chapters in this volume were first presented at a workshop entitled 'Health Care in Malaysia', held at the National University of Singapore from 9–11 September 2004. We are grateful for the support we received from the Asia Research Institute (ARI), National University of Singapore, for the organization of the workshop as well as for the preparation of this volume.

We would like to thank the many individuals who contributed to the success of the workshop, in particular the chairpersons and participants, and the Events Team at ARI. Adela Baer, Angelique Chan, Chan Chee Khoon, Joel Kahn, Phua Kai Hong, Volker Schmidt, Vineeta Sinha and Wong Mee Lian very generously spent time reading the various papers and giving their comments as discussants at the workshop. We would also like to place on record our appreciation for the participation of Mary Cardosa, Chua Hong Teck, Kumar Devaraj and Ooi Giok Ling.

From the conception of the workshop to the completion of this volume, we benefited from the support and input of many individuals. The idea for a workshop on health care in Malaysia, from which an edited volume would result, came initially from Anthony Reid, Director of ARI, without whose encouragement this volume would never have been produced. We also wish to thank Gavin Jones, Research Leader of the Changing Family in Asia Research Cluster at ARI for his help at various critical junctures.

Early on, Chan Chee Khoon and Jomo Sundaram were involved in the conceptualization of this volume; they also read and commented on various chapters, with Chee Khoon contributing to an early draft of the Introduction. M.K. Rajakumar who gave a keynote address at the workshop, and who has also kindly graced us with a Foreword, provided many invaluable comments. In this regard, we also wish to thank Gerald Bloom, who also gave a keynote address at the workshop, for his critical comments and insights. Tan Boon Kean lent his editing expertise for the Introduction and the Epilogue, and provided support and encouragement during the long and arduous process of editing. Nonetheless, as editors, we bear the responsibility for the final shape and contents of this volume. And to all the contributors of the volume, *ribuan terima kasih* for collaborating with us in bringing this project to fruition.

The Editors

Foreword

M.K. Rajakumar

Health is a requirement for fitness to earn a living, to attract a mate and to raise children, indeed for life itself: it is a special good that you cannot do without. Shared health care, and education, are the principal sources of social solidarity and social cohesion between peoples sharing a land in the modern state. This is more strongly a factor in new states such as Malaysia.

Health investment also reflects the distribution of political power. Equity in access to health care is a measure of the effective functioning of democracy. Rapid economic growth in Asia has reduced poverty, but we need measures of equity that incorporate timely access to health care and education, to give direction to further economic growth.

In a complex plural society like Malaysia, continued ethnic harmony is contingent on the acceptance of a reasonable degree of economic and social inequities, and on an electoral consensus based on the assurance of progress in remedying these inequities.

It is useful to consider the development of health services in Malaysia in several phases, as determined by the governing power:

- Foreign administration
  British colonial period, before and after the Second World War
  Japanese military administration
  Postwar British administration
- Independence, elected government
  'Malayanization'
  Modernization
  Privatization

British colonialism

Modern scientific medicine, so-called 'western medicine', was introduced during the colonial period. It was directed towards the health care of the British and, separately, for preserving a fit workforce in the plantations and tin mines. The principal cause of disability and death was malaria: rushed felling of the forests for plantations created a favourable environment for the mosquito vector of the malarial parasite; and in reclaiming land for Port Swettenham, nearly half the indentured labour from India died every year so that constant replacement of imported labour was needed. On the plantations and mines, where British personnel were also exposed, anti-malarial work to keep the environment free of the mosquito vector was conducted vigorously.

As populations became concentrated into townships, prevention of epidemics of water-borne infections, typhoid and cholera necessitated investment in providing safe water. The health services moved into the hands of professionals who brought a degree of professionalism and conscientiousness to their work.

Only low status employment was given to Asian doctors, nurses and lab technologists, who were discouraged from acquiring postgraduate qualifications. In Singapore, the determination of the Chinese community was shown when it funded a medical school. Its graduates, as well as doctors qualified in India and elsewhere, were designated 'assistant medical officers' ranking below British matrons. This included a few who had acquired postgraduate qualifications on their own initiative from the United Kingdom (UK) royal colleges. (This formed the basis of a long, friendly, professional association with the royal colleges that lasted beyond British colonial rule.) Nevertheless, on returning home, they were denied specialist status, remaining 'assistants'. Asian doctors held low rank in the hierarchy but were doing major surgery and managing all illnesses. Some resigned in disgust and entered private practice, which gave general practice a wide range of skills, high status and acceptance in the community that has lasted.

Japanese military administration

The Japanese faced a hostile population. Their brutality in China had earned the hostility of the Chinese in Southeast Asia. The British, when abandoning their territories, armed the Communists, mainly Chinese, to provide a resistance. The Japanese sought to subdue the people by terror, brutality and killing, particularly targeting the Chinese.

Japanese doctors and medicines were needed for their soldiers, and the care of the population was relegated to Asian doctors. Overnight, Asian doctors found themselves running hospitals, and training their younger colleagues in managing severe illness and doing major surgery. A medical school was started in Malacca by the Japanese administration, and its students were to become the first entrants – mature, tough and experienced – to the medical school in Singapore when it reopened after the war.

A cadre of self-confident and experienced Asian doctors was in existence when the British returned to re-establish colonial administration. They would not accept reverting to being the juniors to inexperienced British doctors.

Postwar British administration

Events in Asia reflected a vastly different political climate. Malay nationalism was a powerful force and the civil servants and professionals moved to push out the British officers who remained. The reluctance to allow Asian doctors to acquire higher specialist qualifications in the UK was now remedied by sending their younger colleagues, with much experience and skills, but lacking formal qualifications, to the UK for the royal college diplomas.

'Malayanization'

With Independence in 1957, the drive to replace British staff with locals became effective. The new ministers went along with their influential professional staff. The driving force behind Malayanization were the medical alumni from Singapore. They moved systematically to replace the British doctors, although they personally liked some of them. In Kuala Lumpur, a medical school was started, which soon became a university. Demand for tertiary education – the principal channel for upward mobility, apart from politics – resulted in rapid proliferation of universities, both public and private, many of which set up medical schools.

The leaders of the health professions retained their orientation to British education, and doctors turned to the royal colleges for postgraduate training and certification. Soon local medical schools created their own postgraduate specialist programme in response to demands for Malays to be trained as medical specialists. The success of this policy can be seen in the preponderance of Malay doctors of all grades in public hospitals now. The same process took place in the civil service.

There was for the first time a preoccupation with the needs of our people. A rural health service was initiated, new specialties created, including the speciality of family medicine/general practice, and generous allocations of research funds became available. Even larger numbers of young doctors were sent abroad, still mainly to the UK, for training and certification.

Modernization

Following 'Malayanization', a high degree of professionalism emerged. Advanced training developed which was in time offered to other developing countries. The first new universities achieved high standards, and entered postgraduate training and qualifications. A self-confident generation of experts filled posts in the public services, gently replacing their local seniors who had risen by seniority out of the old colonial service.

In medicine, an emphasis on science and expertise, and keeping up to date with research became the paradigm. Research was regarded as important, and public health research, beyond malaria, received attention and funding.

New specialty institutions began to appear at the Kuala Lumpur General Hospital.

The public health services, underpaid and over-extended, remain the mainstay of health care for the majority of people. They are further strained by VIP pressure for privileged access and expensive care. Health care is virtually free to anyone willing to wait, and to overlook the shabbiness of facilities and shortage of staff. Some 80 per cent of those hospitalized are in public hospitals, and half of all outpatients attend public clinics and the outpatient departments of public hospitals. The numbers increase sharply when the economy slows.

The public sector trains all categories of medical staff, and does all research. It is the exclusive source of care for perhaps half the population and provides a safety net for those whose incomes fluctuate with the economy. It is also provider of last resort for patients who are very ill and whose savings have been exhausted, or who have been admitted as emergencies.

Our health indices are very good. For example, in 2005, life expectancy was 76 years for women, and 71 years for men, and the infant mortality rate was 5.8 per 1000 live births. Since Independence, the public health services have performed brilliantly in dealing with the principal causes of mortality and morbidity associated with a poor colonial territory. The challenge to improve further will be more difficult.

The 'developed' country pattern of disease is the price of rising living standards. The new causes of morbidity and mortality, replacing malaria, tuberculosis, infant gastroenteritis and respiratory infection, are hypertension, diabetes, ischaemic heart disease/atherosclerosis and cancer. Increasingly important are the consequences of 'lifestyles' – tobacco smoking, alcohol excess, excess fat and calorie intake, physical inactivity and obesity, and sexually transmitted infections. Infections spread by international travel are a new phenomenon, including HIV and SARS. More research will be required to design new public health approaches, and a high degree of personalized intervention will be needed to reduce morbidity and mortality from the new causes of death.

Public hospitals and ambulatory care provide open access to all Malaysians. No financial barrier exists for ambulance services, receiving emergency or normal treatment, or for admission to open wards, that is 'Third Class', where conscientious care will be given by overworked and underpaid nurses and doctors. Government servants have assured medical care, and ward accommodation allocated according to rank. There is continuity with the colonial practice of East India Company employees in 'Company' hospitals!

The public health care system is the 'safety net' for the great majority of Malaysians, and they are fiercely protective of this right to free access. It is now in a bad state, unable to deter all categories of staff from leaving for the private sector. Nevertheless, resources continue to be diverted to private contracts for building more hospitals that are beyond the available staffing capacity.

Privatization

Privatization was heralded by the 'corporatization' of profitable government departments and agencies. In reality, it was not a straightforward transfer of public assets to the successful corporate bidder in an open competition. Public assets were secretly allocated to powerful political interests.

For the first time citizen activist groups have appeared. Their hostile reaction to the possible 'corporatization' of public hospitals pressured the government to give a categorical assurance, before the general elections, that this would not happen. An unanticipated consequence was that the good idea of giving more management power to individual hospitals, instead of them being controlled by ministry officers, was scuttled. A sensible way out would be to establish statutory trusts, by Act of Parliament, mandated to manage the hospitals efficiently in the public interest.

Emerging issues

There are multiple tiers of care. The private sector looks after the better-off, and access is slowly being extended to senior public servants. Government servants are separated from the community, in the colonial tradition, by privileged access to public heath care services, and to some private hospitals. Employees of statutory authorities may also have access to private hospitals.

The urban workforce has limited access to health care as part of their employment benefits. Relatively small numbers have private insurance. The majority are outside the sphere of organized care, and they move between the public and private sectors for episodic care, depending on their income at a particular time.

The take-over of health decision-making by politicians means that projects can be awarded without assessment by the expert professionals in the Ministry of Health. This cost is hidden, noticeable post hoc in the accounts and budgets, or from reliable leaks that have become the principal source of information. There is a cost to the community.

The persistence of low relative incomes amongst the majority of the population, with increased urbanization, has generated high levels of stress among people, with predictable consequences. The Malays remain the largest number amongst the underprivileged, in spite of a half century of privileges which never reached small Malay businesses and rural Malays. This is ominous for our future.

With increased commercialization of health care, and diversion of health funds to private interests, a multi-tiered quality of care has become entrenched. The better-off in our society have sustained a parallel health system (as with education), from ambulatory care to tertiary centres, funded and managed by foreign investors under liberalized access claimed under free-trade agreements and supportive government policies. There are also World Trade Organization (WTO) concessions and an Association of Southeast

Asian Nations (ASEAN) services network agreement. Foreign investors already own most private hospitals and they are now moving into primary care through so-called 'ambulatory care' centres. (In education, too, there is a fast growing parallel system with numerous foreign investors, from kindergarten to university, offering overseas qualifications, taught by visiting teachers from overseas.) The middle and upper classes have seceded from the national stream!

The commercialization of health care, and neglect of rural health, have serious consequences for the management of diabetes, hypertension and cardiovascular disease, which require continuing care, not merely episodic care. The rural population bypasses good government rural facilities and goes to the cities for private care, believing they will get better care. The urban poor, who cannot afford the loss of income that the long wait for care at government facilities entails, either neglect their health or make visits to private doctors when they can afford it.

There is under-investment in public health facilities and failure to retain skilled staff. It is more rewarding for politicians to build costly, unnecessary hospitals with expensive equipment that carry costly maintenance contracts. Training nurses, doctors and technologists has become a subsidy to the private sector, which is growing fast and pressing for more skilled doctors and nurses.

Malaysia has targeted 2020 to be a 'developed country'. The collapse of the public sector in health (and education) gives rise to forebodings of a highly inequitable future, with health services transferred to foreign investors and their local partners.

Dr. MK Rajakumar is Past-President of the Malaysian Medical Association and was Chair of the MMA Committee that produced the landmark 1980 report 'The Future of the Health Services in Malaysia'. His previous positions include President of the Malaysian Science Association, Vice-Chair of the Malaysian Academy of Sciences and President of the World Association of Primary Health Care Physicians. He was also the last acting chair of the Labour Party of Malaya, and he is frequently consulted on health care policy in Malaysia.

Abbreviations and glossary of Malay terms

ABC	Alternative birthing centres
ADL	Activities of daily living
AIG	American International Group, Inc.
APHM	Association of Private Hospitals of Malaysia
AZT	Zidovudine
BAPPENAS	Badan Perencanaan dan Pembangunan Nasional/ National Development Planning Agency (Republic of Indonesia)
BCIC	Bumiputera Commercial and Industrial Community
BPS	Biro Pusat Statistik/Central Statistics Bureau (Republic of Indonesia)
Bumiputera	Official Malaysian category for 'indigenous', literally the word means 'sons of the soil'
CAHCP	Coalition Against Health Care Privatization
CalPERS	California Public Employees' Retirement System
CAP	Consumers' Association of Penang
CARE	Cooperative for Assistance and Relief Everywhere
CBR	Crude birth rate
CCM	Chemical Company of Malaysia
CEDAW	Convention for the Elimination of Discrimination Against Women
CHI	Citizens' Health Initiative
CHM	Citizens' Health Manifesto
CI	Composite index
CIROAP	Consumers International Regional Office for Asia and the Pacific
CNR	Crude rate of natural increase
CPM	Columbia Pacific Management
CTG	Cardiotocograph
CUSO	Canadian University Services Overseas

DAP	Democratic Action Party
DBKL	Dewan Bandaraya Kuala Lumpur/Kuala Lumpur City Hall
DOSH	Department of Occupational Safety and Health
DST	Drug substitution treatment
EPF	Employees' Provident Fund
EPI	Expanded Programme for Immunization
EPU	Economic Planning Unit
FDS	Flying Doctor Service
FELDA	Federal Land Development Authority
FFPAM	Federation of Family Planning Associations of Malaysia
FOMCA	Federation of Malaysian Consumers Associations
GATS	General Agreement on Trade in Services
GDP	Gross domestic product
GMPPK	Gabungan Membantah Penswastaan Perkhidmatan Kesihatan or CAHCP
GNI	Gross national income
GNP	Gross national product
HAART	Highly active antiretroviral therapy
HIV/AIDS	Human immunodeficiency virus/Acquired immune deficiency syndrome
HMI	Health Management International
HMO	Health maintenance organization
HTS	Healthcare Technical Services Pte. Ltd
HUKM	Hospital Universiti Kebangsaan Malaysia
HUSM	Hospital Universiti Sains Malaysia
IADL	Instrumental activities of daily living
ICPD	International Conference for Population and Development
IFIs	International financial institutions
IJN	Institut Jantung Negara/National Heart Institute
IKIM	Institut Kefahaman Islam Malaysia/Institute of Islamic Understanding
ILO	International Labour Organization
IMF	International Monetary Fund
IMR	Infant mortality rate
IRPA	Intensification of Research Priority Areas
IUD	Intra-uterine device
JHEOA	Jabatan Hal-Ehwal Orang Asli/Department of Orang Asli Affairs
JOA	Jabatan Orang Asli/Department of Aborigines
KLSE	Kuala Lumpur Stock Exchange
KPJ	Kumpulan Perubatan Johor

LGBT	Lesbian, gay, bisexual and transgender
LIAM	Life Insurers Association of Malaysia
LTC	Long-term care
MAC	Malaysian AIDS Council
MCA	Malaysian Chinese Association
MCH	Maternity and child health
MCQ	Midwife clinic cum quarters
MDA	Malaysian Dental Association
MMA	Malaysian Medical Association
MMC	Malaysian Medical Council
MMR	Maternal mortality rate
MOF Inc	Ministry of Finance Incorporated
MOH	Ministry of Health
MPAJ	Majlis Perbandaran Ampang Jaya/Municipal Council of Ampang Jaya
MPKSM	Majlis Pusat Kebajikan Semenanjung Malaysia/ Central Welfare Council of Peninsular Malaysia
MRI	Magnetic resonance imaging
MSCI	Morgan Stanley Capital International
MTUC	Malaysian Trade Union Congress
NEP	New Economic Policy
NGO	Non-governmental organization
NHFA	National Health Financing Authority
NHI	National Heart Institute
NHMS 1	National Health and Morbidity Survey (1986–87)
NHMS 2	National Health and Morbidity Survey (1996)
NPFDB	National Population and Family Development Board
NPP	New Population Policy
OECD	Organization for Economic Cooperation and Development
PAS	Parti Islam SeMalaysia
PDC	Penang Development Corporation
Pernas	Perbadanan Nasional Berhad
PIC	Preliminary Investigation Committee
PKR	Parti Keadilan Rakyat
PLI	Poverty line income
PLWHA	People living with HIV/AIDS
PMC	Penang Medical Centre
PNB	Permodalan Nasional Berhad
PPP	Purchasing power parity
PROAP	Principal Regional Office for Asia and the Pacific
PROSTAR	Program Sihat Tanpa AIDS untuk Remaja/The Healthy Programme Without AIDS for Youth

PRSPs	Poverty reduction strategy papers
PSM	Parti Sosialis Malaysia
RHS	Rural Health Service
RPS	Rancangan Perkumpulan Semula/Regroupment Scheme
SAPs	Structural adjustment programmes
SARS	Severe acute respiratory syndrome
SEAMEO-TROPMED	Southeast Asian Members on Education Organization & Regional Centre for Tropical Medicine Network
SEDC	State economic development corporation
SIHAT	Sistem Hospital Awasan Taraf
SOCSO	Social Security Organisation
STDS	Sexually transmitted diseases
Syariah	Islamic law
UEM	United Engineers Malaysia
UMNO	United Malays National Organization
UN	United Nations
UNAIDS	Joint United Nations Programme on HIV/AIDS
UNDP	United Nations Development Programme
UNESCO	United Nations Educational, Science and Cultural Organization
UNGASS	United Nations General Assembly Special Session
UNICEF	United Nations Children's Fund
VHP	Village health promoter
VHT	Village health teams
WB	World Bank
WHO	World Health Organization
WTO	World Trade Organization
Yayasan Pelaburan Bumiputera	Bumiputera Investment Foundation

Introduction

The transformation of health care in Malaysia

Chee Heng Leng and Simon Barraclough

After Independence in 1957, the health care system in Malaysia was for many years practically a national health service. Although primary care was provided by both the public and private sectors, the rural areas were almost entirely served by a wide network of government health clinics and hospitals rapidly developed in the 1960s. The private sector general practitioner was an important feature, but was usually only found in urban areas. As the country was predominantly rural, the importance of government health services was therefore unquestioned. Hospital care was primarily provided by the public sector, although there were non-profit Christian mission hospitals and charity hospitals that had been established by the Chinese community. Other than the ubiquitous general practitioners in the towns, health care services were almost totally provided by the federal government, and funded through the national budget.

In the 1980s, this began to change, with health care demand and utilization fuelled by rising incomes and the emergent middle classes, as well as increasing urbanization. International influences and governmental policy also supported private sector growth, resulting in a health care system that is now much more complex. Although primary care is still balanced almost equally between the private and public sectors (in terms of numbers of doctors in service), the hospital sector is seeing the rapid rise of the corporate, investor-owned entity, and the growing presence of specialist clinics. In financing the use of private sector medicine, out-of-pocket payments have ballooned, and there is increasing resort to health insurance and managed care organizations.

Meanwhile, the government is in the process of working out the details of a proposed national health financing scheme, which will essentially transform health care financing from a taxation-based system into a social insurance system. Whether supplementary private financing will be needed, and how much, will depend on the extent of population coverage, as well as the breadth and depth of services covered. Nevertheless, it appears that this is a crucial time for Malaysian health care, and decisions taken at this time could take the health care system down a number of different paths.

This edited volume examines a range of issues shaping the Malaysian health care system. It has come about through a collective enquiry into the state of health care in Malaysia today. The issues addressed by the chapters are by no means comprehensive, but they represent some of the most salient issues posed from the standpoint of the citizens, the users and the people who are the beneficiaries of the national health care services, and who therefore also have the most to lose if the health services were to change for the worse. To provide a context for the discussion, we will briefly describe in this chapter the health care system in Malaysia, and its development since the time of Independence. It is not the aim of this chapter to provide a comprehensive account of the health care system, rather, the intention is to focus on the components and aspects that are relevant to the discussion in the subsequent chapters.

Definition of a health care system

The World Health Organization (WHO) defines a health system as including all the activities whose primary purpose is to promote, restore or maintain health (WHO 2000). This is a very broad definition that would include all the resources, actors and institutions related to the financing, regulation and provision of health actions. In clarifying further, it is explained that this would not include actions that may influence health (for example educating girls) if their primary intent is not to improve health. Within these boundaries, then, the WHO definition does not question the importance of the determinants of health that are outside the health system. While the primary objective of a health system is to promote health (*intent*), this does not imply that it is the most important contributor to improving health status. Although this caveat is important, it is also the case, however, that population health outcomes such as mortality and morbidity rates are often used as a general overall assessment (or reflection) of the health system of a country.

In his classic tome, Roemer (1991: 31–2) defines a health system as the 'combination of resources, organization, financing, and management that culminates in the delivery of health services to the population'. This definition is based on the description of a specific set of structural arrangements, with a specific purpose. He then goes on to describe the five basic components of a health system (consisting of the production of resources, organization of programmes, economic support mechanisms, management methods and delivery of services) and their relationships to each other. One important point made by Roemer is that the economic support mechanism, or the health care financing system – whether from tax revenues, social security, voluntary insurance, out-of-pocket payments or charitable donations – should be considered as a medium of exchange, not a resource as such. Based on his detailed definition, Roemer then describes the health systems in over a quarter of the countries in the world, categorizing them in a four by four matrix according to the country's economic level and its health system policies.

Writing about the mid-1980s, Roemer characterized Malaysia as having a welfare-oriented health system in a transitional economy. His volume contains a detailed description of the organizational structure and the various components of the system (Roemer 1991: 395–411). He also describes, though succinctly, certain particularities of the Malaysian health system. For example, he points out that it is particularly significant that governmental health sector planning does not include in its purview the private hospitals – where they are located, what their size should be, what standards they should abide by, nor are there schedules governing the inspection of these hospitals. Such anomalies are recognized by the World Health Organization's caveat that its definition of a health system 'does not imply any particular degree of integration, nor that anyone is in overall charge of the activities that compose it' (WHO 2000: 6).

A definitional description of the Malaysian health care system in the mid-1980s is also found in Chee (1990), while the Malaysian Medical Association has a description of the system in the mid 1970s (MMA 1980). A more recent official account may be found in MOH (*c.* 2000).

Roots of the Malaysian health care system

The specific characteristics of Malaysia's health care system may be explained by the history of the country. It is not the aim to provide a comprehensive historical account of the development of Malaysian health care here but, nevertheless, it is important to provide some historical background, and point out a few of the most important features.

The different states of the Malay Peninsula were under British colonialism until 1957, while the eastern states of Sabah and Sarawak became independent in 1963 when they joined with the Federation of Malaya and Singapore to form Malaysia.[1] Although the Portuguese, the Dutch and the British had successively had a colonial presence in the peninsula, it was only after 1870 that the British began to gradually extend their control over the Malay sultanate states.

The indigenous peoples had their own medical beliefs and practices, and there were also practices in the medical traditions of the Arabs, the Hindus and various other peoples who were either settled or sojourning in the Malay Peninsula at the time. The large-scale immigration of Chinese and Indian labourers at the turn of the century brought with them their healing systems as well as healers, herbalists and other practitioners. Nevertheless, with the advent of the colonial state, it was western medicine that soon predominated and has since been privileged to be the only system of medicine sanctioned and practised in state-provided services.

Thus by the early years of the twentieth century, the basic structure of the current health care system was already set in place. By 1910, general hospitals were established in each of the states. The civil service, which was one of the outstanding features of the administration set up by the British, had as part of its privileges an entitlement to free health care; and government hospitals had different classes of service to which different ranks of the civil service were entitled. Sanitary boards and health departments were organized to take care of environmental sanitation. The Institute for Medical Research, which became a key research centre for tropical diseases, was established in 1900, while a medical college that was later to become the Faculty of Medicine in the country's first university was set up in 1905. Meanwhile, the Chinese charitable hospitals also had their beginnings during this time, when small clinics and hospitals providing traditional Chinese medicine were set up primarily for the poor and the indigent population using funds from specific taxes on the Chinese community and donations from Chinese businessmen.

Labour legislation enacted in this period also required the profitable rubber and tin companies to provide health care for their employees, but the estate hospitals generally did not provide a high level of care. Subsequently, town dispensaries and maternal and child health clinics were also set up in some areas. Most of the health care structures established before the Second World War, however, were in urban centres.

During the Second World War, the communists formed the main organized resistance to the Japanese invasion, and when the war ended, there was contestation for power. Eventually, the British re-established control, and from 1948 to 1960, fought a guerilla war (called the 'Emergency') with the Malayan Communist Party, whose bases were in the forests. The strategy that proved decisive in defeating the communists was the resettlement of the mainly Chinese rural population into 'New Villages', planned settlements where the residents' freedom of movement was restricted, thereby cutting them off as a source of food and support to the communists. As part of the strategy to win over the population, the colonial government often provided midwifery clinics and first-aid facilities in these settlements. Catholic missionaries were also encouraged to establish the Fatimah Hospital in Ipoh and the Assunta Hospital in Petaling Jaya to service relocated Chinese populations. Likewise, health services played a key role in the strategy to win over the Orang Asli (the indigenous people) and to prevent them from providing assistance to the communists.

It was during the Emergency therefore that the attention of the state focused on the rural population, and the provision of health care services began to be extended beyond the urban population and the working class (in the estates as well as the towns). Although the Malay villages were not under the purview of the security or military forces during the Emergency, nonetheless, attention also shifted to the need to provide health care services to this population. Eventually, the rural health services scheme was started in 1953.

Establishment of a national health care system

In the aftermath of the Second World War, the main ideological current in the world, especially in Western Europe, was liberal welfarist. For health systems this meant an emphasis on universal provision, and equity in financing and access. In Britain, a national health service was established by the Labour Government. In newly independent Malaya, the national health care system that was envisioned, and eventually came into being, was welfare-oriented.

When Britain granted independence to Malaya in 1957, it bequeathed a public hospital system originally developed for the care of expatriate and local government officials, but subsequently inclusive of the general population. Hospitals were, however, concentrated in urban areas, and a feature that would persist was the prevailing ethos of access by entitlement for the civil service. Government servants enjoyed free or heavily subsidized hospital care in wards strictly stratified according to rank. Nevertheless, the public hospitals also embodied a welfare model for the general population. The general public could seek free or heavily subsidized inpatient and out-patient care or choose to pay more for higher class wards.

An element of plurality was represented by the presence of charitable hospitals, which was welcomed by the government. Originally catering to the poor, these institutions later also catered to better-off patients, using revenues to cross-subsidize the cost of treating the poor. The Chinese charitable hospitals provided traditional Chinese medicine together with western medicine. Other systems of medicine (besides western medicine) proliferated in the private sector, and traditional Chinese medicine was provided not only in the Chinese charitable hospitals, but also in the herbal medicine shops.

Until well into the 1970s, there were no corporate, for-profit, hospitals in Malaysia, although some small maternity and nursing homes were established by entrepreneurs. Under the continuation of British colonial labour laws, the plantation sector continued to provide basic primary care to its workers, but such care was often of lower quality than that available at government institutions.

In the cities and towns, primary care (provided by general practitioners) and dental services were largely located in the private sector on a for-profit basis, and paid for out-of-pocket. In contrast to the British National Health Service (NHS), established a decade earlier, these services were not integrated into the state-provided services and, hence, the resulting system was not a national health service as such. Nevertheless, costs of state-provided services were largely met from consolidated taxation revenue, as in the British NHS.

At the time of Independence, therefore, the fundamentals of the hospital and primary care system were already in place. The basic skeleton of the public health infrastructure, separately administered from the hospitals, had also been established. There were important centres for training (the production of human resource) and health research. Most important, however, were the rudiments of a rural health service. The strong nationalist sentiment at the time, supported by international ideological currents, provided the impetus for this to develop into a full-fledged rural health service.

Primary health care as an element in national development

In the first two decades of Independence, health care policy was a major priority and closely dictated by the national government. Soon after Independence, the federal government had centralized control over health policy by using its constitutional powers to take over the health functions previously exercised by the states. Health care policy was presented as being inseparable from the imperatives of national development, rural development and, after the inter-communal violence of 1969, socio-economic equity between ethnic groups. Policy goals were articulated in five-year economic plans, in the New Economic Policy (NEP) and related policy documents.

The political support that gave the United Malays National Organization (UMNO) the power it needed to gain independence, and to become the dominant political party in the ruling coalition, came from the rural Malay populace. Right up to the 1980s, the population was predominantly rural, with the proportion of the rural population being 73 per cent in 1970 and 66 per cent in 1980 (Department of Statistics 1977: 275; Malaysia 1986: Table 5-4). UMNO could be said to be a populist party. Reflecting the power of this major electoral base, and the ideological drift at that time, the newly independent state was liberal capitalist, and had a developmental orientation, as reflected in the development planning approach.

The limited number of rural clinics at the time of Independence had been rapidly expanded under the national economic and rural development plans, and further developed under the New Economic Policy in the 1970s. In 1960, there was one main health centre for every 638,000 rural dwellers, one health sub-centre for every 319,000 and one midwifery clinic for every 121,000; by 1965, these figures had improved to 1 : 150,000, 1 : 36,000 and 1 : 7,300. By 1986, the sub-centres had been upgraded to main health centres, and there was one for every 21,697 rural inhabitants, while the ratio for midwifery clinics was 1 : 5,147 (MMA 1980; MOH 1986).

Access is much better in Peninsular Malaysia, where in 1986, 74 per cent of the population lived within 3 kilometres of a health facility, and 89 per cent within 5 kilometres; with corresponding figures of 86 per cent and 93 per cent in 1996 (Public Health Institute 1999). Up to today, the rural health service forms the backbone of the country's primary health care infrastructure. No less important was the referral system that was established in the public sector; a line that extended from the primary care clinics to district hospitals, then state hospitals, regional hospitals and finally the general hospital in the capital city of Kuala Lumpur.

The welfarist trend in international health policy circles culminated in the 1970s in the Alma-Ata Declaration, which touted primary health care as a strategy toward achieving 'Health for All'. Malaysia was one of the signatories of this landmark declaration.

During this period, Malaysian health care policy, unlike policies on the economy, culture and education, was free of serious political conflict. Policy-making was largely directed by the national political leadership and relevant ministries, with some consultation with the Malaysian Medical Association. In comparison with other countries, Malaysia enjoyed comparatively good health indicators achieved with low levels of public expenditure on health care. Expanded state intervention to provide primary health care had been balanced with the continuation of private medical practice. There was access to hospital care for all Malaysians, including the indigent, albeit with marked differences in the quality of accommodation; and health care was part of the social wage.

Health care reforms and the present stage in health care

In its report on health systems, WHO identified three overlapping stages of health reforms (World Health Organization 2000). In the first stage, universal national health care systems were established. For many newly independent nations, this involved extending the health care system beyond one that had been created primarily for the use of colonial administrators, with second class provision for most of the local population and charitable institutions providing for the poor. In the second stage, primary health care was promoted in order to extend care to wider sections of the population, largely due to a realization that rising costs of hospital care were not being matched by improved health status indicators. For newly independent states, the care of rural populations was of particular concern.

The third and most recent stage of health care reforms originated from the ideological shift in the 1980s away from a welfare-orientation and reliance on state institutions towards a focus on market mechanisms and the role of the private sector. The world economic crisis of the late 1970s (sparked off by a rise in oil prices and a fall in prices of raw materials and goods) had led to fiscal and debt crises in developing countries. The World Bank spearheaded, and in many cases mandated, structural adjustment policies leading to cutbacks in welfare and social spending.

In the health care sector, these took the form of limiting direct health care provision by governments and privatizing certain components of government health services. There was greater concern with how a more pluralistic system should be financed, generally followed by a move towards using social insurance. The neo-liberal outlook emphasized the advantages of fostering greater individual choice and responsibility that came with the move towards market solutions (World Bank 1987; World Bank 1993; World Health Organization 2000: 13–17).

Decreasing the public, increasing the private

With some variations, a similar overlapping pattern has been seen in the development of the Malaysian health care system. Many of the features of the first and second stages of Malaysia's health system development described above persisted to varying degrees. In the hospital sector, these include universal access to government hospitals funded largely from general taxation, a strong civil service culture in the public health care services and a rigid hierarchy in terms of the accommodation entitlements of different categories of patients. Although the network of rural government clinics has been consolidated and expanded, most urban primary health care continues to be provided by private practitioners.

In the past two decades, however, the principle of universal access has been increasingly subjected to third stage health system reforms. The 1970s was a decade of rapid transformation for the Malaysian nation. The New Economic Policy, with its twin-pronged objectives of eradicating poverty and restructuring the economy so as to eradicate the identification of race with economic sectors, was instituted in the aftermath of racial riots, and political and social crisis. While the rest of the world faced an economic crisis, Malaysia discovered petroleum; the main earners of the economy shifted from rubber and tin to oil palm and petroleum, while manufacturing, and later tourism, also became important.

Rapid economic growth led to a concomitant rise in national income, and the growth of the middle classes. From the 1970s onwards, rapid urbanization occurred.[2] Urbanization among the Malays in Peninsular Malaysia was most pronounced, with the NEP playing a major role. The percentage of Malays living in urban areas grew from 11 per cent in 1960, 15 per cent in 1970, to 25 per cent in 1980, 43 per cent in 1991 and 54 per cent in 2000 (Jones 1990).[3]

In the wake of sustained economic growth in 1983, the incoming Mahathir Administration announced a privatization policy. At an ideological level, no doubt influenced by the neo-liberal reforms in the United Kingdom and the United States, the government promulgated the Malaysia Incorporated policy, under which the state would cooperate with, and foster, the private sector. At the same time, the Caring Society policy was popularized, through which individual and family self-sufficiency was promoted as preferable to any form of welfare statism. The 21 years of this administration were eventually characterized primarily by the ascendance of the Malay corporate class.

However, the hospital system that existed up till the early years of the 1980s did not fit into these new policy perspectives. There were few private hospitals, most of which were registered charities. There was a lack of capital for the expansion of the hospital system. Within the government hospital system a highly regulated civil service culture prevailed. Hospital support services, including maintenance and waste disposal, were regarded as being inefficiently run. Welfare through heavily subsidized, or free, care to patients was no longer seen as a public entitlement, but as a drain on public funds (with the inevitable future escalation of costs) and an undesirable legacy from colonial rule.

In line with the new direction in economic policy, and fuelled by rising incomes and urbanization, from the mid-1980s onward, the health care system has been subject to profound changes. Twenty years on, in the mid-2000s, the basic structure of Malaysian health care remains a mixed private-public system. The ratio of public to private doctors has fluctuated from 59 : 41 (1972) to 42 : 58 (1986), and has been increasing again since then to 54 : 46 in 2000.[4] Most of the private doctors, however, are at the primary care level – general practitioners – serving the urban areas. Rural primary care is still delivered primarily through the public rural health system.

In the hospital sector, however, the private sector has grown manifold, and with it, private specialist services. Where before, private hospital beds made up only 5 per cent of total acute beds (1980), they now constitute 25 per cent (2002).[5] There is no official specialist registration system for the private sector, but as an indication, official estimates place the number of private oncologists about twice that in the public sector.[6] The same official source estimates that over 70 per cent of specialist services in radio-therapy, magnetic resonance imaging, CT scanning, mammography and cardio-thoracic treatment over 1999–2001 are in the private sector.

The growth in private hospitals has provided an attractive alternative for public sector health care workers, exacerbating the exodus of medical specialists, physicians, nursing personnel and other allied health staff from the public sector. The government health services have had to resort to ameliorative efforts through the recruitment of foreign doctors and, recently, through the purchase of specialist services from the private sector.

The official thinking on this matter is that this exodus can only be stemmed if the medical sector is removed from the civil service, which will enable salary structures to rise above levels permitted under the civil service remu-neration structure. In other words, corporatization – restructuring govern-ment hospitals into corporate-type entities – is seen as the way forward. This has the potential to increase user charges greatly, as seen in the payments charged by the corporatized National Heart Institute (Institut Jantung Negara, IJN), and risks being an unpopular, and perhaps unacceptable, political move.

Health policy planners, therefore, have been considering setting up a social health insurance scheme, which will effectively be an alternative funding source for both public and private sectors. A proposal for the National Health Financing Authority has been submitted by the Ministry of Health (MOH) to the Prime Minister's Department begun in 2006 and a study is currently being conducted.[7]

These third generation reforms in the health care system, and further impending changes, give rise to many issues that need to be analysed and discussed. The changes have significant longer term implications for all Malaysians, including their access to good quality health care. In the sub-sequent, and final, section of this chapter, we will highlight these issues and give a summary of the each of the chapters in this book in relation to them.

Current health care issues

Role of the state

International debate on health care reforms has shifted in the last two decades. The formal inception of what are called third generation health care reforms in the 2000 World Health Report (WHO 2000) can be traced to the 1987 World Bank document, *Financing Health Services in Developing Countries: An Agenda for Reform* (World Bank 1987), which unabashedly called for a reduction in governmental involvement in health care and an increased private sector role. This was followed by the 1993 World Development Report *Investing in Health* (World Bank 1993), which contains a refinement of the arguments for expanding the private sector's role in health care, and limiting the involvement of the state.

While many developing countries have taken this direction in health care policy, there is more debate regarding what has been undertaken in Europe. In countries with a national health service, such as the United Kingdom and the Scandinavian countries, the role of the state in financing, planning, managing and providing services has remained unquestioned throughout, and the reforms have taken the form of introducing market-type mechanisms (such as the internal market in UK) within the public sector. Portugal and Spain have in fact moved towards the direction of greater state involvement through the setting up of taxation-based health care financing.

In countries with social insurance, such as Germany, France, Belgium and Austria, where the state does not play a major role in either financing or providing health care, the reforms may have led to more state involvement in some aspects, and less in others; but in general, there has been greater state regulation particularly for the purpose of cost-containment. An argument that emerges from this is that the advent of the market does not necessarily lead to withering of the state. In other words, the greater the reliance on market mechanisms, the greater the need for a strong role for the state in regulation.

The question, therefore, for countries like Malaysia, which has embarked on a privatization programme, is whether or not the state regulatory mechanisms are in place. The Seventh Malaysia Plan clearly outlines the future of the role of the government in health care: it will reduce its provider role and increase its role in regulating, coordinating and monitoring. The intention has been backed up by the passing of the Private Health Care Facilities and Services Act (1998), through which the regulation of the private sector will be intensified. Eight years on, the Minister of Health finally announced that the Act will be implemented effective from 1 May 2006 (*Bernama*, 24 April 2006).

The first two chapters in this volume grapple with these issues. Chee and Barraclough's chapter on the growth of corporate health care charts the growth of the private (corporate) hospital sector and examines the contradictions faced by the Malaysian state as the supporter of capitalist expansion into the health care sector on the one hand, and as the principal welfare provider for the Malaysian people on the other. It shows that the Malaysian state is directly involved in investor-led private health care provision through the state economic development corporations and the state investment holding companies, and also, indirectly, through political patronage of well-connected companies that are the beneficiaries of health care privatization. While this reflects the working of the Malaysia Incorporated concept, the authors argue that it also reflects an ironical edge to the policy of state withdrawal from health care provision. Finally, they show that the tension between the two conflicting roles of the state is reflected in weak attempts to ameliorate the ill-effects of an insufficiently regulated private health care sector.

The second chapter, Nik Rosnah's 'Regulating Malaysia's private health care sector', examines the functioning of the regulation of Malaysia's private health sector in accordance with the government's stated objectives to gradually reduce its role in the provision of health services and increase its regulatory and enforcement functions. The chapter assesses the degree to which regulatory agencies successfully influence private providers to meet the government's health priorities. It investigates the role of local government and the Ministry of Health in licensing new hospitals, and that of the Malaysian Medical Council and the Malaysian Medical Association in regulating doctors. The performance of the regulatory agencies in regulating the health sector is also discussed and key issues and problems in establishing and operating these regulatory functions, including issues of management and analysis of information, are examined. The author concludes that many of the government's objectives for regulating the private health sector are not being realized due to an insufficient legal framework and a lack of coordination among relevant agencies.

Financing health care

We have mentioned earlier that the Malaysian Government is on the verge of transforming the system of health care financing from tax-based to social insurance. Foremost among the arguments for this is that public health expenditure has been rising, and will soon become unsustainable. The national health security fund, when set up, is expected to be the second largest fund after the Employees' Provident Fund (EPF). Rumours are rife that various corporate entities are vying for the management of this fund, while details are lacking in government announcements.

Three chapters in this volume deal with issues related to the financing of health care. Phua's 'Rising health care costs: the contradictory responses of the Malaysian state' examines the trend in public health care expenditures, and notes that although expenditures have generally increased in nominal and absolute terms, they have remained fairly constant in relation to the national budget and to GDP (gross domestic product). He questions the validity of the government's claim that public health care costs have risen and, indeed, points out that the government's policy of privatization, as well as allowing private hospitals to proliferate, has been shown to lead to increased total health care costs. Phua's main contention is that the continued pursuance of the privatization policy, as well as increased funding allocation under the Eighth Malaysia Plan for building more public hospitals, are contradictory responses, if, indeed, health care costs have risen, because they all lead to increasing costs.

In the fourth chapter, 'Malaysian health policy in comparative perspective', Ramesh takes an outsider's comparative point of view, and puzzles over what the Malaysian government hopes to achieve by promoting the private provision and financing of health care. He points out that the large state involvement in health care has served the country well at a cost per GDP that may be considered low compared to other developed and developing countries, yet the government has been planning major health care financing reforms since the mid-1980s. He argues that it is the large presence of the public sector in health care provision that has kept total health care costs low, and that promoting private provision without first having adequate regulations that can check providers' activities will inevitably raise expenditures. He points out that increased private funding will not necessarily lead to reduction in government expenditures, even if it reduces the government's share, because private funding is often accompanied by increased overall expenditure. Furthermore, costs are set to spiral if expanded private provision is accompanied by compulsory insurance, as envisaged in the forthcoming national health insurance scheme.

In 'The welfarist state under duress: global influences and local contingencies in Malaysia', Chan's main issue of contention is that even as the government is on the verge of starting a national health care financing scheme, private health insurance has already been allowed to establish a foothold, contradicting the principles of social risk management and undermining the role of government in social insurance and social protection. In his analysis, Chan observes that the rise of global finance capital coincides with the imperatives of Malaysian domestic politics to drive the privatization programmes, including the privatization of the health care sector. Although privatization has primarily involved some aspects of hospital care provision and various support services, it is the privatization of health care financing that is most at odds with the exigencies of a welfarist state in socializing risks. Chan gives an account of how the EPF, the employee social security fund, is ironically being used as a Trojan Horse to institutionalize risk-profiling in health insurance. Even while deliberating on the establishment of a new health care financing scheme, the government has allowed, even encouraged, a plethora of private medical insurance schemes to emerge, apparently implementing a *de facto* policy in health care financing which will rely on a patchwork of profit-driven health insurance and managed care schemes as a supplement to the national health financing scheme.

Access and equity

The chapters in the second half of this volume delve deeper into issues related to equity and access. They highlight current problems faced by a particular social group, or the current inadequacies in a particular aspect of health care. A common thread running through them is the concern that these problems will be worsened with increasing privatization of health care. Likewise, a change in the structure of health care financing could also have distributional and equity effects, as well as consequences for access and the related issue of quality of health care.

The chapter by Wee and Jomo ('Equity in Malaysian health care: an analysis of public health expenditures and health care facilities') is a bridge between the chapters on health care financing and provision, and the subsequent chapters dealing with access and equity, and other specific issues pertaining to particular sectors. The chapter examines the issue of equity in governmental health care expenditure and provision. Although governmental spending on health care has increased over the years, the authors argue that the priority accorded to health care has decreased relative to other sectors. They also show that despite favourable overall statistics for the whole nation, inequities exist in the distribution and utilization of health care services, with rural states and the lower social classes at a disadvantage.

Nicholas and Baer's chapter ('Health care for the Orang Asli: consequences of paternalism and non-recognition') is a powerful indictment of the inadequacy of state-provided health care services for the Orang Asli, the indigenous people of Peninsular Malaysia, during both the colonial period and the post-colonial, developmental period. They contend that the Orang Asli health care services were set up and delivered within a paternalistic framework, which also led to the establishment of laws and institutions that treated the Orang Asli as 'wards of the state' and not as an indigenous people with particular rights to land and resources. Nevertheless, their criticism of the post-independence state's attitude towards the Orang Asli is even stronger. They allege that the Malaysian state's continued non-recognition of the Orang Asli as an indigenous people with rights is the basic cause underlying the inadequate and poor quality health services provided to them. The lack of cultural sensitivity with which Orang Asli patients are often treated is a barrier to their access and utilization of health care services.

The chapter by Chee and Wong ('Women's access to health care services in Malaysia') also examines the question of access to health care. Women's access to health services is assessed in the context of the country's institutional and social constructs of 'women's health'. They make the case that women's access to reproductive health care, within the context of the conventional marriage and family, is generally high, but women who fall outside the conventional boundaries have greater difficulties in gaining access. Patriarchal constructs of what constitutes 'women's health' form institutional and structural barriers to access, and effectively exclude certain groups of women from easily accessing care.

Huang and Mohd Nasir's chapter ('HIV/AIDS health care policy and practice in Malaysia') also examines the issue of access, but from the perspective of HIV/AIDS prevention. In this case, the authors show that the overriding moralistic agenda of the state forms an institutional barrier to implementing the pragmatic and more effective approach of making condoms and clean needles accessible to the social groups that are at high risk. The authors argue that state agencies' promotion of moralistic messages related to sexual abstinence and zero tolerance of drug abuse is unrealistic, and is a barrier to an effective prevention strategy. The authors hold up neighbouring Thailand as an example of an effective way of confronting the epidemic, which is to be realistic and not moralistic. So far, the prevention strategy in Malaysia has yet to show effect, and HIV/AIDS now has the potential to escalate into a major and costly epidemic.

Ong's chapter ('Health care and long-term care issues for the elderly') deals with an increasingly important aspect of health care. Malaysia is fast transforming into an ageing society, due to a faster rate of growth of the elderly population than the younger age groups. Nevertheless, the country lags behind in planning and providing for this, particularly in terms of long-term care facilities and expertise. The issue of equitable access is highlighted, because many geriatric services are still not available in the rural areas. Furthermore, Ong shows that public health care remains an important service provider for the elderly, primarily because cost is a major consideration. In light of rising health care costs, much of the panic over the ageing population relates to the burden said to be placed on the health care system. Ong provides a discussion of the various options, suggesting that more consideration be given to community-based care and programmes supporting informal caregivers.

Khoo Khay Jin's chapter ('Health care in Sarawak: model of a public system') provides a positive account of public health care in Sarawak, a very large state with a small and unevenly distributed population, half of whom live in areas that are difficult to access. Despite these difficult circumstances, the health care system is well run and has achieved close to universal coverage for basic health care and preventive services. These positive outcomes have been achieved at relatively low cost, although with some inevitable inefficiencies. According to Khoo, two important contributory factors have been (i) the quality of human resources in health care provision at the lower levels, which is the front line in preventive work, and (ii) the way that the state health system has been able to exercise a significant degree of flexibility and autonomy from the central health administration of the country. The most important factor, however, is that both financing and provision are public. In this regard, Khoo points out that the growing privatization of health care is the greatest threat to the continued success of Sarawak's health care system. The private sector will not find it profitable to set up clinics and hospitals in geographically inaccessible rural areas. Given the geographical distribution of the population, Khoo's contention is that any health care system will have to carry a certain burden of inefficiency in order to achieve universal coverage and accessibility. This, the private sector will most certainly not be able to tolerate.

Finally, we close with an epilogue which gives a brief description of the current efforts made in civil society in response to the threat that privatization poses to health care access for broad segments of society. The dangers of health care privatization have been a common theme in the chapters of this volume; it is therefore fitting that we conclude with some observations on the responses that it has elicited from its affected public.

Together, these chapters identify salient issues on the agenda for the future of the Malaysian health system. The chapters in Part I deal with the macro-level issues of public and private provision, and health care financing, while those in Part II present some fundamental concerns about access and equity, in particular aspects of health care practice and policy. Juxtaposed, these two sections provide an insight into the macro-level issues, as well as a sense of the complexities at the micro-level. As a whole, this volume serves to raise some questions regarding the direction in which the country is heading in health care policy – in relation to privatization, regulation, the role of the state in welfare provision, implications of public and private financing, and what health care access and quality mean for certain sectors of the population. No solution is presented here, but a start is made by asking the necessary questions.

Notes

1 Singapore had joined the Federation in 1963, and then left in 1965.
2 In 1957/60, the urban population, defined as the population living in gazetted areas with 10,000 people and more, was 27 per cent in Peninsular Malaysia, 13 per cent in Sabah and Sarawak, with very little change until 1970, when the urban population was 27 per cent for Malaysia (29 per cent for Peninsular Malaysia, 16 per cent for Sabah and Sarawak) (Department of Statistics 1977: 275). In 1980, the urban population in Malaysia jumped to 34 per cent and in 1990 to 41 per cent (Malaysia 1986: Table 5-4). In the 2000 population census, Malaysia has become predominantly urban, with 62 per cent of its population living in urban areas (Department of Statistics 2002).
3 The figures for 1991 and 2000 were for the whole of Malaysia, and were calculated from population census data (Department of Statistics 1991 and 2000) by Gavin Jones, 18 November 2005, personal communication.
4 Ratios calculated from the Ministry of Health *Annual Report*, various years.
5 Ratios calculated from the Ministry of Health *Annual Report*, various years.
6 In 2003, there were 23 oncologists in the private sector, and 11 in the public sector (seven in Ministry of Health hospitals, four in Ministry of Education hospitals)

(personal communication between Chee Heng Leng and Ministry of Health officer in 2003).

7 The proposal was submitted in March 2001, *The Sun* 4 March 2001, page 1. Plans for an alternative health financing source have been 20 years in the making, during which time numerous consultant reports have been commissioned, but not one has been publicly released. The current study, commissioned by the government and funded by UNDP, is for examining how the proposed health financing scheme can be implemented. An interim report has been submitted to the government, but it has not been publicly released.

References

Bernama, 24 April 2006, 'Six months for medical practitioners to get used to new Act'.

Chee Heng Leng (1990) *Health and Health Care in Malaysia: Present Trends and Implications for the Future*, Institute for Advanced Studies Monograph Series SM No. 3, Kuala Lumpur: University of Malaya, Institute for Advanced Studies.

Department of Statistics (1977) *Population Census of Malaysia 1970: General Report (Volume 1)*, Kuala Lumpur: Department of Statistics, Malaysia.

—— (1991) *Population Census of Malaysia 1991: General Report (Volume 1)*, Kuala Lumpur: Department of Statistics, Malaysia.

—— (2000) *Population and Housing Census of Malaysia 2000: Population Distribution and Basic Demographic Characteristics*, Kuala Lumpur: Department of Statistics, Malaysia.

—— (2002) *Yearbook of Statistics 2002*, Kuala Lumpur: Department of Statistics, Malaysia.

Jones, Gavin (1990) 'Fertility transitions among Malay populations of South-East Asia: puzzles of interpretation', Working Papers in Demography, Research School of Social Sciences, The Australian National University, Canberra.

Malaysia (1986) *The Fifth Malaysia Plan 1986–1990*, Kuala Lumpur: Economic Planning Unit, Prime Minister's Department, Malaysia.

Malaysian Medical Asssociation (MMA) (1980) *The Future of the Health Services in Malaysia: A Report of a Committee of Council of the MMA*, Kuala Lumpur: MMA.

Ministry of Health (MOH) (various years) *Annual Report*, Kuala Lumpur: MOH.

—— (1986) *Annual Report 1986*, Kuala Lumpur: MOH.

—— (c. 2000) *Health in Malaysia: Achievements and Challenges*, Kuala Lumpur: MOH.

Public Health Institute (1999) *National Health and Morbidity Survey 1996*, Volume 3: *Recent Illness/Injury, Health Seeking Behaviour and Out-of-pocket Health Care Expenditure*, Kuala Lumpur: Public Health Institute, MOH Malaysia.

Roemer, Milton (1991) *National Health Systems of the World*, Volume 1: *The Countries*, Oxford: Oxford University Press.

World Bank (1987) *Financing Health Services in Developing Countries: An Agenda for Reform*, a World Bank Policy Study.

—— (1993) *World Development Report 1993: Investing in Health*, New York: World Bank.

World Health Organization (2000) *The World Health Report 2000: Health Systems: Improving Performance*, Geneva: WHO.

Part I

The state and the private sector in the financing and provision of health care

1 The growth of corporate health care in Malaysia

Chee Heng Leng and Simon Barraclough

It is widely accepted that markets in health care are subject to failures, and the 'health care market' is therefore a theoretical anomaly.[1] Despite acknowledging their problems, however, 'market solutions' and privatization in health care continue to be pursued by economists and policy-makers (Evans 1997; Light 2000). The belief is that market competition will lead to greater cost-effectiveness and efficiency, while state involvement is mired in inefficiencies and lack of responsiveness to users, besides not allowing for consumer choice.[2] Nevertheless, since health care markets are expected to fail in other ways, the debates therefore centre on the ways in which they should be managed and regulated.

In the marketplace, health care as private industry will logically strive to achieve optimal returns, maximum profits and long-term growth. The higher the health care expenditure, the greater the demand for health care, and the larger the market, the better its interests are served. There is therefore an obvious and fundamental contradiction in a state that promotes capitalist investment and corporate growth in health care, while also seeking to fulfil its role to provide welfare and to ensure more equitable distribution of benefits within public budgetary constraints.

Analyses uncovering the social forces that benefit from health care markets and privatization could reveal the reasons for the persistent pursuit of markets in health care (Evans 1997; Light 2000). Using just such an approach to analyse the United States health care system, Evans (1997) incisively points out that the beneficiaries (of private health care) are the suppliers – physicians, drug companies, private insurers and the wealthy, who pay less in a private system of financing while able to purchase better quality health care for themselves. As such, competition and privatization redistribute national income in favour of these social groups. Likewise, Freund and McGuire (1999)[3] examine the structural power of health care businesses, which has been responsible for the dramatically increased scale of profits leading to the current crisis in the United States health care system.

Malaysia – the interventionist state

In Malaysia, state interventionist policies have predominated since Independence in 1957. Nevertheless, from the mid-1950s to late 1960s, the development strategy placed the role of the state primarily in the development of the infrastructure of the country and to provide the enabling environment, leaving the development of commerce and industry to private enterprise (Rugayah 1995). Progressively from the mid-1960s on, and particularly after the 1969 communal riots and the 1970 New Economic Policy (NEP), public (or state-owned) enterprise came to be seen as the vehicle of industrialization and the mechanism to ensure that manufacturing growth was evenly distributed along ethnic lines.[4] From 1970 onwards, there was an expansion of the public sector and state intervention in the economy (Jomo 1995).

In the health care sector, the state played the predominant role in the provision and financing of health care up until the 1980s. There was a concentration of general practitioners providing primary care in urban centres and small towns, while the rural population relied on the wide network of rural health clinics and district hospitals, and hospital care was overwhelmingly provided by the government. Health care policy was welfare-oriented and health care one of the institutions through which the state gained legitimacy among the rural Malay electorate.[5]

The push toward privatization and a greater role for the private sector began with Mahathir's administration in the early 1980s. The privatization policy was announced in 1983, marking a departure from previous governmental policy. At the same time, Mahathir expounded 'Malaysia Incorporated', his concept of the country as a corporate entity in which the government provides the enabling environment – infrastructure, deregulation, liberalization and overall macroeconomic management – but the private sector acts as the main engine of growth (Malaysia 1986; Jomo 1995: 81). This shift in economic policy was in line with international ideological trends and pressures from international and regional financial institutions such as the World Bank, the International Monetary Fund and the Asian Development Bank.

Privatization was slow to reach the Malaysian health care sector, however, with the privatization of the Government Medical Stores (the main public drug manufacturing, procurement and distribution centre) and the five hospital support services occurring more than a decade after the promulgation of the privatization policy.[6] The 1991 Privatization Masterplan had included little about the health care sector other than identifying the Government Medical Stores as privatizable within the medium term. Significantly, in this document, general hospitals had been relegated to the bottom category, as being *potentially* privatizable, and even so, only after five years (Economic Planning Unit 1991: 65, 71, emphasis added). It has been argued that the delay has been due in part to political considerations and the constraints facing the populist Malay ruling party in withdrawing from the provision of welfare-type public services (Barraclough 2000; Chan 2003).

While privatization of public health services became a politically sensitive issue, state encouragement of private health sector development was less contentious. Consequently, the number of private hospitals, particularly corporate investor-owned hospitals, increased markedly from the mid-1980s onwards. In this chapter, we chart the growth of the private (corporate) hospital sector, and examine the contradictions faced by the Malaysian state as the supporter of capitalist expansion into the health care sector on the one hand, and the principal welfare provider for the Malaysian people on the other.

State policy on private hospitals

Overall, state encouragement of private hospitals took the form of inaction, rather than action. Even as private hospitals proliferated, no effective measures were taken to control the rapid growth in their numbers, or even to modulate the distribution and consequences of this growth. Policy inaction was most obvious in the realm of regulation. A virtual laissez-faire regulatory policy prevailed for most of the period when private hospital investment was rapidly expanding. A slender piece of legislation[7] that came into force in 1971 was the only regulatory instrument at a time of unprecedented expansion in the private hospital sector. It was not until 1998 that comprehensive regulatory legislation was enacted and, even so, not until 2006 that this new legislation was implemented.[8]

Nevertheless, strong encouragement for the expansion of private hospitals is contained within economic policies on the development of the private sector and the market as a whole, and is reflected in the tax incentives that are available for the health care industry. These include an industrial building allowance for hospital buildings, exemption from service tax for expenses on medical advice and use of medical equipment, and tax deduction for expenses for pre-employment training (Ministry of Health 2002: 107).

Encouragement is also implicit in official statements that the government would like the private sector to share in the provision of health care, and that the private sector should cater to those who can afford their services, freeing public resources for those who cannot afford private medical care. Actual steps taken to encourage demand are in the form of personal income tax concessions for medical expenses for oneself, spouse, children and parents.[9]

When the then Prime Minister Mahathir Mohamad presented the Seventh Malaysia Plan (1996–2000) in Parliament, he emphasized that in the future, private funding would be necessary to pay for hospital care – even in government hospitals. Larger companies would be expected to provide health insurance for their employees, and the private sector would be expected to cross-subsidize the costs of health care for those unable to afford market prices. At the same time, he argued that low-cost hospital care would be a financially lucrative field for investors (Mahathir 1996).

Official encouragement for the role of private hospitals in Malaysia's health care system has also been evident at the symbolic level. The private hospital sector has successfully sought elite patronage for its activities. Health ministers and senior civil servants involved in health planning have been guest speakers at Association of Private Hospitals of Malaysia (APHM) annual conferences, while Ministers of Health regularly attend private hospital functions, and royal princes officiate at the opening of private facilities (Barraclough 1997: 646).

Health care financing – moving from public to private?

Since the country's Independence, public health care services have been funded almost wholly from taxation, while private services are paid privately from out-of-pocket or by employers through employee benefit schemes. Private health insurance has, until recently, been an insignificant source of health financing. The government's intention is to shift into a compulsory health insurance system of financing, but this drawn-out process has already taken more than 20 years.[10] Meanwhile, there are signs that health care financing in the country has been silently shifting from public to private sources.

The Second National Health and Morbidity Survey (NHMS 2) reported that from 1989 to 1996, out-of-pocket expenditure increased by 40 per cent, estimating this to be RM3.82 billion in 1996, almost equivalent to the total public sector expenditure of RM3.99 billion in the same year (Public Health Institute 1999: 103–4, 111). As such, in 1996, out-of-pocket health expenditure constituted 1.35 per cent of GNP (or 1.28 per cent of GDP), while total public sector expenditure was 1.41 per cent of GNP (or 1.34 per cent of GDP).

Considering that 'out-of-pocket' is not the only private source of health financing, it is likely that total private health expenditure would have been higher than public health expenditure. Although the NHMS 2 did not provide any estimates for total private health expenditure, the country-representative population survey found that while the majority (64 per cent) financed their health care from out-of-pocket, there were substantial proportions whose health care (or some part of it) was paid for by employers (17.8 per cent) or by health insurance (4.5 per cent) (Public Health Institute 1999: 76).[11]

On the other hand, according to World Health Organization (WHO) estimates, public health expenditure is still higher than private, with the private share of Malaysia's total health expenditure even decreasing slightly from 48.4 per cent (1998) to 46.2 per cent in 2002 (WHO 2005). It has been reported that an unpublished study in 1983 showed private health expenditure to be 24 per cent of total (total health expenditure was RM1.8 billion or 2.8 per cent of GNP) (Economic Planning Unit 1996).[12] Taking this at face value would mean that the private share of total health expenditure increased by about 24 per cent in the period 1983 to 1998, and then decreased slightly between 1998 and 2002. The recent decrease may have been a consequence of the financial crisis of 1997, as well as an increase in governmental spending on health care.[13]

State policy, or its lack, has therefore resulted in a shift towards private sources of financing health care, but it is unclear whether this trend will continue. As it stands, however, the private share of total health expenditure in Malaysia is much higher than Thailand (30.3 per cent), and developed countries such as the United Kingdom (16.6 per cent), New Zealand (22.1 per cent), Germany (21.5 per cent) and Japan (18.3 per cent), although it is comparable to Sri Lanka (51.3 per cent).[14]

There is no evidence that the state is acting to limit the growth of private health insurance. On the contrary, state encouragement may be implied from personal income tax relief allowed on the purchase of medical insurance.[15] Furthermore, a medical savings scheme was introduced through the Employees' Provident Fund (EPF) in 1994,[16] and in 2000, it was announced that this account may be drawn upon for a risk-rated medical insurance scheme offered by the Life Insurers Association of Malaysia (LIAM) (*The Star*, 18 January 2000).

The increasing trend in out-of-pocket health expenditure[17] charted by the NHMS 2 occurs concomitantly with an increasing demand on private hospital care, in the context of steadily rising national income (see next section). The felt need to use increasingly expensive private health care will translate into a rising demand for private insurance. This kind of milieu, particularly in an absence of regulatory curbs on private health insurance or private health care, is conducive to the proliferation of private hospitals.

Proliferation of private hospitals

In the space of two decades, from 1980 to 2000, the number of private medical facilities in Malaysia grew from 50 to 224 (Table 1.1). Although private medical facilities include nursing and maternity homes in addition to hospitals, the bulk of this growth has been in private hospitals, which increased from 10 in 1980 to 32 in 1983, and then to 128 in 2003.[18] Within two decades, therefore, the number of private hospitals increased by four times, while the number of maternity and nursing homes registered with the MOH has remained stable since 1983.

The private sector's share of hospital beds increased from 5.8 per cent to 28.4 per cent in 2001, subsequently dropping to 26.7 per cent in 2003 (Table 1.1). In the period 1985 to 1997, the utilization of private inpatient services more than doubled, and that of private outpatient services almost tripled (Table 1.2). In comparison, public inpatients in the same period fluctuated between 68.2 per 1,000 population (1985) and 73.6 per 1,000 population (1990), while public outpatients dropped slightly from 1,308 per 1,000 in 1985 to 1,219 per 1,000 in 1997.

Table 1.1 Private medical facilities and national income

Year	Facilities (no.)	Hospital beds		Per capita GNP (at purchasers' value, in 1978 prices, RM)
		(no.)	(% of total)[1]	
1980	50	1171	5.8	3221
1985	133	3666	14.5	3758
1990	174	4675	15.1	4426
1995	197	7192	19.4	5815
1998	216	9060	25.1	—
2001	224	10348	28.4	7593[2]
2003	219	10405	26.7	—[3]

Source: Ministry of Health Annual Report, various years; GNP figures from Fifth and Seventh Malaysia Plan (Malaysia 1986; Malaysia 1996).

Notes
[1] Total of acute beds in MOH hospitals and private hospitals.
[2] For the year 2000.
[3] For 2002, GNP per capita at purchasers' value in 1987 prices is RM8,418 (calculated from Malaysia 2003).

Table 1.2 Utilization of private and public medical facilities

Year	Hospital admissions (per 1,000 population)		Outpatients (per 1,000 population)	
	Private	Public	Private hospitals	Public facilities
1980	n.a.	66.2	n.a.	1369
1985	9.8	68.2	62	1308
1990	12.8	73.6	120	1340
1995	18.1	72.9	151	1208
1997/8	20.8	69.6	179	1219
2000	n.a.	69.3	n.a.	1186

Source: Computed from Ministry of Health *Annual Report*, various years.

The rapid rise in utilization of private facilities has been fuelled primarily by the rapid rise in national income. Between 1980 and 2000, per capita gross national product (GNP) more than doubled, from RM3,221 to RM7,593 (Table 1.1). Nevertheless, the majority of the population (78 per cent) still depend on the public hospitals for hospital care, and only 18 per cent utilize private hospitals (4 per cent others) (Public Health Institute 1999: 68). For acute care, the private clinic is utilized by most people (54 per cent), with 39 per cent going to public facilities, 2 per cent to private hospitals and 5 per cent others (Public Health Institute 1999: 54).

Not-for-profit hospitals

The breakdown of the numbers shows that out of the 214 private facilities registered with the Ministry of Health (MOH) in October 2003, 83 are maternity homes, 3 are nursing homes and 128 are private hospitals.[19] Out of the 128 hospitals, more than half (75 hospitals) have 50 beds or fewer, 19 (15 per cent) have more than 50 but fewer than 100 beds, 21 (16 per cent) have more than 100 but fewer than 200 beds, and 13 (10 per cent) have more than 200 beds. Out of the 13 large private hospitals, four are not-for-profit hospitals – Lam Wah Ee Hospital (the largest at 437 beds), Assunta Hospital, the Penang Adventist Hospital and Tung Shin Hospital.

Not-for-profit hospitals are not investor-owned, so they are usually governed by a board of directors who give their service voluntarily, or do so because they are part of a church or religious group (as in Adventist Hospital and Assunta Hospital). They generally operate on the same basis as any other for-profit private hospitals, except that they have a charitable mission. Therefore, there is provision for collecting donations, which may be exempt from tax, subject to governmental approval, and also for providing free or discounted treatment to people who cannot afford to pay.

The not-for-profit hospitals have earlier origins than the for-profit hospitals. The Tung Shin Hospital and the Lam Wah Ee Hospital are firmly embedded in the history of the Chinese community, tracing their beginnings to the late nineteenth century. The Penang Adventist Hospital, run by Seventh Day Adventist Christians, was started before the Second World War, while Assunta Hospital, Hospital Fatimah and Mount Miriam Hospital were established by Christian missionaries in the postwar period. Recent growth in the number of non-profit hospitals is limited, particularly since the proliferation of for-profit hospitals.

Conglomerates

Most major private hospitals are for-profit. Some of them were originally small ventures begun by a group of medical doctors, but have since been sold to large public-listed companies. Examples of this are the Penang Medical Centre (PMC), started by a group of doctors in 1973, later sold to the Gleneagles group, and Pantai Hospital, established in 1974 with 68 beds and 20 medical specialists, later sold to the Pantai conglomerate, and which today has 264 beds and more than 130 medical specialists. Other examples are Tawakal Hospital (150 beds), established in 1984 by a group of doctors with only 66 beds, and the Ipoh Specialist Hospital (210 beds), established in 1981 by 16 consultants, operating 100 beds, both eventually taken over by Kumpulan Perubatan (Johor) Healthcare (KPJ Healthcare).

Some private hospitals were established in conjunction with the interests of property developers who developed housing estates as large as townships. To make the township attractive as a residential centre, hospitals and colleges were also developed in the township. Subang Jaya Medical Centre is owned and operated by Sime Darby, the conglomerate that also developed the Subang Jaya housing estate, while Sunway Medical Centre is managed by Sunway City Bhd, a corporation involved in housing development.

Another property development company that acquired hospitals is Tan and Tan Development Bhd, a family-owned conglomerate which is a leading developer of residential condominiums, serviced apartments, hotels and holiday resorts. Tan and Tan acquired a 35 per cent interest in two associate companies, Gleneagles Medical Centre (KL) and Gleneagles Hospital (KL). In 1989, the Singapore-based Gleneagles International Group took over the Penang Medical Centre, renamed the Gleneagles Medical Centre, with Tan and Tan as a major partner.

The chain of Gleneagles hospitals is now under Parkway Holdings, a health care conglomerate which not only owns hospitals in Singapore, Malaysia, Brunei and India, but also owns a general practitioners' group practice and companies providing radiology services, laboratory services and clinical research services. The Tan family (and the Ang family, also original investors) sold their equity, and the biggest shareholder is now Newbridge Capital, a United States private equity firm (*The Straits Times*, 11 June 2005). Net profits for the fiscal year 2004 were reported to be SGD50.5 million, a 50 per cent increase compared to the fiscal year 2003.

One characteristic of the conglomerates that have entered the hospital industry is that they have broad investments, and health care is not their sole interest or speciality. Sime Darby, for example, which owns and runs the Subang Jaya Medical Centre, was originally a plantation-based company that had diversified into tyres, tractors, insurance, property development, oil and gas, paint manufacturing, travel services, motor vehicle distribution and then into hospitals. Likewise, Columbia Pacific Healthcare, part of the Columbia Asia group, was initially a joint venture between Columbia Pacific Management (CPM) and Chemical Company of Malaysia (CCM), a major conglomerate involved in the manufacture and marketing of industrial chemicals and pharmaceuticals, and agrochemicals.[20]

State corporations

The most prominent investor in private hospitals is a state corporation. Kumpulan Perubatan (Johor) (KPJ) Healthcare, owned by the Johor State Economic Development Corporation, the investment arm of the Johor State Government, has become Malaysia's leading owner of private hospitals. It owns and operates 13 hospitals in Malaysia, with a combined capacity of over 1,500 beds, 260 resident specialist consultants and 100 visiting specialists, the largest in any group outside the MOH. In addition to running hospitals, KPJ also owns companies in laboratory services, marketing and retailing pharmaceuticals, hospital support services and human resource training.[21] In 2004, it reported a net profit of RM32 million, almost 10 per cent higher than the previous year (*The Edge Malaysia*, 20 June 2005).

State governments have also entered into joint ventures with health care companies to operate private hospitals. The Southern Hospital, for example, is a joint venture between the health care division of the state government of Melaka and the United Medicorp Pte Ltd of Singapore and a group of medical professionals under Mediquest and Apex Pharmacy (APHM website). This joint grouping is currently operating two private hospitals, one in Melaka and another in Batu Pahat.

The Penang Development Corporation (PDC), the state economic development corporation of Penang state, is another major player, having entered into a joint venture agreement with KPJ Healthcare to operate and manage the Bukit Mertajam Specialist Hospital, and to develop the Bayan Baru Specialist Hospital (Penang Development Corporation website). Yet another example is the Sclesa Medical Center, the only fully equipped private hospital in the oil producing town of Miri, jointly owned by Permodalan Amanah Saham Sarawak, the Sarawak state investment-holding company, and Columbia Asia, Boaz Holdings and a group of doctors (APHM website).

Globalized expansion of health care companies

The trajectory of the Penang Medical Centre, which started as a small local-based private hospital, to Gleneagles Medical Centre, owned by Parkway Holdings, illustrates very well the globalized nature of hospital ownership today. Parkway, listed on the Singapore stock exchange, is now the biggest listed hospital operator in Southeast Asia (*The Straits Times*, 14 September 2005). It owns the Gleneagles chain of hospitals in Malaysia and Singapore, Mount Elizabeth Hospital and East Shore Hospital in Singapore and a cardiac centre in Brunei, and recently acquired a majority stake in Pantai Holdings, which owns the Pantai group of hospitals and other subsidiary health care companies in Malaysia. It also jointly runs a hospital in India with the Apollo Group, and has plans to expand into Vietnam and China.

The flow of capital is occurring both ways: foreign capital entering into the Malaysian health care market, as well as Malaysian capital expanding overseas. Newbridge Capital, which owns the controlling equity in Parkway Holdings, is an American company. In 2005, the Malaysian KPJ Healthcare was reported to have agreed to build, own and manage a hospital in Indonesia, where it is already managing two hospitals owned by its parent company, Johor Corporation (*The Edge Malaysia*, 20 June 2005). It is currently in a joint venture to set up a hospital in Dhaka, Bangladesh, and is planning to expand its hospital management services to the Middle East, Pakistan, Myanmar and Vietnam. Another example is Khazanah Nasional Holdings, the Malaysian government's investment agency, which has acquired stakes in Apollo, a major hospital services group in India (*The Star*, 17 September 2005).

Other examples of international capital investment are HMI and the Columbia Group. Mahkota Medical Centre in the state of Melaka is owned by Health Management International (HMI), which is listed on the

Singapore stock exchange. HMI has provided consultancy services for setting up a new hospital in the Riau province of Indonesia, and it also carries out training and education for allied health professions, including nurses, in China as well as Malaysia (HMI 2004). The Columbia Group from Seattle, USA set up Columbia Asia, which owns the Columbia Asia Medical Centre in Seremban and two other hospitals in Malaysia, two hospitals in Vietnam and three medical centres in Bangalore, two of which are currently being developed.[22]

Medical tourism

The regional and global expansion of health care companies is a logical outcome of the need for businesses to increase revenue and profits. In their quest to increase their customer base, each business will have to compete with rival health care companies. One way in which the pie can be expanded for all is to expand the market, or to create new markets. It is primarily for this reason that 'medical tourism' or 'health tourism' is now touted as an important growth industry.[23]

Medical tourism has been targeted by the Malaysian government as a strategy for increasing revenue from tourism (which is already the second largest revenue-earner after manufacturing) as well as an industry that should be developed in its own right. The impact of the 1997 Asian financial crisis on the economy provided much of the impetus for this. Following the crisis, the number of patients at private hospitals decreased, as users shifted back to government hospitals. Facing the prospects of declining revenue, private hospitals turned to overseas markets to promote their services (MOH 2002: 107).

In 1998, the government convened a national committee on health tourism (MOH 2002: 104–7). The Ministry of Health has been charged with the task of accrediting and assisting selected private hospitals to provide services for foreign patients, as well as regulating advertising and fees. The Association of Private Hospitals of Malaysia (APHM) is the private sector partner cooperating with the MOH, and the 34 private hospitals selected for medical tourism promotion are marketed on its website. This cooperation is in keeping with the policy of Malaysia Incorporated, under which the government encourages a partnership approach with private capital to further national economic goals.

Governmental efforts are not limited to the Health Ministry. Trade missions organized by the Ministry of International Trade and Industry regularly place health care services on the agenda (*The Business Times*, 12 June 2003). The Prime Minister, Datuk Seri Abdullah Ahmad Badawi, identified health care services as one of five key sectors of core business areas of cooperation with China at the Malaysia–China Business Dialogue (*The Star*, 29 May 2004). Furthermore, generous tax incentives have been proposed for private hospitals engaging in medical tourism.[24]

Available statistics indicate an increasing trend in revenue from foreign patients in Malaysian private hospitals (MOH 2002: 108). Eight private hospitals reported an increase of 197 per cent in revenue from foreign patients between 1989 and 2001. From 2000 to 2001, ten private hospitals reported an increase in number of foreign patients from 56,133 to 75,210 (an increment of 34 per cent), and a corresponding increase in income generated from RM32.6 million to RM44.3 million (an increment of 36 per cent).

These statistics do not represent the total revenue generated from foreign patients. One estimate puts the total at about RM90 million in 2002.[25] The majority of medical tourists in Malaysia are from Indonesia, Brunei, Thailand and Singapore, with Indonesians constituting the largest group, accounting for 72 per cent of total foreign patients in 2003 (SERI 2004). Nevertheless, other countries, including developed countries as well as Middle Eastern countries, are targeted in the country's marketing strategies (MOH 2002: 106).

Although medical tourism is currently advocated by and for private hospitals, there are no official sanctions against the involvement of public hospitals. The corporatized National Heart Institute is already one of the hospitals listed for medical tourism promotion. Furthermore, in 2003, the then Health Minister Datuk Chua Jui Meng was quoted as saying:

> Although none of our Health Ministry hospitals has yet to be promoted as a provider of health tourism services, the setting up of many new, sophisticated and ultra-modern hospitals under the ministry have been identified as prime movers of health tourism in the future [sic]. Our public hospitals have the potential of raking in at least RM2 billion a year in health tourism earnings by the year 2010.
>
> (*The Star*, 28 October 2003)

More recently, during a visit to the Universiti Malaya Medical Centre, the incumbent Health Minister, Chua Soi Lek, said, 'There is a need for a concerted effort by university hospitals and private hospitals to raise their services to international standards so that more foreigners will come here for operations and hospital care' (*The Star*, 6 April 2004).

Consequences and contradictions

In the years of the NEP (1970–1990), public enterprises were set up to mobilize resources and accumulate capital on behalf of the *Bumiputera/* Malays. The state economic development corporations (SEDCs) were one such type of public enterprise, and Johor Corporation, which owns KPJ Healthcare, is one such SEDC. To advance the aim of increasing *Bumiputera* corporate equity, the Malaysian Government also set up investment holding companies and trust agencies which held shares on behalf of the *Bumiputera*.

In 1969, the investment holding company, Perbadanan Nasional Bhd (Pernas), was incorporated; it was controlled by Ministry of Finance Incorporated (MOF Inc.), the Treasury's holding company. When PNB (Permodalan Nasional Berhad) was established in 1978 to be the investment house and fund manager for the Yayasan Pelaburan Bumiputera (Bumiputera Investment Foundation), headed by the Prime Minister, Pernas transferred its major companies to PNB. Among these companies was Sime Darby, the parent company of the Subang Jaya Medical Centre.

While the NEP gave rise to state involvement in capital accumulation through public enterprises and state investment holding companies, the privatization policy in the mid-1980s sought to divest state assets to private entities. There was apparent irony in the fact that the most prominent investors in private hospitals – KPJ Healthcare, PNB – were themselves part of the Malaysian state at a time when national policy dictated a retreat from government ownership of commercial enterprises.

Nevertheless, it has been argued that there is no contradiction between the two sets of policies, as the primary objective of both is to increase the *Bumiputera* share in corporate equity (Gomez and Jomo 1999) While the NEP accumulated and held in trust corporate equity on behalf of the *Bumiputera*, the privatization policy divested state assets to *Bumiputera*-owned corporations, i.e. private *Bumiputera* capital accumulation. In reality, both sets of policy involve political patronage in determining access to and allocation of rents, and therefore the elite which controlled the state trust agencies and the corporations that benefited from privatization were not only those defined as *Bumiputera*, but had to be politically well connected as well. In creating a new business class mutually dependent on the political elite, the NEP and the privatization policy were therefore not inconsistent with each other.[26]

In the health care sector, the first government entity to be privatized was the government pharmaceutical procurement and distribution centre, the Government Medical Stores.[27] The award includes a 15-year concession to manufacture, procure and distribute drugs to all government hospitals and clinics. In 1994, this was privatized to Remedi Pharmaceuticals, wholly owned by United Engineers Malaysia (UEM), a company linked to UMNO (Gomez and Jomo 1999: 97).[28]

Subsequently, the five hospital support services, which collectively constituted the second largest expenditure category (after remuneration) in government hospitals, were privatized to three companies. Again, this involved a 15-year contract for cleansing, linen and laundry, clinical waste management, biomedical engineering maintenance and facility engineering maintenance for all MOH hospitals and clinical facilities. The three beneficiary companies were Tongkah Medivest, Faber Mediserve and Radicare.

Tongkah Medivest, later renamed Pantai Medivest, belonged to the conglomeration of companies which was at that time owned by the then Prime Minister's son, Mokhzani Mahathir.[29] Faber Medi-Serve is part of the Faber

Group, a member of the UEM and Renong group of companies, which are closely linked to UMNO interests (Gomez and Jomo 1999: 50, 52; Barraclough 2000).

The Malaysian state is therefore intricately involved in private sector health care: directly through the state economic development corporations and the state investment holding companies, and indirectly through political patronage of well-connected companies that are the beneficiaries of health care privatization. It may be argued that in a system of multiple players in health care provision and financing, and where regulation is weak, the growth of private health care is detrimental to the viability of a robust public health care service.

Insofar as health care provision is a primary welfare function of the state, state involvement in private health care as well may well be seen as a conflict of interests. However, since the Malaysian state is a major investor in private hospitals and other private health care activities, it is therefore not surprising nor inconsistent for state agencies to support the growth of private health care and the development of the health tourism industry. In fact, state agencies' promotion of private hospital interests represents the Malaysia Incorporated concept at its most ascendant. Nevertheless, assigning to the MOH the two conflicting functions of ensuring population health as well as private hospital (and medical tourism) industry development reflects most clearly its contradiction.

Consequences

The official rationale for the expansion of private health care is that it will cater for those who can afford it, thereby freeing the public health care services for those who cannot afford to use private health care. This policy has directly exacerbated the most critical and intractable problem facing the public health care services: the drain of public medical personnel into the expanded and more lucrative private sector. The loss of public sector doctors and nurses to the private sector has for some years caused serious problems for public health care. In desperation, the health minister had at one time proposed that private doctors and specialists be required to serve a stipulated number of hours in government hospitals each year (*The Star*, 11 June 2004). This was of course rejected by the 10,000-strong Malaysian Medical Association (*The New Straits Times*, 12 June 2004).

There are other consequences, primarily for equity. Private health care facilities are concentrated in the richer urban areas, and there are no regulatory provisions for encouraging private facilities to be more evenly distributed, thereby exacerbating the problem of geographical equity. By virtue of the fact that private hospitals are established to turn a profit, they are priced above the reach of the majority of patients, and are accessible only to those who can pay their prices. While public health care is funded by taxation, thereby ensuring some form of financial equity and cross-subsidization, private health care in Malaysia is largely funded by out-of-pocket payments, and partly by employers, medical savings and private insurance, financing mechanisms that do not ensure financial equity nor cross-subsidization.

The privatization of hospital support services has not been without its problems. An official report found that maintenance services were underperforming and concluded that 'a much more concerted effort is required on the part of the concession companies to plan their activities in order to fulfill service and thereby fulfill customer satisfaction' (Ministry of Health 1999: 133–8). An evaluation of the pharmaceutical supply services noted improvements in the ordering process due to high investment in information technology but cautioned that 'there is a need to improve customer satisfaction especially with regards to quality, availability of stocks and greater initiative in replacing recalled products' (Ministry of Health 1999: 126–32).

Contradictions

The role of the state in investor-led private health care provision is in direct contradiction to its role of ensuring the welfare and security of citizens. This tension between the two roles is reflected in weak attempts to ameliorate the ill-effects of a dominant private health care sector. It is manifestly evident in the then Prime Minister Mahathir Mohamad's speech when launching the Seventh Malaysia Plan. He exhorted the private sector:

> Hospitals for poorer sections of the population should be put up by the private sector. The present private hospitals tend to stress five-star accommodation which the majority of patients cannot afford. An ordinary class private hospital should be lucrative for Malaysian investors. Even within private hospitals there must be elements of cross-subsidy, so that those who cannot afford can have equally good medical treatment without the need for luxurious accommodations. Doctors working in five-star hospitals should also spend time in ordinary private wards where fees and charges should be low. Medicine is a noble profession and financial considerations alone should not determine its practice. Society owes a lot to the practitioners of medicine but the affluence of the professionals also owes a lot to the kind of society we have. There must always be gratefulness and charity in our hearts.
>
> (Mahathir 1996)

The Budget for 1996 revealed that the government was no longer relying on the private for-profit hospitals to voluntarily play a social role; rather it signalled the intention to make the provision of low-cost wards mandatory. In the following year's Budget a tax-offset of 60 per cent was given to private hospitals constructing wards for low-income earners (Barraclough 1999: 60). Once more, the contradiction in public policy was evident – the social role of private sector investors was to be subsidized by the state.

The burgeoning private hospital sector has also created a situation where traditional not-for-profit hospitals have to compete with for-profit hospitals. While it has been the stated practice of not-for-profit hospitals to cross-subsidize the treatment of poor patients, this practice is probably becoming more difficult to sustain since these hospitals must compete with profit-oriented commercial hospitals which are not encumbered by any substantial charitable role.[30]

In 2002, the government set up the National Health Welfare Fund to receive public donations on behalf of needy patients, who have to go through an application and vetting process by the MOH. In early 2003, the Director-General of Health announced that the fund held a total of RM5.5 million, and since its inception in September 2002 had received 102 applications, among which 63 had been approved (*The Sun*, 27 February 2003). In rationalizing and safeguarding the use of public donations for poor patients, the health fund appears to be a device used by the government to marginalize its own welfare role, from its previous position as a central role. Not only that, as a source of health care financing, the health fund represents the state institutionalizing of health care as charity.

Another contradiction may be pointed out. Sime Darby is a conglomerate that was established on the rubber industry. As a large plantation owner it is responsible for the health care facilities on its estates, and it is among the plantation companies whose estate health care services have been of such low quality (MMA 1988) that their health care functions have had to be taken over by the government. Sime Darby, as previously mentioned, owns and runs the premier Subang Jaya Medical Centre that provides high quality health care, and is itself owned by PNB, the government's investment agency.

Concluding observations

In the Eighth Malaysia Plan it was announced that the government would decrease its role in the provision of health care, while increasing its regulatory role (Malaysia 2001). The intention is for government hospitals to be corporatized. In order for this to happen, a financing mechanism has to be in place. The proposal for a social insurance scheme is currently being decided upon. The fund will provide the necessary financing for the increased costs that will be transferred to the patients. In effect, it will be a transferring of financing from taxation to social security. It will also mean an improvement in financial equity insofar as a large part of health care financing is now out-of-pocket. Nevertheless, the social security fund also represents a large pool of money for financing the utilization of private health care. Depending on how the fund is structured, it could significantly increase the capacity of Malaysians to use private hospitals and thereby boost their profitability.[31]

While withdrawing from the provision of health care, the government's stated intention is to increase its regulatory role. This expansion of regulation is not yet evident. For example, when the five hospital support services were privatized in 1996, a private consultant company, Sistem Hospital Awasan Taraf (SIHAT), was awarded a contract to supervise and monitor the concessionaires.

Furthermore, while the Private Healthcare Facilities and Services Act was passed in 1998, it was only enforced from 1 May 2006. The seemingly haphazard and slow way in which the regulatory control of private hospitals has so far developed contrasts with the systematic approaches to planning and social engineering in other areas of the economy. The contrast reflects an ambiguity that has been thrown up from the battle that is being fought between the conflicting functions and interests of the state.

Notes

1 There is a considerable body of literature which explains the market failures. See, for example, 'Arguments in economics and justice for government intervention in health insurance and health service markets', Chapter 2 in Flood (2000).
2 Although, in the United Kingdom, the initial experiments in managed competition have been pulled back and in Europe, there is caution in pursuing further privatization and marketization (Saltman *et al.* 1998; Hunter 2002).
3 Chapter 12, 'Economic interests and power in health care'.
4 The NEP involved a two-pronged strategy, one, to eradicate poverty irrespective of race, and two, to restructure the economy so as to eradicate the identification of race with economic sectors. Although the NEP embodied a broad range of socio-economic objectives – employment, housing, education – the cornerstone was the distribution of corporate asset ownership as the indicator of wealth distribution (Jomo 1995).
5 The population was predominantly rural in 1957/1960 (74 per cent in Malaya, 87 per cent in Sabah and Sarawak), with very little change until 1970 (73 per cent for Malaysia). Since then, however, the rural population has shrunk to 66 per cent in 1980, 59 per cent in 1990 and 38 per cent in 2000 (Department of Statistics 1977: 275; Malaysia 1986: Table 5–4; Department of Statistics 2002).
6 The privatization of the five support services was announced in 1993, but was only effected in 1996. The Government Medical Store was privatized in 1994. See Chee (2004) for a brief review of the privatization of health care services in Malaysia.
7 The Private Hospital Act 1971 Act 43.
8 The Private Healthcare Facilities and Services Act 1998 Act 586. The regulations that pave the way for its implementation were finally enacted with effect from 1 May 2006 (Bernama, 24 April 2006).
9 Tax concessions for the costs of medical treatment for a taxpayer's parents were raised from RM1,000 to RM5,000. Medical treatment for serious illnesses such as cancer, renal failure, AIDS, heart disease, for oneself, spouse or child has a concession up to a maximum of RM5,000, RM500 of which could be used for medical examination (Inland Revenue Board, Explanatory notes for year of assessment 2004. Online. Available at <http://www.hasilnet.org.my/english/eng_index.asp>, accessed 15 October 2005).

10 The intention to seek an alternative scheme for financing medical and health services was first announced in the Mid-term Review of the Fourth Malaysia Plan (Malaysia 1984: 376). Numerous studies have been commissioned since then. See Chee (2004), also Chan (this volume).

11 It is important to note that the NHMS 2 estimate is confined to out-of-pocket expenditure only. As noted in the NHMS 2 (Public Health Institute 1999: 102–3), information on private health expenditure in Malaysia is incomplete due to lack of data on expenditure by private sector companies and private health insurance. The NHMS 2 defines health expenditure as annual expenditure on ambulatory care including transport and hospitalization, as well as expenditure on traditional and alternative medicine, pharmaceuticals and health appliances, self-treatment, dental care and eye care.

12 The same study estimated that (in 1983) cost per admission in public hospitals was RM537, while in private hospitals, cost borne by the consumer was RM1,703.

13 Malaysian public sector health expenditure increased between 1998 and 2002, not only as a proportion of total health expenditure, but also as a percentage of total government expenditure (from 5.1 per cent to 6.9 per cent), while total expenditure on health increased as a percentage of GDP from 3.0 per cent to 3.8 per cent (see Statistical Annex Table 5 in WHO 2005). For an explanation of the WHO method of assessment, see Statistical Annex Explanatory Notes in WHO (2005).

14 The figures here are for 2002, and are taken from Statistical Annex Table 5 in WHO (2005). Thailand is attempting to establish social insurance, and governmental health spending jumped between 2001 and 2002 resulting in private spending dropping from 41.1 per cent to 30.3 per cent.

15 Tax relief on medical (or education) insurance is up to a maximum of RM3,000 (Inland Revenue Board, Explanatory notes for year of assessment 2004. Online. Available at <http://www.hasilnet.org.my/english/eng_index.asp>, accessed 15 October 2005).

16 The EPF is the national social security organization, with 10.23 million members (of which 4.82 million are active members). It operates a compulsory retirement savings scheme, to which employees contribute 11 per cent of their wages and employers 12 per cent. Under the medical savings scheme, 10 per cent is put into a separate account, which could be drawn upon for treatment (of a list of 'critical illnesses' and conditions) in either the public or private sectors. It may also be used for family members – spouse, children, parents and siblings (EPF 2002).

17 Likewise, there is an increasing trend in using the medical savings scheme – the number of withdrawals for health and medical reasons increased from 643 (constituting RM4.75 million) in 1996 to 8,510 (RM36.13 million) in 2002 (EPF 2000, 2001 and 2002).

18 Data for 1980 and 1983 from MOH Annual Reports 1980 and 1983/84. Data for 2003 is computed from a list of private hospitals obtained from the Corporate Unit of the MOH.

19 Data from a list of private hospitals obtained from the Corporate Unit of the MOH. The number of nursing homes is very low because they are normally registered with the Department of Social Welfare (under the Ministry of Women, Family and Community Development since 2004), although those with inpatient beds should be registered with the MOH. Currently, however, the MOH have not yet implemented the legal provision for compulsory registration.

20 CCM has since divested its stake, while the Employees' Provident Fund acquired major shares in the company in 2005 (*The Business Times*, 10 June 2005 and 13 June 2005).

21 From a listing of the principal activities of the KPJ Group in a circular to shareholders dated 24 May 2005, posted at the Bursa Malaysia (Malaysian stock exchange) website, available at <http://announcements.bursamalaysia.com/EDMS/subweb.nsf/o/f50faa0ee45afbfd4825700b0018c005/$FILE/KPJ-circular.pdf> (accessed 19 October 2005).

22 Such globalized expansions are not limited to hospitals. Pharmaniaga, the Malaysian company that holds the concession to supply drugs to government hospitals until 2009, is venturing into Indonesia (where it acquired a controlling share in a leading pharmaceutical distributor), China (where it is setting up a joint venture to produce injectibles) and South Africa (where it is bidding for a contract to build a pharmaceutical procurement and distribution system) (*The Edge Malaysia*, 15 August 2005).

23 In this chapter, the term 'medical tourism' will be used to denote travelling to another country to seek medical treatment, including medical screening, from the health care services in that country; 'health tourism' will be used to encompass a broader range of travel activities such as spa, massage, or just to avail oneself of another type of climate for the purposes of health. This follows a similar use of the terms in MOH (2002: 104).

24 These include exempting from tax all revenue from foreign patients in excess of 5 per cent of total hospital revenue (MOH 2002: 110).

25 Total revenue cannot be computed because the other private hospitals have not complied in providing statistics (MOH 2002: 108). The estimate given here is provided by the Socio-economic and Environmental Research Institute (SERI), the research think-tank of the Penang state government (SERI 2004).

26 In fact, the policy of corporatization entails refashioning certain governmental entities into corporate structures which nevertheless remain under the ownership of the government. In certain key sectors, such as petroleum and heavy industries, the government remains firmly entrenched.

27 There is a detailed explanation of the corporate interests behind the privatization of government health care entities in Chan (2004).

28 UMNO, the United Malays National Organization, is the dominant political party in Barisan Nasional, the ruling coalition. After many changes, Remedi Pharmaceuticals is now known as Pharmaniaga, while the parent company is UEM World, which is owned by Khazanah Nasional Holdings, the government's investment agency.

29 Pantai Medivest and Fomema (the monopoly holder of the government contract for monitoring the medical examinations of foreign workers in Malaysia) are subsidiary companies of Pantai Holdings Limited, which also owns Pantai Medical Centre and six other hospitals. The controlling stake in Pantai Holdings was previously held by Tongkah, the flagship company of Mokhzani Mahathir. In April 2001, Mokhzani Mahathir sold his controlling stake to Lim Tong Yong (*The Edge Daily*, 5 December 2003). In September 2005, it was reported that Parkway Holdings had acquired a 31 per cent stake in Pantai Holdings, making it Pantai's largest shareholder (*The Straits Times*, 14 September 2005). This gave rise to much dissatisfaction among UMNO members, following which *Khazanah Nasional* has engineered a scheme to buy back majority ownership of Pantai (*The Edge Malaysia*, 21 August 2006).

30 Under the 1998 Private Healthcare Facilities and Services Act, private hospitals will be required to provide some social welfare contribution.

31 The MMA, in representing the interests of its members in the private sector, has advocated vociferously for the social insurance model. The model also has the support of the APHM, whose honorary secretary has been quoted as saying, 'Having a national health care financing scheme similar to social insurance schemes

found in the US and Australia is one way to go about it . . . We're all for this as it allows everyone to have equal access to health care services' (Gayathri 2004: 30).

References

Association of Private Hospitals of Malaysia (APHM) website. Available at <http://www.hospitals-malaysia.org/index.cfm> (accessed 19 October 2005).

Barraclough, Simon (1997) 'The growth of corporate private hospitals in Malaysia: policy contradictions in health system pluralism', *International Journal of Health Services* 27(4): 643–59.

—— (1999) 'Constraints in the retreat from a welfare-oriented approach to public health care in Malaysia', *Health Policy* 47: 53–67.

—— (2000) 'The politics of privatization in the Malaysian health care system', *Contemporary Southeast Asia* 22(2): 340–59.

Bernama, 24 April 2006, 'Six months for medical practitioners to get used to new Act'.

The Business Times, 12 June 2003, 'Trade missions to promote healthcare services overseas'.

The Business Times, 10 June 2005, 'EPF acquires stakes in hospital operators'.

The Business Times, 13 June 2005, 'Columbia Asia to invest RM135m in hospital'.

Chan Chee Khoon (2003) 'Privatizing the welfarist state: health care reforms in Malaysia', *New Solutions* 13(1): 87–105.

—— (2004) 'Market development in healthcare services in Malaysia: a political economic and institutional analysis', paper presented at the UNRISD International Conference on Commercialization of Health Care: Global and Local Dynamics and Policy Responses, in the UNRISD Programme on Social Policy and Development, Geneva, March.

Chee Heng Leng (2004) 'Current health care financing issues in Malaysia', Asia Research Institute Working Paper Series No. 18, February. Online. Available at <http://www.ari.nus.edu.sg/docs/wps/wps04_018.pdf> (accessed 2 November 2005).

Department of Statistics (1977) *Population Census of Malaysia 1970: General Report (Volume 1)*, Kuala Lumpur: Department of Statistics, Malaysia.

—— (2002) *Yearbook of Statistics 2002*, Kuala Lumpur: Department of Statistics, Malaysia.

Economic Planning Unit (1991) *Privatization Masterplan*, Kuala Lumpur: Government Printers.

—— (1996) 'Health sector development', in R., Haas, Sulaiman Mahbob and Tham S.Y. (eds) *Health Care Planning and Development: Conference Proceedings*, Kuala Lumpur: Malaysian Institute of Economic Research (MIER).

The Edge Daily, 5 December 2003, 'Lim Tong Yong Keeps Pantai stake'. Online. Available at <http://www.theedgedaily.com> (accessed 9 December 2005).

The Edge Malaysia, 20 June 2005, 'KPJ given clean bill of health'.

The Edge Malaysia, 15 August 2005, 'Pharmaniaga a coup for UEM World'.

The Edge Malaysia, 21 August 2006, 'The Pantai conundrum'.

Employees' Provident Fund (EPF) (2000) *Annual Report 2000*.

—— (2001) *Annual Report 2001*.

—— (2002) *Annual Report 2002*.

Evans, Robert G. (1997) 'Going for the gold: the redistributive agenda behind market-based health care reform', *Journal of Health Politics, Policy and Law* 22(2): 427–65.

Flood, Colleen M. (2000) *International Health Care Reform: A Legal, Economic and Political Analysis*, London: Routledge.

Freund, Peter E.S. and McGuire, M.B. (1999) *Health, Illness and the Social Body: A Critical Sociology*, Englewood Cliffs, NJ: Prentice Hall.

Gayathri, S. (2004) 'Social insurance for all', *Personal Money* 39 (November).

Gomez, Edmund T. and Jomo K.S. (1999) *Malaysia's Political Economy: Politics, Patronage and Profits*, Cambridge: Cambridge University Press.

Health Management International Ltd (HMI) (2004) *Annual Report 2004*.

Hunter, David J. (2002) 'Health systems reforms: the United Kingdom's experience', in Andrew C. Twaddle (ed.) *Health Care Reform around the World*, London: Auburn House.

Jomo K.S. (ed.) (1995) *Privatizing Malaysia: Rents, Rhetoric, Realities*, Boulder, CO: Westview Press.

Light, Donald W. (2000) 'The sociological character of health-care markets', in Gary L. Albrecht, R. Fitzpatrick, and S.C. Scrimshaw (eds) *Handbook of Social Studies in Health and Medicine*, London: Sage.

Mahathir bin Mohamad (1996) Speech by Prime Minister Datuk Seri Mahathir Mohamad presenting the motion for the tabling of the Seventh Malaysia Plan in the Dewan Rakyat (full text reprinted in *The New Straits Times*, 7 May 1999).

Malaysia (1984) *Mid-term Review of the Fourth Malaysia Plan 1981–1985*, Kuala Lumpur: Economic Planning Unit, Prime Minister's Department, Malaysia.

——— (1986) *The Fifth Malaysia Plan 1986–1990*, Kuala Lumpur: Economic Planning Unit, Prime Minister's Department, Malaysia.

——— (1996) *The Seventh Malaysia Plan 1996–2000*, Kuala Lumpur: Economic Planning Unit, Prime Minister's Department, Malaysia.

——— (2001) *The Eighth Malaysia Plan 2001–2005*, Kuala Lumpur: Economic Planning Unit, Prime Minister's Department, Malaysia.

——— (2003) *Mid-Term Review of the Eighth Malaysia Plan 2001–2005*, Kuala Lumpur: Economic Planning Unit, Prime Minister's Department, Malaysia.

Malaysian Medical Association (MMA) (1988) 'A study on the current health care delivery system in the estates and plantations in Peninsular Malaysia', unpublished report, Kuala Lumpur: MMA.

Ministry of Health (MOH) (various years) *Annual Report*, Kuala Lumpur: Ministry of Health.

——— (1999) *Malaysia's Health 1999: Technical Report of the Director-General of Health Malaysia 1999*, Kuala Lumpur: Ministry of Health.

——— (2002) *Malaysia's Health 2002: Technical Report of the Director-General of Health Malaysia 2002*, Kuala Lumpur: Ministry of Health.

The New Straits Times, 12 June 2004, 'Medical association rejects proposal'.

Penang Development Corporation (PDC) website. Available at <http://www.pdc.gov.my/article.cfm?id=40> (accessed 19 October 2005).

Public Health Institute (1999) *National Health and Morbidity Survey 1996*, Volume 3: *Recent Illness/Injury, Health Seeking Behaviour and Out-of-pocket Health Care Expenditure*, Kuala Lumpur: Public Health Institute, MOH Malaysia.

Rugayah Mohamed (1995) 'Public enterprises', in Jomo K.S. (ed.) *Privatizing Malaysia: Rents, Rhetoric, Realities*, Boulder, CO: Westview Press.

Saltman, Richard B., Figueras, J. and Sakellarides, C. (eds) (1998) *Critical Challenges for Health Care Reform in Europe*, Buckingham: Open University Press.

Socio-economic and Environmental Research Institute (SERI) (2004) 'Economic briefing to the Penang State Government: health tourism in Penang', *Penang Economic Monthly* 6(11), November. Online. Available at <http://seri.com.my/oldsite/EconBrief/EconBrief2004-11.PDF> (accessed 6 September 2006).

The Star, 18 January 2000, 'Health option: EPF members can use Account III for health insurance scheme from June'.

The Star, 28 October 2003, 'Hospitals set fees for health tourism'.

The Star, 6 April 2004, 'Move to boost health tourism'.

The Star, 29 May 2004, 'PM identifies areas of cooperation with China'.

The Star, 11 June 2004, 'National service for private doctors'.

The Star, 17 September 2005, 'Pantai gets a dose of excitement'.

The Straits Times, 11 June 2005, 'Four directors replace Parkway founders'.

The Straits Times, 14 September 2005, 'Parkway pays $139m for stake in Malaysia's Pantai'.

The Sun, 27 February 2003, 'Welfare fund is above board'.

World Health Organization (2005) *The World Health Report 2005*. Online. Available at <http://www.who.int/whr/2005/en/index.html> (accessed 2 November 2005).

2 Regulating Malaysia's private health care sector

Nik Rosnah Wan Abdullah

The unprecedented growth of the private medical sector since the 1980s has had wide-ranging implications for the Malaysian health care system. In particular, it is well known that leaving health care to market forces does not necessarily lead to an effective and efficient health care system (Rosenthal and Newbrander 1996). Therefore, there has to be a robust regulatory framework to ensure equity and access, and also to ensure that private health services are of acceptable quality. The Malaysian Government, in the *Mid-Term Review of the Sixth Malaysia Plan 1991–1995*, states:

> While the government will still remain a provider of basic health services, the role of the Ministry of Health will gradually shift towards more policy making and regulatory aspects as well as setting standards to ensure *quality, affordability* and *appropriateness of care*. At the same time the Ministry of Health will ensure an *equitable distribution* in the provision of health services and health manpower between the public and private sectors.
>
> (Malaysia 1993: 244, emphasis added)

According to the Seventh Malaysia Plan (1996–2000), the government 'will gradually reduce its role in the provision of health services and increase its regulatory and enforcement functions' (Malaysia 1996: 544).

This chapter considers the role of the regulatory agencies in addressing these aims, and focuses on two important aspects of regulation: regulating private health facilities and regulating the medical profession. Of particular concern are issues of equitability and accessibility and the quality of health care services. The degree to which regulation achieves the government's objectives of ensuring quality of health care services, and is seen to do so, will be assessed.

The findings of this study are mainly drawn from a review of documentary sources and interviews carried out from August to December 1999.[1] The author conducted a series of interviews with informants from the Ministry of Health (MOH), the Malaysian Medical Council (MMC), members of the Preliminary Investigations Committees (PICs), the Medico-Legal Society of

Malaysia, the Malaysian Medical Association (MMA), the Municipal Council of Ampang Jaya, or Majlis Perbandaran Ampang Jaya (MPAJ), and Kuala Lumpur City Hall, or Dewan Bandaraya Kuala Lumpur (DBKL). Officials of non-governmental organizations, including the Federation of Malaysian Consumers Associations (FOMCA), the Malaysian Trade Union Congress (MTUC) and the Institute of Islamic Understanding (IKIM), were also interviewed.

In addition, interviews were conducted with managers of six private hospitals, one in the Federal Territory of Kuala Lumpur and five in the state of Selangor.[2] The hospitals selected for detailed study included relatively newly established ones and those which have existed for a number of years. Personnel of Healthcare Technical Services Pte. Ltd (HTS),[3] a private company owned by Kumpulan Perubatan Johor (KPJ), the largest health care conglomerate in the country, were also interviewed. Other interviewees included advocates and solicitors, doctors from both public and private sectors, academics and some members of the general public. In all, 105 persons were interviewed. The author also observed an inspection tour that was carried out by district-level Ministry of Health inspecting officers in a newly established hospital for the purpose of issuing a hospital licence.

Issues in regulation

In social sectors, such as health care, there is imperfect information since consumers have only a limited understanding of what will or will not restore health. By contrast, the provider has much better information on what the patient requires and usually has considerable influence over what is supplied and consumed. The key issue, therefore, is how the regulatory system deals with the problem of information asymmetry and the logistics of collecting and processing information to regulate private providers (Mills *et al.* 2001).

Another concern is the hazard of regulatory capture[4] (Stigler 1971; Laffont and Tirole 1991; Soderlund and Tangcharoensathien 2000; Mills *et al.* 2001). Freidson (1970a, 1970b, 1988a, 1988b) suggests that there is an implicit understanding between the professions and the state that the professions will ensure safe and competent services in exchange for the exclusive right to provide these services. Other authors have pointed out that the professions use their powers to further their own interests, rather than the general public interest (Stigler 1971; Posner 1974; Peltzman 1976; Hancher 1990). The challenge for the state, therefore, is to identify regulatory mechanisms and structures, including monitoring systems, that are effective in protecting public interest.

Regulation of private health facilities

The stated concerns of the government with regard to private hospitals may be summarized as (a) quality in terms of health services and manpower, and

(b) equity in terms of geographical location and cost of services.[5] An analysis of the regulation of private health facilities should therefore take into account the extent to which these objectives are addressed.

Regulatory framework

The main Acts under which private hospitals are regulated are the Local Government Act 1976 (Laws of Malaysia Act 171), the Private Hospitals Act 1971 (Laws of Malaysia Act 43) and the Atomic Energy Licensing Act 1984 (Laws of Malaysia Act 304).

The Local Government Act 1976 confers on local governments a wide array of powers and functions. However, these laws and regulations are about standard local government planning and building regulation procedures and are not specific to health facilities. The Private Hospitals Act 1971 is the existing Act governing private hospitals and is still in force. It provides for control through registration, licensing and inspection of existing private hospitals, nursing homes and maternity homes. A licence issued or renewed is valid for a year. It sets the basic service standards and minimum requirements for the operation of clinics or hospitals.

However, this Act and its associated regulations (the Private Hospitals Regulations 1973) do not provide adequate provisions to regulate the private health facilities. The Atomic Energy Licensing Act 1984 provides for the control and licensing of radiation equipment and radioactive materials and for the establishment of standards, liability for nuclear damage and related matters. Other than this, many services and facilities, including medical and dental clinics, day surgeries, and screening and diagnosis services, are not covered under these Acts. Neither are ambulance services, clinical laboratories, haemodialysis centres and hospices. These limitations and omissions are addressed in a new Act, the Private Healthcare Facilities and Services Act 1998 (Laws of Malaysia Act 586, hereafter, Private Healthcare Act 1998).[6]

The two main institutions involved in regulating private hospitals are the municipal or local authorities, and the MOH. Government control of private health facilities is effected primarily through licensing. Before new private health facilities may commence operations, the licences that are required are (i) the 'Development order and building licence or certificate of fitness for building occupation', issued by the relevant municipal council or local authority in whose jurisdictional areas the private hospitals are situated, (ii) the 'Licence to operate' issued by the Licensing Unit of the Medical Practice Division of the MOH, and (iii) the 'Licence for installation and usage of radiation equipment' issued by the Radiation Safety Unit of the MOH.

Implementation

Siting of hospitals

The degree to which the government's objective of equity through the siting of hospitals has been achieved can be evaluated by reference to relevant government directives, circulars and guidelines. The 'Guidelines to application for planning approval', issued by the Muncipal Council of Ampang Jaya (MPAJ), for example, has no requirement for the siting of health facilities.

Local council officers interviewed suggested that no guidelines were issued regarding the siting of facilities. According to one of them, 'there are no directives from the higher authority or the MOH on the issue of siting of facilities'. Hence he does not see the relevance of taking the siting of facilities into account when licensing hospital buildings. He recounted that when reviewing the application for the planning approval of a proposed health facility, information such as the population to be served and distance from the nearest health facility for the siting of facilities was not requested. Issuance of the 'Certificate of fitness for building occupation' was based mainly on the quality and safety of the building.

Under the Private Healthcare Act 1998, approval to establish or maintain private health care facilities or services other than private clinics would consider matters such as the extent to which the health care facilities or services are already available in an area, and the need for the health care facility and services. However, the local council officers interviewed implied that any ruling requiring the siting of hospitals in rural areas would be difficult to impose; nor were they aware of any survey made on the location of new facilities over the past few years.

Personnel from the private company HTS suggested that factors that were taken into account in their planning to set up a hospital pertained mainly to the viability of the business. They said it would not be economical to site hospitals in rural areas. According to one CEO, 'the private hospitals are meant for those who can afford to pay, not for the poor ... It is therefore the responsibility of the government to take care of (the health services for) the poor.'

Control of hospital charges

Interviews with key informants of the six study hospitals suggested that no relevant information on fees and hospital charges were required when applying for a hospital licence. The Private Healthcare Act 1998 states that the Minister may make regulations prescribing a fee schedule for private health facilities or services, but since this Act has yet to be implemented, the relevant regulation is the Private Hospitals Act 1971, which governs the 'Checklist for inspections of private hospitals regarding the requirement

Table 2.1 Number of hospitals providing social or community services by hospital size, Malaysia, 1999

Forms of social service	Hospital size (number of beds)					Total no. of hospitals providing social or community services
	≥ 10	11–50	51–100	101–200	>200	
Special fund			2	3	3	8
(Amount in funds)			(RM4,099 –30,000)	(RM94,000 –600,000)	(RM207,730 –1 million)	
Discount for charges	1	9	14	13	9	46
(Amounts given out)	(RM1,000)	(RM150 –44,000)	(RM3,594 –143,000)	(RM5,220 –700,000)	(RM65,000 –2,349,237)	
Welfare ward			2	1		3
(No. of welfare beds)			(51 beds)	(28 beds)		(79 beds)

Source: Compiled from raw data obtained from the Medical Practice Division, MOH, 1999.

Note:
Figures do not include responses from maternity homes.
( ) Numbers in brackets show the range of contributions.

under the Hospital Act 1971 and Regulations 1973'. In this checklist, no information was required on fees and hospital charges.

An MOH officer who had researched private hospital charges said that the charges in private hospitals for services[7] (which ranged from 15 to 28 per cent of the total hospital bill) and medication (which made up about 15 per cent of the bill) were not broken down into various items when patients were billed. Often, fees for services and medication were increased to compensate for lowering charges for accommodation and food.

On the positive side, some private hospitals have provided some form of social or community services in response to the government's call for the private sector to shoulder some social responsibilities (Table 2.1). The amounts that have been set aside in the special funds and the discount charges were not mandated, and were up to the individual hospitals. Other forms of community service include public education, free medical services for special groups (including inmates of old folks homes and the disabled), medical screening and accident and emergency services.

Review of the regulatory conduct and processes of the regulatory agencies

Officials at the district level of the MOH faced difficulties in carrying out inspection of private facilities due to the lack of guidelines. The inspection of the technical requirements of a facility relied upon the planning made by the consultant engaged by the corporate body of the private hospital. Furthermore, the medical consultants who headed the various medical disciplines were the ones who determined the hiring of qualified personnel. There was heavy reliance on information supplied by the proprietors in decision-making that would ensure quality in technical aspects and medical care.

On the other side, personnel of HTS confirmed that decisions made by many large hospitals to engage well-known medical consultants for their hospitals were based primarily on business considerations. Interviews with municipality (MPAJ) officers revealed that there was not much capacity to assess technical information received from the private sector on the establishment of hospitals. Mostly, the technical departments gave their agreement to the plans submitted by the proprietors, which suggests a lack of technical appraisal on the part of the government agencies.

Monitoring and enforcement

Decisions with regard to the issuing of licences for the use of radiation and medical equipment in newly established health facilities are heavily based on the reports of testing made by the physicist engaged by the supplier. The Radiation Safety Unit of the MOH, which monitors the performance of x-ray machines, record-keeping, radiation leakage and dark room facilities, makes random visits to premises in response to requests or complaints from the public. From 1996–1999, it was found that less than 10 per cent of the premises visited complied fully with the Acts and Regulations. Warnings were issued to non-compliant hospitals and clinics. However, due to the shortage of manpower, follow-up visits could not be made. Despite the low compliance rate of private facilities to regulation standards, there were very few complaints. Only 10 complaints were made in 1998 and two in 1999.[8]

Sanctions for violations and non-compliance

In two cases of violation brought to court in 1999 the defendants were found guilty of employing unqualified persons to operate the x-ray machine and providing examinations such as intravenous pyelogram[9] on patients. Section 40(2) of the Atomic Energy Licensing Act 1984 provides for a penalty of imprisonment for a term not exceeding 10 years or a fine not exceeding RM100,000[10] or both. However, despite the strong provisions of the Act, the two cases were brought to a magistrate's court and the offenders were fined only RM5,000 and RM3,000 each.[11]

A number of hospitals operate without a hospital licence, for various reasons.[12] These hospitals were advised not to accept inpatients, but instead to operate as clinics. Currently, under the Private Hospitals Act 1971, the penalty for hospitals operating without a valid hospital licence is only RM1,000.[13] The MOH does not have the power to close these premises and it is restricted in its powers to regulate private hospitals. Under the new Private Healthcare Act 1998, the proprietor of an unlicensed private health care facility would be liable to a fine of RM300,000[14] or six years imprisonment or both.

Regulation of medical professionals

Currently there are three regulatory institutions with varying degrees of authority over Malaysian medical professionals: the Malaysian Medical Council (MMC), the Malaysian Medical Association (MMA) and the Ministry of Health (MOH). Each has its own disciplinary committees: the MMC has three Preliminary Investigation Committees (PICs), the MMA has its Ethics Committee and the MOH has its Board of Enquiry.

The MMC is the core regulatory body of the medical profession, as it is provided with a legal framework. The Medical Act 1971 and Medical Regulations 1974 place the MMC as the custodian of the medical profession (MMC 1993). It has jurisdiction over doctors in both public and private sectors. The functions of the MMC are to register medical practitioners intending to practise in Malaysia and to ensure that medical practice is of reasonable and acceptable standards (MMC 1994). In exercising its powers to protect the public from malpractice and negligence, and in disciplining transgressors, the MMC convenes one of the PICs to make preliminary investigations into complaints or information touching on disciplinary matters (Medical Regulations 1974).

Under the Medical Act 1971, the Director-General of Health is the President of the MMC. The members of the MMC are drawn from three main sources: nomination by universities, election by registered medical practitioners and appointment from the public services. Out of the 24 members, 20 represent the medical profession and medical organizations, while three represent the public services. There is no representation of advocacy groups, the users, the general public or any other stakeholder groups. Since its inception, the membership of the MMC, including the public service representatives, has consisted solely of doctors. There have not been any 'lay' or non-medical members. Therefore, the viewpoints of doctors and their interests have an important bearing in the MMC.

The President of the MMC appoints members to the PICs from among the medical practitioners (Medical Regulations 1974). All complaints to the MMC are considered first by a PIC. It holds a formal inquiry to establish whether there is a prima facie case of professional misconduct which would then be referred to the MMC (Medical Regulations 1974). There are three PICs, each consisting of not fewer than three and not more than six members (Medical Regulations 1974). All PIC members are doctors, most of whom are in senior positions and are specialists. Much depends on the way complaints are dealt with by the PICs, and NGO representatives and academics interviewed in this study raised concerns that the PICs are not large enough to reflect a wide range of opinions and to allow for differences of opinion.[15] This problem is exacerbated by the fact that these committees do not include lay members.

Doctors in the public sector are regulated under three tiers of regulatory structure: the state level, the ministerial level (MOH) and ultimately the Public Services Department. They are also subject to regulation by the MMC and, if they are members of the MMA, the regulation of the MMA. The MOH establishes the Board of Inquiry to look into ethical and disciplinary matters of doctors in public service, but does not play a role in regulating medical professionals in the private sector. The MOH Board of Inquiry comprises two specialists in a specialty relevant to the case in question, a third member from another specialty and any other co-opted members deemed necessary.

The MMA, on the other hand, is a representative body of the medical profession. Its Ethics Committee considers complaints by its members or members of the public. The Constitution of the MMA empowers it to expel its members in accordance with the procedure prescribed by the Code of Ethics and Rules of the Ethics Committee (MMA 1997).

Membership of the MMA is open to medical practitioners in both private and public sectors. It is financially strong, self-funded and owns properties. Many of its members are from the influential elite of society (see MMA 1999a). As an indication of relative strength, the MMA's secretariat is staffed by 25 people of whom four are medical practitioners, in comparison to the MMC's secretariat, which is staffed by seven people including two medical officers. The MMA has wide influence, for example the MMA-established fee schedule, which is annually reviewed and revised, is used by most private hospitals and private practitioners.

The MMA has a close relationship with the government – it names representatives to sit on various government boards, such as the Atomic Energy Licensing Board, and the organization is often consulted by government agencies on issues pertaining to health such as in the Health Dialogue Council 1998 and the Budget Council 1999 (MMA 1999a). Given these resources and political influence, the MMA is placed in a very influential position.

The nine members of the MMA Ethics Committee are elected from among the registered members of the medical profession (MMA 1997). As with the PICs and the MOH Board of Inquiry, there are no lay members or representatives of advocacy groups or other stakeholders in this disciplinary committee.

Channels for complaints

The power of the MMC lies in its control of the registers for licensing medical professionals since it can de-register, temporarily or permanently, those found unfit to perform their professional duties. It published a statement on Medical Ethics in 1975, replaced by the Code of Professional Conduct in 1987 (MMC 1987), which is similar to that issued by the UK General

Medical Council. The code outlines minimum standards. Breaches of these standards are referred to as 'infamous conduct in professional respect' or 'serious professional misconduct'. The MMA produced its own Ethical Code in 1998, similar to that of the MMC. It includes brief guidelines on good medical practice, the relationship of doctors with other professionals, dealings with commercial undertakings, advertising and canvassing, and setting up practices (MMA 1999b).

Beyond these two codes, however, there is not much else that regulates the clinical competence of practising doctors to ensure that doctors keep up with developments in their area, or to ensure doctors, particularly those in the private sector, do not slacken in their performance. There are no other specific guidelines to define the minimum benchmark of an acceptable standard of competence. In the public sector, the government addresses this issue by sending government doctors overseas for training and to attend conferences, while most public hospitals and teaching hospitals have adopted medical audit, whereby doctors of the specialty or department meet to review complicated cases, deaths or unusual cases. The aim is for the doctors to learn from each other and improve the quality of service.

The MMA: complaints by colleagues and peers

The MMA considers complaints about professional conduct of its members through its Ethics Committee, which is empowered to investigate and take action, as it deems fit, on complaints about breach of ethics by members of the Association (MMA 1997). Following investigation, it may decide that (i) the case be dismissed; (ii) the doctor has committed an error of judgment but the conduct does not call for censure; (iii) the doctor be censured; (iv) a recommendation be made to the MMA for expulsion from its membership; or (v) a complaint be made to the Malaysian Medical Council, in which case, the Ethics Committee will act as a complainant by filing a report to the MMC for further action.

The report 'The handling of complaints against doctors' (Allen *et al.* 1996) provides a useful dichotomy for assigning complaints to (i) those primarily of professional interest (e.g. unacceptable behaviour) but not principally detrimental to the medical treatment of patients, and (ii) those primarily concerned with the public interest (the personal behaviour of doctors towards patients which either lead to criminal convictions or raise issues of serious professional misconduct that relate principally to the medical treatment of patients).

In the 10 years commencing 1987/88, 43.5 per cent of complaints received were on issues which may be categorized as primarily of professional interest, with the largest number being concerned with advertising, while 56.5 per cent of complaints were on issues of public interest, with the largest number concerning 'clarification and advice' (Table 2.2). Among the issues categorized as primarily of professional interest, complaints relating

Table 2.2 Number of complaints received by the Malaysian Medical Association Ethics Committee, 1987–1997

Complaint/Year	87/88	88/89	89/90	90/91	91/92	92/93	93/94	94/95	95/96	96/97	Total
Primarily of professional interest											
Advertising	39	24	14	17	15	6	11	8	8	16	158
Exorbitant charges	2	2	6	9	9	5	4	10	6	12	65
Medical certificate	2	2	2	2	1	5	7	5	6	4	36
Total	43	28	22	28	25	16	22	23	20	32	259 (43.5%)
Primarily of public interest											
Unsatisfactory treatment	15	14	8	12	17	5	1	4	9	4	89
Alleged negligence	—	—	10	4	4	6	15	6	4	8	57
Clarification/advice	15	12	8	13	10	11	19	10	11	16	125
Unprofessional conduct	—	—	3	—	14	4	6	6	4	4	41
Refusal to label drugs	—	—	—	2	1	—	2	1	—	—	6
Refusal to give medical report	—	—	—	1	—	2	3	—	3	5	14
Refusal to make house call	—	—	—	—	—	2	—	—	3	—	5
Total	30	26	29	32	46	30	46	27	34	37	337 (56.5%)
Grand total	73	54	51	60	71	46	68	50	54	69	596 (100%)
Cases referred to MMC	11	7	10	5	—	1	—	—	2	1	37

Source: Adapted from various MMA Annual Reports.

principally to personal behaviour of doctors which could raise serious professional misconduct were fewer in comparison to those pertaining to advertisement. Regulation of advertisements might deter quacks from advertising; however, it may also reduce competition between medical service providers. This sentiment seems to be raised by many interviewees from the advocacy groups and also from among doctors interviewed.

The MMC: complaints by the public

The MMC's primary mode of regulating the profession is by maintaining the register of qualified medical practitioners, so that the public may be able to distinguish to whom they may safely go for advice and treatment. However, the MMC has not established an inspectorate to carry out its responsibilities by ensuring, for example, that those registered with the MMC are practising in accordance with the conditions on their licensing certificates and that they practise competently. According to some doctors and a CEO of a private hospital interviewed, practitioners can continue to practise incompetently as long as they are not caught. The authorities are alerted about breaches in the standard of competence only when a complaint is lodged.

The MMC receives complaints from many sources, including written complaints and those made by telephone or through hospitals. Complaints made by readers writing to newspapers are also followed up by the MMC. Following a complaint to the MMC, a PIC is convened to inquire into it. Of the three PICs, one is specially assigned to look into matters pertaining to advertisements, whilst the other two look into matters of ethics and conduct. The conduct of disciplinary inquiries is governed by the Medical Regulations 1974 and guided by the Code of Professional Conduct. The PICs can summarily dismiss an allegation if it is found to be unsustainable (Medical Regulations 1974). If a PIC finds there are grounds to support a charge it may recommend an inquiry by the MMC.

In conducting investigations, the MMC usually goes by the decisions of the PIC. Therefore, the first hearing of a case before the PIC is crucial. However, the decision is by a majority (Medical Regulation 1974), with no right to a dissenting opinion. Any person who is aggrieved by the decision of the MMC may appeal to the High Court (Medical Act 1971). Ranjan (1998) argues that it would be extremely difficult to set aside the findings or decision of the tribunal unless it can be shown that there is a substantial error of law or procedure, or that the findings are inconsistent with the evidence.

However, as emphasized by an interviewee from the MMC, this body deals with complaints of ethics and professional behaviour, not cases of malpractice or negligence, as cited from its Code of Professional Conduct:

> The Council is not ordinarily concerned with *errors in diagnosis or treatment, or with the kind of matters which give rise to action in the civil courts*

for negligence, unless the practitioner's conduct in the case has involved such a disregard of his professional responsibility to his patients or such a neglect of his professional duties as to raise a question of infamous conduct in a professional respect.

(MMC 1987: 12, emphasis added)

Between 1993 and 1994, from a total of 18 cases that were summarily dismissed, 13 were related to medical incompetence or neglect of professional responsibilities. The cases were summarily dismissed on the grounds that those complaints were not ethical matters (MMC *Annual Reports* 1993 and 1994). The complainants were advised that they could pursue the matter before other forums, such as the civil courts (MMC 1994: 22).

Table 2.3 indicates the number and nature of complaints received by the MMC from 1986–1994. According to two PIC members, a significant number of complaints received by the MMC were from the medical professionals themselves, with some referred by the Ethics Committee of the MMA. As in the case of complaints received by the MMA, most complaints from medical professionals were related to advertisements, and these number more than those related principally to the personal behaviour of doctors.

Of 246 complaints received by the MMC, 95 (38.6 per cent) were primarily of professional interest, 94 (38.2 per cent) were primarily of public interest and 57 (23.2 per cent) were obscure cases. Out of the 95 complaints of professional interest, 60 (24.4 per cent of the total of 246 complaints) pertained to advertising. On the other hand, out of the 94 complaints of public interest, only 11 complaints (4.5 per cent of the total of 246 complaints) pertained to incompetence. This gives the impression that significant resources in terms of time and manpower have been allocated for issues of professional interest rather than for issues of public interest.

The MOH: doctors in the public sector

Complaints about doctors in public hospitals and clinics are dealt with by the MOH Board of Inquiry at the state level. Following investigations by the Board of Inquiry, a report is sent to the ministerial level – the Medico-legal Unit for complaints on doctors in public hospitals and the Public Health Division of the MOH for complaints against the government's health clinics. At the ministerial level, the report of the findings is then submitted to the Disciplinary Board for its action.

The Medico-legal Unit of the MOH handles disciplinary cases as well as cases filed in court against the government hospitals, the MOH or government doctors. Apart from these, there were also cases that were obviously medical negligence, which were settled out of court. From 1993 to 2002, there were 102 medico-legal cases involving compensation of some RM6,490,649.[16]

Table 2.3 Number of complaints received by the Malaysian Medical Council, 1986–1994

Nature of complaints	1986	1987	1988	1989	1990	1991	1992	1993	1994	Total
Primarily of professional interest										
Advertising	17	8	6	7	7	3	2	3	7	60
Association with unregistered and/or unqualified persons	3	5	1	2	1	1	3	3	2	21
False claim/medical reports (including selling of medical certificates)	0	3	1	3	0	0	0	4	3	14
Total	20	16	8	12	8	4	5	10	12	95 (38.6%)
Primarily of public interest										
Abuse of relationship with patients/relatives	1	0	2	0	0	0	1	0	2	6
Prescribing drugs without care and control, inclusive of poison item	1	5	4	0	0	0	0	0	2	12
Neglect/disregard of professional responsibilities	4	3	0	7	8	7	14	4	4	51
Convicted by court	0	2	0	0	0	1	1	1	1	6
Incompetent to practise	—	—	—	—	—	—	—	7	4	11
Standard of care/management	—	—	—	—	—	—	—	5	3	8
Total	6	10	6	7	8	8	16	17	16	94 (38.2%)
Others	3	4	1	10	7	7	9	10	6	57 (23.2%)
Grand Total	29	30	15	29	23	19	30	37	34	246 (100%)

Source: Malaysian Medical Council, *Annual Reports* 1993 and 1994.

The courts

Medical negligence cases may be filed in court against public or private practitioners and providers. Information on the number of private cases settled out of court or private cases brought to court is, however, unobtainable. Cases brought to the civil court can take up to seven years to be settled, and many private practitioners and private hospitals usually settle their cases out of court to avoid bad publicity. This was confirmed in the interviews conducted with managers of private hospitals, and with lawyers who deal with medico-legal cases. An out-of-court settlement is not made public. Hence, colleagues do not necessarily know about the alleged malpractice and are therefore not discouraged from referring patients.

According to an advocate and solicitor, it can be very difficult to establish medical negligence. First, the courts recognize that there are differences of opinion in the medical profession, and so long as the actions taken are in accordance with the standard of an informed body of medical opinion, the doctor cannot be held negligent. Second, for the plaintiff to succeed, it must be shown that the injury was foreseeable at the time that the breach of duty was committed. This would depend on the state of medical knowledge about the patient at the time of the incident. A frequent problem is that many patients would already have been suffering from some pre-existing ailment at the time of being seen or treated by the doctor. As such, it would be difficult to say if the injury that was the subject of the complaint was caused by the doctor's action.

Ranjan (1998) observes that in Malaysia, patients often face difficulties as the law relating to disclosure of and access to their medical records is inadequate for them to obtain a complete clinical picture of their case and to obtain expert opinion before their case goes to court. This situation is exacerbated by the doctor's ethical and legal duty of confidentiality:

> A practitioner may not improperly disclose information which he obtains in confidence from or about a patient.
>
> *(The Code of Professional Conduct of the MMC 1987,*
> paragraph 2.22)

According to Ranjan (1998) and another legal specialist interviewed, medico-legal cases in Malaysia are on the rise but there are no official statistics. The majority of the claims are filed against doctors in the private sector, with an average of approximately 13–15 per cent of the claims filed annually being against government doctors.

Channels for patients' grievances

A joint meeting of principal office bearers of the MMA, the Malaysian Dental Association (MDA), the Bar Council and the Medico-legal Society was reactivated in October 1998 to provide a channel for communication between doctors, dentists and lawyers. The joint meeting occurs every six months to discuss matters affecting doctors, dentists and lawyers, and, in particular, problems doctors face when they are required to attend court as witnesses. It was noted that lawyers also faced problems in obtaining the services of doctors to provide a medical opinion or to attend court as witness as 'most doctors were not prepared to come forward to give medical evidence against another doctor' (Medico-legal Society 1999: 10–11).

There are no organizations in Malaysia specifically concerned with patients' problems or with victims of malpractice, such as the 'Victims of Medical Accidents in Britain'. Aggrieved parties have not attempted to work as a group to pursue justice from the regulatory institutions of the medical profession. Individual victims most often make use of newspapers to publicize their complaints. There is no institutional support or channel for patients who need to utilize the legal system to consult on their cases except to rely on their counsel.

The Patients' Charter, which states the right to redress of grievances, has not been effective and lacks supportive sanctions. According to the President of the Federation of Malaysian Consumers Associations (FOMCA), the Patients' Charter is not effective because of the absence of a platform to address health matters. He explained that there is no entity that deals with grievances on health matters, nor is there institutional support from the government's health sector institutions to handle such grievances, which can therefore only be redressed through a court of law. He added that although the Patients' Charter was embraced by consumer representatives more than seven years ago, it has been reported in the media that the Charter still has not seen formal implementation.[17]

In October 1999, the Ministry of Domestic Trade and Consumer Affairs became responsible for enforcing the newly passed Consumer Protection Act 1999 (Laws of Malaysia Act 599). The Act aims to protect consumers, especially those from the low-income group, by means of a tribunal comprising lawyers appointed by the Ministry. Under the Act, the tribunal would conduct civil claims of RM10,000 and below and would handle cases other than those linked to the medical profession. However, cases concerning medicines that are not officially registered as official medicines and not prescribed by hospitals can be taken to the tribunal. The omission of medical cases leaves consumers without redress to the tribunal and reliant upon private legal action.

Conclusions

Regulation involves complex issues of gathering and processing information. As we have seen in this study, the Malaysian Government has little information upon which to base a regulatory or control function, and its implementation of regulation has many weaknesses. For example, one of the basic aspects of regulation is the gathering of information on fees and charges, and this was lacking. Maintenance of records on the location of new facilities and a definition of what constitutes poor patients for the purpose of the social function of private hospitals were also lacking.

The government needs to establish effective systems of record-keeping in the private sector. The regulatory units within the MOH do not register private facilities routinely. Some facilities have been operating without a hospital licence. This examination of the regulation of both private health facilities and the medical profession has demonstrated the weak implementation of regulations. Despite the strong provisions of the Acts, the two cases uncovered by the Radiation Safety Unit indicate not only that its monitoring is at a low level, but also that its enforcement of the law is weak.

The predominance of the medical profession in the key regulatory institutions raises concerns about the objectivity of these agencies and the impartiality of judgments in the cases brought to their committees. It also suggests that the viewpoints of the doctors and their interests are influential. This bias seems to be reinforced by the procedures and processes of the MMC.

There is lack of proper machinery to deal with poorly performing doctors except through the courts of law. Cases of medical negligence or malpractice are excessively difficult to prove and may take years to settle. The inadequacy of laws relating to access to medical records exacerbates this problem.

In the cases reviewed, both the Radiation Safety Unit and the MMC tended to adopt a passive approach to regulation, waiting for the users to complain and failing to inform the general public of what is considered a breach of care, how and to whom to complain. The MMC appeared to play a minimal role in controlling poor conduct by professionals. Although the MMC organizes disciplinary hearings and the initiation of procedures to revoke the licence to practice, the use of such sanctions is rare.

The findings from this study of medical regulation suggest that there is a need for a review of the composition of the regulatory bodies and their disciplinary committees so that they represent all relevant stakeholders. Similarly, inspection needs to be more rigorous to ensure that those registered are practising according to conditions stipulated in the licensing certificates.

The broader social and cultural context is also an important influence on the effectiveness of government legislation. In Malaysia, the imbalance is marked; consumer protection laws and consumer voice are weak compared to the well-informed, organized medical profession. There are no organizations in Malaysia specifically concerned with patients' grievances or with victims of malpractices. There is no institutional support or channel to provide patients with legal guidance, unless they seek this privately. The Patients' Charter has not been effective and lacks sanctions. The Consumer Protection Act 1999 does not permit claims in cases linked to the medical profession. Consumers have little protection apart from the existing provision governing the licensing of medical professionals.

The findings suggest a number of ways to improve the functioning of the current regulatory environment. Adequate laws relating to disclosure and access of medical records are needed. The dominance of the medical profession in the regulatory bodies contributes to the general perception that it acts for its own interests. The government needs to institute a fair representation of interest groups in the professional regulatory bodies to ensure that their decisions are in the interests of both the professionals and the users. In this connection, consumers can play a significant role in promoting regulatory effectiveness, but the role needs to be developed within the context of a stronger regulatory framework.

Notes

1 This chapter draws from the author's doctoral dissertation, 'The private health sector in Malaysia: an assessment of government regulation', Institute of Development Studies at Sussex University, 2002.
2 In 1999, the year of the study, Kuala Lumpur had 43 private hospitals, the highest number in the country, and the state of Selangor had 40, the second highest number. The municipal councils in Selangor, of which the MPAJ is one, and the Kuala Lumpur City Hall have had more experience in regulating private hospitals than other local authorities in the country.
3 This company was involved in establishing the Damansara Specialist Hospital, a 140-bed hospital, also owned by KPJ.
4 There is considerable literature on 'regulatory capture' by interest groups – that regulation was designed initially to serve public interests, but over time, the regulatory agency is 'captured' and private goals then predominate. The theory emphasizes the role of interest groups in the formation of public policy. The proponents of this theory (Stigler 1971; Posner 1974; Peltzman 1976; Hancher 1990; Laffont and Tirole 1991) hypothesize that regulatory capture enables what would be a competitive industry to act as though it were a monopoly. Capture of the regulatory agency enables the industry to charge higher prices, restrict its output, increase its profits and protect itself from competitors (Posner 1974; Peltzman 1976; Laffont and Tirole 1991).
5 See the keynote address by Tan Sri Dato' Seri Ali Abul Hassan bin Suleiman, then Director-General of the Economic Planning Unit, in a seminar, 'The Future of Health Services in Malaysia', 19–20 October 1996, Kuala Lumpur. See also EPU (1996).
6 This Act was not implemented during the period that the research and writing of this chapter was undertaken. In the early part of 2006, it was announced that this Act will be implemented from 1 May 2006.
7 This would include rental of operation theatre, labour room/nursery, equipment such as monitors, ECG (electrocardiograms) and CTG (cardiotocograph, a procedure to measure the fetal heart rate and contractions in labour), ambulance, other personnel charges (nursing services, x-ray, on-call fees, physiotherapy) and sundry (consumables and procedure sets).
8 The number of complaints for previous years was not available.
9 Or intravenous urogram, where a dye injection is used to observe excretion by the kidneys.
10 Equivalent to US$26,315 (exchange rate: US$1.00 equivalent to RM3.80).
11 Equivalent to US$1,316 and US$789 respectively.
12 According to an MOH officer, there may be various reasons for this, for example the hospital's staff strength having been reduced but the number of beds being retained; the waiting period for the hospital licence to be released took too

long as it is dependent on the recommendation certificate from the Fire Services Department; the hospital staff did not have the Annual Practicing Licence; or the information in the application form was not complete.

13 Equivalent to US$263.
14 Equivalent to US$79,000.
15 The MMC and its PICs are dominated by male doctors. For example, at the time of this study, there were two female members out of the 17 members in the three PICs.
16 Equivalent to US$1,708,066.
17 In October 2000, consumers' representatives, including FOMCA and the Consumers International Regional Office for Asia and the Pacific (CIROAP) organized a National Consumers' Seminar. One of the items on the agenda was to re-examine ways to make the Charter an operational document (*The Sun*, Sun Valley Section, 21 October 2000).

References

Ali Abul Hassan bin Sulaiman (Tan Sri Dato' Seri), keynote address at the seminar 'The Future of Health Services in Malaysia', organized by the Malaysian Medical Association, 19–20 October 1996.

Allen, I., Perkins, E. and Witherspoon, S. (1996) 'The handling of complaints against doctors', report by Policy Studies Institute for the Racial Equality Group of the General Medical Council, London: Policy Studies Institute.

Economic Planning Unit (EPU) (1996) 'Policies and objectives under the Seventh Malaysia Plan', paper presented at the 1996 National Healthcare Conference, Kuala Lumpur, 13–14 June 1996.

Friedson, E. (1970a) *Professional Dominance: The Social Structure of Medical Care*, New York: Atherton Press.

—— (1970b) *Profession of Medicine: A Study in the Sociology of Applied Knowledge*, New York: Dodd Mead.

—— (1988a) *Professional Powers: A Study of the Institutionalization of Formal Knowledge*, London: University of Chicago Press.

—— (1988b) *Profession of Medicine*, 2nd edn, Chicago: University of Chicago Press.

Hancher, L. (1990) *Regulating for Competition*, Oxford: Clarendon Press.

Laffont, J.-J. and Tirole, J. (1991) 'The politics of government decision-making: a theory of regulatory capture', *Quarterly Journal of Economics* 106(4): 1089–127.

Malaysia (1993) *Mid-Term Review of the Sixth Malaysia Plan 1991–1995*, Kuala Lumpur: Percetakan Nasional Malaysia Berhad.

—— (1996) *Seventh Malaysia Plan, 1996–2000*, Kuala Lumpur: Economic Planning Unit, Prime Minister's Department, Malaysia.

Malaysian Medical Association (1997) *The Constitution, Articles and By-Laws*, Kuala Lumpur: Malaysian Medical Association.

—— (1999a) *Annual Report 1998/99*, Kuala Lumpur: Malaysian Medical Association.

—— (1999b) *Ethical Code*, Kuala Lumpur: Malaysian Medical Association.

Malaysian Medical Council (MMC) (1987) *Code of Professional Conduct*, Kuala Lumpur: Malaysian Medical Council.

—— (1993) *Annual Report*, Kuala Lumpur: Malaysian Medical Council.

—— (1994) *Annual Report*, Kuala Lumpur: Malaysian Medical Council.

Medico-legal Society (1999) *Annual Report 1998/1999*, Kuala Lumpur: Medico-legal Society, Malaysia.

Mills, A., Bennett, S. and Russel, S. (2001) *The Challenge of Health Sector Reform: What Must Governments Do?*, Basingstoke: Palgrave.

Peltzman, S.L. (1976) 'Towards a more general theory of regulation', *Journal of Law and Economics* 19(2): 211–40.

Posner, R.A. (1974) 'Theories of economic regulation', *Bell Journal of Economics and Management Sciences* 5(2): 335–58.

Ranjan, P.S. (1998) 'The law and practice relating to medical negligence', unpublished document, Malaysian Medical Association, May.

Rosenthal, G. and Newbrander, W. (1996) 'Public policy and private sector provision of health services', *International Journal of Health Planning Management* 11(3): 203–16.

Soderlund, N. and Tangcharoensathien, V. (2000) 'Health sector regulation: understanding the range of responses from government', *Health Policy and Planning* 15(4): 347–8.

Stigler, G.J. (1971) 'The theory of economic regulation', *Bell Journal of Economics and Management Sciences* 2: 3–21.

The Sun, Sun Valley Section, 21 October 2000, 'Healthcare at the crossroads: consumer representatives meet today to discuss implementation of proposals on such services'.

Malaysian laws and documents

Laws of Malaysia Act 43 Private Hospital Act 1971 and Regulations 1973.

Laws of Malaysia Act 50 Medical Act 1971 Medical Regulations 1974.

Laws of Malaysia Act 133 Uniform Building By-laws 1984 (Revised).

Laws of Malaysia Act 171 Local Government Act 1976.

Laws of Malaysia Act 172 Town & Country Planning Act 1976.

Laws of Malaysia Act 304 Atomic Energy Licensing Act 1984:
Radiation Protection (Basic Safety Standards) Regulations 1988.
Radiation Protection (Licensing) Regulations 1986.
Radiation Protection (Transport) Regulations 1989.

Laws of Malaysia Act 586 Private Healthcare Facilities and Services Act 1998.

Laws of Malaysia Act 599 Consumer Protection Act 1999.

The Town Planning Department of MPAJ, *Panduan permohonan kelulusan perancangan* (Guidelines for planning approval), enforced on 20 May 1993 in accordance with the Town Planning Act 1976.

Majlis Perbandaran Ampang Jaya (MPAJ) 'Guidelines on application for development order', enforced on 1 January 1997.

—— *Sijil layak menduduki* ('Certificate of fitness for building occupation').

Dewan Bandaraya Kuala Lumpur (DBKL) *Panduan pengemukaan pelan untuk kelulusan DBKL* (Guidelines to submit plan for approval by Kuala Lumpur City Hall).

Ministry of Health (MOH) *Borang A – Permohonan untuk lesen/pembaharuan lesen bagi hospital swasta, peraturan 3(2)* [Form A – Application form for a licence/renewal of a licence for a private hospital, regulation 3(2)].

—— *Senarai semak untuk pemeriksaan di hospital swasta* (Checklist for inspection of private hospitals).

—— *Borang permohonan untuk mendapatkan, meminda atau membaharui lesen (Peraturan 13 dan 14) LPTA3* [Application form to obtain, amend or renew licence (Schedule 13 and 14) LPTA3].

3 Rising health care costs
The contradictory responses of the Malaysian state

Phua Kai Lit

All developed nations are facing the challenge of rising health care costs today. One extreme example is the United States where total health spending as a percentage of the gross domestic product (GDP) rose from 6.9 per cent in 1970, to 13.3 per cent in 2000, 14.1 per cent in 2001 and then to 14.9 per cent in 2002. Between 2001 and 2002, national health expenditures rose 9.3 per cent to reach the astonishing figure of US$1.6 trillion (Sethi and Fronstin 2004). Many West European governments also perceive rising health care costs to be a major problem and have responded by introducing various cost containment strategies (Mosslalos and Le Grand 1999).

As a result of phenomena such as population ageing and changes in disease patterns (especially in the middle income countries), developing nations are also facing the challenge of rising health care costs (Schieber and Maeda 1997). It has been claimed that Malaysia is also being affected by this challenge (Raj 2000; Ministry of Health 2002; Rohaizat Yon 2002). In fact, one of the reasons used to support privatization in Malaysia (including privatization of health care) was that it would help to relieve the financial burden on the government.[1] The Malaysian government has also declared that it plans to gradually reduce its role in the provision (and therefore financing) of health care services in the country while increasing its regulatory and enforcement activities (Malaysia 1996).

This chapter will focus on health care financial trends in Malaysia with the following objectives in mind: (i) to critically analyse Malaysian health care financial trends to determine if a problem really exists, (ii) to discuss possible factors that may be affecting these trends, and (iii) to discuss the reasons for the often contradictory responses of the Malaysian state to this articulated problem.

Are health care costs rising?

First of all, it is necessary to determine if there is actually a problem with rising health care costs in Malaysia. The estimation of a nation's total annual health care expenditure is fraught with difficulties. Definitions of health care expenditure can differ by country. Also, health expenditure data – especially data related to private sector spending – are often unavailable, incomplete or unreliable (Schieber and Maeda 1997). This is certainly true of data pertaining to private sector health spending in Malaysia (Rozita Halina Tun Hussein 2000).

Trends in government health expenditure

Financial data from the Ministry of Health (MOH) can be analysed to show trends in public spending over time. These trends may be taken as a proxy for trends in total public sector spending on health (bearing in mind that other ministries such as the Ministry of Defence and the Ministry of Education also engage in health-related spending).

Table 3.1 shows that costs seem to be rising for the Malaysian government in terms of the ever increasing operating budget, development budget and overall budget of the MOH.[2] Indeed, when the figures for 'per cent increase over the previous year' are examined, it can be seen that they can be quite significant. For example, there was an increase of 25.2 per cent for the 1990 overall budget as compared to the 1989 budget, and an increase of 22.6 per cent for the 1996 overall budget as compared to the 1995 overall budget. When the figures for the operating budget are examined, one can see that year to year increases (in percentage terms) can be quite significant.

The impact of the Asian financial crisis of the late 1990s on Malaysian government expenditure is reflected by no increase in the MOH budget for 1999 as compared to 1998 (Table 3.1). However, the recent figures (1990 onwards) for the MOH budget as a percentage of the national budget are relatively constant and range from 5.22 per cent to 6.61 per cent.[3] This implies that although the MOH budget keeps rising over time, the national budget has also been rising and the government has been allocating a relatively constant share of the national budget to the MOH. Thus, although some will argue that the government is facing a problem of rising health care costs in the public sector, it can also be argued that it is not really a problem as the Malaysian state can actually afford it. Analysis of the data calculated in terms of constant (inflation adjusted) *ringgit* support these conclusions (see the last two columns of Table 3.1).

Recent total health expenditure and health care cost inflation

The World Bank has been encouraging its member states to develop a system of national health accounts to facilitate health policy and planning (as well as to facilitate comparisons of expenditure on health between countries). Table 3.2 presents data extracted from Malaysia's national health accounts showing that total health expenditure (nominal costs), both in per capita terms as well as a percentage of GDP, has been rising steadily over time. Nevertheless, total health expenditure as a percentage of GDP remains

Table 3.1 Ministry of Health allocated budget, and health care cost inflation, Malaysia, 1980–2001

Year	MOH budget (nominal RM)	Percentage increase over previous year	Percentage of national budget	MOH operating budget (nominal RM)	Percentage increase over previous year	MOH development budget (nominal RM)	Percentage increase over previous year	MOH budget (constant 2000 RM)[1]	Percentage increase over previous year[1]	Health care cost inflation[1,2]
1980	895,579,857	—	5.27	759,307,400	—	136,272,457	—	1,749,179,408	—	—
1981	1,011,686,375	12.9	4.38	891,918,100	17.5	119,768,275	−12.1	1,800,153,692	2.9	9.1
1982	1,075,043,070	6.3	3.35	924,676,700	3.7	150,366,379	25.5	1,809,836,818	0.5	4.8
1983	1,034,468,227	−3.8	3.58	856,126,000	−7.4	178,342,227	18.6	1,679,331,537	−7.2	13.7
1984	1,126,810,440	8.9	4.07	966,738,600	12.9	160,071,840	−10.2	1,757,894,602	4.7	1.1
1985	1,256,333,300	11.5	4.30	1,094,117,000	13.2	162,205,300	1.3	1,953,862,052	11.2	2.4
1986	1,273,622,440	1.4	4.13	1,114,345,000	1.8	159,277,440	−1.8	1,968,504,544	0.8	1.6
1987	1,174,786,100	−7.8	4.29	1,081,695,700	−2.9	93,090,400	−41.6	1,807,363,230	−8.2	−0.3
1988	1,264,729,700	7.7	4.50	1,142,741,900	5.6	121,987,800	31	1,898,993,543	5.1	1.4
1989	1,470,384,550	16.3	5.00	1,248,230,600	9.2	222,153,950	82.1	2,146,546,788	13.0	1.7
1990	1,840,321,780	25.2	5.51	1,335,325,500	6.9	504,996,280	127.3	2,606,688,073	21.4	2.7
1991	2,178,672,370	18.4	5.66	1,492,222,400	11.7	686,449,970	35.9	2,960,152,676	13.6	5.3
1992	2,487,821,000	14.2	5.47	1,798,404,800	20.5	689,416,200	0.4	3,226,745,784	9.0	3.5
1993	2,513,981,010	1.1	5.69	1,964,507,100	9.2	549,473,910	−20.3	3,146,409,274	−2.5	5.1
1994	2,462,149,700	−2.1	5.22	2,085,066,900	6.1	377,082,300	−31.4	2,973,610,748	−5.5	3.5
1995	2,793,731,000	13.5	5.73	2,365,765,000	13.5	427,966,000	13.5	3,259,896,149	9.6	3.1
1996	3,424,778,000	22.6	6.17	2,880,134,000	21.7	544,644,000	27.3	3,861,080,945	18.4	3.6
1997	3,786,834,900	10.6	6.31	3,236,047,600	12.4	578,538,000	6.2	4,161,357,032	7.8	3.7
1998	4,237,960,000	11.9	6.61	3,494,774,000	8.0	743,186,000	31.1	4,423,757,828	6.3	6.1
1999	4,237,960,000	0	6.61	3,494,774,000	0.0	743,186,000	0.0	4,302,497,461	−2.7	3.0
2000	4,931,315,300	16.4	6.32	4,023,162,300	15.1	908,153,000	22.2	4,931,315,300	14.6	2.0
2001	5,765,553,410	16.9	6.33	4,545,407,400	13.0	1,220,146,010	34.4	5,685,950,108	15.3	2.9

Source: Ministry of Health (Annual Report, Health Facts, various years), Bank Negara Malaysia (2004).

Notes
1 Author's calculations from Malaysian Government data (Ministry of Health Annual Report, Health Facts, various years and Bank Negara Malaysia 2004).
2 Percentage increase in consumer price index for medical care and health expenses over the previous year.

Table 3.2 Total health expenditure and health care cost inflation, Malaysia, 1997–2003

Year	Per capita at international dollar rate[1]	Percentage increase over previous year	Percentage of GDP[1]	Health care cost inflation[2]
1997	237	—	2.8	3.7
1998	237	0.0	3.0	6.1
1999	257	8.4	3.1	3.0
2000	297	15.6	3.3	2.0
2001	345	16.2	3.8	2.9
2002	—	—	—	2.4
2003	—	—	—	1.7

Source: World Bank (2002) and author's calculations from Malaysian government data (Bank Negara Malaysia 2004).

Notes
[1] Data extracted from the World Bank's National Health Accounts; available for Malaysia from 1997 onward only.
[2] Percentage increase in consumer price index for medical care and health expenses over the previous year, figures for 1997–2001 repeated from Table 3.1.

relatively small (3.8 per cent of GDP in 2001, for example) and changes in the consumer price index (CPI) for medical care and health expenses, although relatively high in 1997, and particularly high in 1998, appear to be relatively low after 2000.

Therefore, when total health expenditure (that is, the sum of private and public sector spending on health) in Malaysia is considered, one can argue either way: (i) that health care costs are rising steadily or (ii) that rising health care costs are not a real problem since total health expenditure remains a small and relatively constant percentage of GDP, and annual changes in the CPI for medical care and health expenses have not been particularly high except during the early 1980s and during certain years, notably 1990–1991, 1992–1993 and 1997–1998 (Tables 3.1 and 3.2).

Comparison with other countries

Where does Malaysia stand in terms of total spending on health as compared to other developing nations? To answer this question, one can compare Malaysia's total health expenditure with the expenditure of other nations of comparative wealth (as measured by conventional economic indicators such as gross national income per capita). In the comparison, Malaysia's health care spending actually lies towards the lower end of the range (Table 3.3).[4] Some may therefore argue that Malaysia is underspending on health relative to other countries at similar levels of 'economic development'.

Table 3.3 Government health expenditure and total health expenditure in 2001 for countries with comparable gross national income per capita (in purchasing power parity international dollars)

Country	GNI per capita (2002)	Government health expenditure (as % of total government expenditure)	Total health expenditure (as % of GDP)
South Africa	9810	10.9	8.6
Chile	9420	12.7	7.0
Latvia	9190	9.1	6.4
Trinidad/Tobago	9000	6.4	4.0
Mexico	8800	16.7	6.1
Costa Rica	8560	19.5	7.2
Malaysia	8500	6.5	3.8
Russia	8080	10.7	5.4
Botswana	7740	7.6	6.6
Uruguay	7710	14.9	10.9
Brazil	7450	8.8	7.6
Bulgaria	7030	9.3	4.8
Thailand	6890	11.6	3.7
Namibia	6880	12.2	6.7

Source: World Bank (2002).

However, it should also be pointed out that, taking into account Malaysia's major health indicators such as infant mortality rate and life expectancy at birth, the country is not doing too badly in terms of outcome measures in relation to health spending. One can also argue that 'health' is affected by more than just health care spending alone. Proper nutrition, a clean water supply, proper sanitation, decent housing, basic education, safe jobs that pay reasonable wages, a healthy environment, amongst other variables, are also major determinants of the health of the people.

Furthermore, not all health spending constitutes investment in human capital – medically unnecessary health spending, such as plastic and reconstructive surgery for aesthetic purposes, would be a form of consumption of scarce resources with significant opportunity costs (Rosen 2004). It would therefore be wiser for advocates of higher public sector health spending to call for more spending on specific types of health care (and other social services) that have been shown to benefit population sub-groups that are more vulnerable to ill health than to call for more spending on health care per se by the government.

Relative performance of the Malaysian health system

Recently, the World Health Organization (WHO) attempted to rank national health systems in terms of performance with respect to 'responsiveness' and

Table 3.4 'Health system responsiveness' and 'fairness of contribution to the health system' for 13 countries with comparable gross national product per capita (in purchasing power parity international dollars)

Country	GNP per capita 2001, PPP (international dollars)	Responsiveness of health systems 1997	Ranking for responsiveness 1997 (range is 1 to 191)	Fairness of financial contribution to health system 1997	Ranking for fairness 1997 (range is 1 to 191)
Antigua & Barbuda	9870	0.994	39–42	0.919	116–20
S. Africa	9510	0.844	147	0.904	142–3
Chile	9420	0.918	103	0.864	168
Poland	9280	0.970	65	0.896	150–1
Trinidad & Tobago	9080	0.909	108–9	0.945	69
Botswana	8810	0.905	111–12	0.934	89–95
Mexico	8770	0.909	108–9	0.903	144
Uruguay	8710	0.981	53–7	0.968	35–6
Russian Federation	8660	0.943	86–7	0.802	185
Croatia	8440	0.945	83	0.925	108–11
Malaysia	8340	0.975	62	0.917	122–3
Costa Rica	8080	0.943	86–7	0.948	64–5
Belarus	8030	0.987	45–7	0.937	84–6

Source: World Bank (2002) and World Health Organization (2000).

'fairness of financial contribution' among other things (WHO 2000). Although the effort has been criticized (Wagstaff 2001), the results are worth noting.

In Table 3.4, Malaysia and 12 other countries with roughly similar per capita gross national product (GNP) are compared in terms of performance on the WHO's 'responsiveness of health systems' index.[5] An index score of 1.0 means that there is complete equality of responsiveness to all social groups (such as poor people, women, old people and indigenous groups) within a particular country. Each of the 191 member states of the WHO, including the 13 countries listed in Table 3.4, were also given a ranking (ranging from 1 to 191) based on the index score.

The responsiveness index score, together with the ranks, shows that the health systems of Antigua & Barbuda, Poland, Uruguay, Malaysia and Belarus appear to be more responsive to the needs of less privileged social groups than the health systems of the remaining countries. Malaysia is ranked at position 62 among the 191 WHO member countries.

Table 3.4 also compares the selected countries in terms of the 'fairness of financial contribution to the health system' index.[6] An index of 1.0 means that all households within a particular country contribute equally (financially) to the national health system of that country. Each country is also assigned a ranking ranging from 1 to 191, based on its scoring on this index.

This table shows that in Trinidad & Tobago, Botswana, Uruguay, Costa Rica and Belarus, there is greater equity in the distribution of the burden of financing health care, that is, if one defines equity as all households contributing equally to the financing of the health system. The rankings of these countries are notably better than the rankings of the other countries in the table. Here, Malaysia does not fare as well and is ranked at positions 122–3.

Possible reasons for 'rising health care costs' in Malaysia

Worldwide, the following factors have been identified as potential contributors to increases in total health expenditure over time: new medical technology, population ageing, changes in disease patterns towards greater prevalence of chronic and degenerative diseases, the phenomenon of emerging and re-emerging diseases (such as tuberculosis in HIV/AIDS patients), 'medicalization' of social problems, and rising expectations of the public with respect to service standards (including the 'hotel services' aspect of health care in both the private and public sectors).

Kornai and McHale (2000) note that for the rich OECD (Organization for Economic Cooperation and Development) countries, per capita health spending is strongly related to per capita income. Spending is also related to the elderly dependency rate but the relationship is less strong. In the case of the post-communist countries of central and eastern Europe, even though health spending as a share of GDP seems to be below the OECD average, they conclude that there is evidence of above normal health spending in most of the countries when income and demographics are taken into consideration. Thus, there is the empirical observation that as the national income of a country increases over time, there is the tendency to spend more and more on health care. However, Kanavos and Mossialos (1999) are sceptical. They argue that although this relationship exists, significant problems in the measurement of both health spending and GDP render the observed relationship misleading for health policy.

In Malaysia, we have noted earlier that 'rising health care costs' in the public sector are largely reflected by the absolute increases in the size of MOH budget allocations, whether in nominal or constant *ringgit*, whilst government health spending as a proportion of the total national budget has remained relatively constant.[7] Total health expenditure for public and private sectors combined, however, has been rising steadily in the five years between 1997 and 2001, both in per capita terms as well as a percentage of GDP. Nevertheless, as a percentage of GDP, it remains relatively low when compared to other countries.

A major contributor to the rising health care costs in Malaysia is the inadequately regulated introduction and proliferation of expensive new medical technology in the private sector. For example, the number of private sector magnetic resonance imaging (MRI) scanners in the Klang Valley alone is more than in the whole of Australia (Abdul Razak Chik 2000). Such new medical technology may not only be expensive to purchase – maintenance costs can be significant and highly trained personnel may be required in order to use the equipment properly. The opportunity costs associated with such technology may be quite significant.

The continued growth of the private sector, as exemplified by the increase in the number of private hospitals and private beds, will affect total health expenditure in Malaysia by stimulating the import of costly, advanced medical technology which not only contributes to rising costs but also distorts the allocation of resources between preventive care and curative care, and between primary care and tertiary care.

Population ageing, that is, the percentage of elderly people in the population rising over time primarily because of falling birth rates, has been singled out as another important reason for rising health care costs in Malaysia. However, this is probably a less important factor at the moment because the percentage of elderly people in the Malaysian population is still under 5 per cent, although it is rising over time. According to the National Population and Housing Census carried out in 2000 (Malaysia 2001a), the percentage of Malaysians over age 65 was only 3.9 per cent of the total population of 23.27 million. Nevertheless, the Population Division of the Department of Economic and Social Affairs of the United Nations has projected that this will increase to 9 per cent in 2025 and 15.4 per cent in 2050 (United Nations 2001).

A more significant contributor to rising health care costs is the epidemiological transition currently underway, that is, the shift in disease patterns from acute infectious diseases to more chronic and degenerative diseases. This, however, does not mean that infectious diseases are no longer a problem in Malaysia. In recent years, there have been rising numbers of people with diseases such as HIV/AIDS, and the appearance of new diseases such as Nipah virus and re-emerging diseases such as tuberculosis in HIV/AIDS patients. In September 2004, the cumulative number of HIV positive cases in Malaysia amounted to 61,486, and the cumulative number of AIDS patients was 8,955. During the period from 1986 to September 2004, there were a total of 6,665 deaths as a result of AIDS (Department of Public Health 2004).

Finally, rising expectations of the public can also increase health care costs. For example, although improved 'hotel services' do not contribute strictly to better treatment and management of disease, they are often introduced because they make the patients feel more comfortable. The government has been both 'upgrading' and building more hospitals and it has also been increasing the number of hospital beds. Between 1995 and 2002, public hospital beds increased from 26,896 to 29,068 (MOH, various years). The number of hospitals and hospital beds in the private sector has also been rising over time. Between 1995 and 2002, the number of private medical institutions rose from 197 to 211, and the number of private beds from 7,192 to 9,849 (MOH, various years). These have undoubtedly added to costs since hospitals are both labour-intensive and capital-intensive institutions.

Contradictory responses of the Malaysian state

The policy of privatization of public services was first introduced in Malaysia in 1983. The Economic Planning Unit (EPU)'s definition of privatization is 'the transfer to the private sector of activities and functions which have traditionally rested with the public sector' and it can involve any of the following components: management responsibility, assets or the right to use assets, and personnel (EPU website). Privatization has also affected the government health sector in Malaysia. In the Seventh Malaysia Plan published in 1996, the government announced its intention to corporatize and privatize Malaysia's public hospitals and medical service (Malaysia 1996). In the Malaysian context, 'corporatization' includes a change in status of hospital personnel such that they are no longer considered to be civil servants and the incorporation of formerly public hospitals as government-owned but profit-oriented entities (Barraclough 2000).

Government economic planners claim that corporatization and privatization of public services would lead to gains in efficiency, induce corporations to expand through greater utilization of growth opportunities, relieve the administrative and financial burden of the Malaysian government, and also increase *Bumiputera* participation in the corporate sector (EPU website). In the case of the health sector, the government also presented the view that corporatization would allow the retention of experienced personnel through the payment of more competitive wages. Thus, institutions such as the Institut Jantung Negara (National Heart Institute), and teaching hospitals such as the University Hospital, Hospital Universiti Sains Malaysia and Hospital Universiti Kebangsaan Malaysia were corporatized while the Government Medical Store and hospital support services of the Ministry of Health such as cleansing services, linen and laundry, biomedical engineering maintenance, facilities engineering maintenance and clinical waste management were privatized and contracted out (Chan 2003).

Critics have pointed out that after the privatization of hospital support services, the costs of these services to the government rose from RM143 million in 1996 to RM468.5 million in 1997 (more than a threefold increase after only one year of privatization) and to RM507.9 million in 1999 (Chan 2000). Similarly, privatization of the Government Medical Store resulted in a 3.3 fold increase in prices. It has also been pointed out that many of the contracts have been awarded to private companies that are politically well-connected (Chan 2003). Such rent-seeking phenomena have also been documented with respect to other sectors of the Malaysian economy (Jomo 1995). The question here is whether changes in product or service quality after privatization are worth it in light of the much higher subsequent costs to the government (and to the Malaysian taxpayer).

Hospitals (whether public or private) are major contributors to total health expenditure. The increase in the number of hospitals and hospital beds in both the public and private sectors has earlier been noted. Thus, the government policy of upgrading or building more public hospitals as outlined in the Eighth Malaysia Plan (Malaysia 2001b) and the tolerance of the proliferation of private hospitals in the late 1990s is a contradictory response to alleged 'rising health care costs' in Malaysia on the part of the government (Barraclough 1997). However, it is interesting to note that the Minister of Health Dr Chua Soi Lek declared recently that the construction of nine hospitals under the Eighth Malaysia Plan has now been deferred and the RM10 billion which had been allocated for these hospitals will be used to build more training facilities in order to help alleviate the shortage of support staff in the existing hospitals instead (*The Star*, 2 July 2004).

From the analysis carried out in this chapter, it can be seen that Malaysian health policy (including the response to the trend of steadily rising health care costs) is not consistent in its objectives. While stating its concerns that health care costs are rising, the state nevertheless carries out policy that ostensibly leads to health care costs rising even more. It may be argued that the formulation and implementation of Malaysian health policy are affected and buffeted by factors such as ideological preferences (Phua 2001), rent-seeking, competition for political support (Barraclough 1999), bureaucratic politics and also by populist pressures, for example the establishment in 2002 of a National Health Welfare Fund to help the needy to pay their medical bills (*The Star*, 13 May 2004).

Thus, there has been an ideological preference for adopting a policy of privatization since the early 1980s. The corporatization of certain health-related public institutions and the privatization of the Government Medical Store as well as the contracting-out of hospital support services in the 1990s were accompanied by a rapid rise in costs.[8] Other examples of policy inconsistency include the suspension of ambitious plans formulated earlier to build more public hospitals. The influence of bureaucratic politics is indicated by the pattern of yearly increases in the total budget of the MOH coupled with the fact that this amount remains relatively consistent as a percentage of the national budget over time. The non-establishment of a nationwide health care funding scheme (partly to deal with the issue of rising health care costs) in spite of study after commissioned study by the government indicates the great interest of policy-makers in the issue but also their hesitancy and uncertainty about what to do next. All of these factors will continue to shape and reshape health policy in Malaysia.

Notes

1 From the Economic Planning Unit (EPU) website, webpage on history of privatization programme. Available at http://www.epu.jpm.my/New%20Folder/priva.htm (accessed 6 June 2005).

2 These data are based on annual budget allocations.
3 Interestingly enough, Table 3.1 shows that the MOH budget in nominal *ringgit* increased significantly in 1996 as compared to 1995, that is, from 5.73 per cent of the national budget in 1995 to 6.17 per cent in 1996. One may speculate that this could be due to the economic boom of the mid-1990s, coupled with the Malaysian general elections that took place in 1995.
4 Although there may be differences in how 'Government health expenditure' and 'Total health expenditure' are computed in different countries, there has been some standardization by the international agencies.
5 The index was calculated using the following methodology (WHO 2000: 147–8): 'Respondents in the key informants survey were asked to identify groups who were disadvantaged with regard to responsiveness. The number of times a particular group was identified as disadvantaged was used to calculate a key informant intensity score. Four groups had high . . . scores: poor people, women, old people, and indigenous groups or racially disadvantaged groups . . . The key informant intensity scores for these four groups were multiplied by the actual percentage of the population within these vulnerable groups in a country to calculate a simple measure of responsiveness inequality ranging from 0 to 1.'
6 Household financial contribution is defined as the ratio of total household expenditure spent on health above subsistence and the index is weighted highly on households that spend a very large portion of their income on health (WHO 2000).
7 This could be due to the phenomenon of budget planners responding to bureaucratic politics and keeping to a rule-of-thumb such as 'keep everyone happy by not rocking the budgetary boat', that is, by giving each Ministry a relatively constant percentage share of the National Budget each fiscal year.
8 This led to protests from non-governmental organizations such as the Citizens' Health Initiative. In response, the government delayed implementation of earlier plans to corporatize more public health-related institutions.

References

Abdul Razak Chik (2000) 'New prescription needed', *Malaysian Business*, 1 May: 30–3.
Bank Negara Malaysia (2004) Indeks Harga Pengguna/Consumer Price Index. Online. Available at <http://www.bnm.gov.my/files/publication/msb/2004/9/pdf/vi_12.pdf> (accessed 6 June 2005).
Barraclough, Simon (1997) 'The growth of corporate private hospitals in Malaysia: policy contradictions in health system pluralism', *International Journal of Health Services* 27(4): 643–59.
—— (1999) 'Constraints on the retreat from a welfare-orientated approach to public health care in Malaysia', *Health Policy* 47: 53–67.
—— (2000) 'The politics of privatization in the Malaysian health care system', *Contemporary Southeast Asia* 22(2): 340–59.
Chan, Chee Khoon (2000) 'Privatization, the state and healthcare reforms: global influences and local contingencies in Malaysia', paper presented at the Fourth GASPP Seminar on Global Social Policies and Social Rights, New Delhi, India, 8–10 November. Online. Available at <http://www.stakes.fi/gaspp/seminars/papers/pachan.pdf> (accessed 6 June 2005).
—— (2003) 'Privatizing the welfare state: health care reforms in Malaysia', *New Solutions* 13(1): 87–105.

Department of Public Health (2004) 'HIV infection, AIDS cases and AIDS death reported in Malaysia, 1986 to September 2004'. Online. Available at <http://dph.gov.my/aids/> (accessed 6 June 2005).

Economic Planning Unit (EPU) website, webpage on history of privatization programme. Online. Available at <http://www.epu.jpm.my/New%20Folder/priva.htm> (accessed 6 June 2005).

Jomo K.S. (ed.) (1995) *Privatizing Malaysia: Rents, Rhetoric, Realities*, Boulder, CO: Westview Press.

Kanavos, P. and Mossialos, E. (1999) 'International comparison of health care expenditures: what we know and what we do not know', *Journal of Health Services Research and Policy* 4(2): 122–6.

Kornai, J. and McHale, J. (2000) 'Is post-communist health spending unusual?', *Economics of Transition* 8(2): 369–99.

Malaysia (1996) *The Seventh Malaysia Plan 1996–2000*, Kuala Lumpur: Economic Planning Unit, Prime Minister's Department, Malaysia.

—— (2001a) Press Statement: Population Distribution and Basic Demographic Characteristics Report. Population and Housing Census 2000. Online. Available at <http://www.statistics.gov.my/English/frameset_pressdemo.php> (accessed 6 June 2005).

—— (2001b) *The Eighth Malaysia Plan 2001–2005*, Kuala Lumpur: Economic Planning Unit, Prime Minister's Department, Malaysia.

Ministry of Health (various years) *Health Facts.*

—— (2002) *Proceedings of the National Healthcare Financing Conference*, 19–22 June, Penang. Online. Available at <http://www.moh.gov.my/PnD/nhfc.pdf> (accessed 6 June 2005).

Mossialos, E. and Le Grand, J. (eds) (1999) *Health Care and Cost Containment in the European Union*, Aldershot: Ashgate.

Phua, Kai Lit (2001) 'Corporatization and privatization of public services: origins and rise of a controversial concept', *Akademika* 58: 45–57.

Raj, C. (2000) 'Who will pay for health?', *Malaysian Business*, 1 May: 40–1.

Rohaizat Yon (2002) 'Health care financing in Malaysia: future trends', in Syed Mohamed Aljunid and Nabilla Al-Sadat Abdul Mohsein (eds) *Health Economics Issues in Malaysia*, Kuala Lumpur: University of Malaya Press.

Rosen, C. (2004) 'The democratization of beauty', *The New Atlantis* 5: 19–35.

Rozita Halina Tun Hussein (2000) 'Estimating health expenditures in Malaysia', in *Malaysia's Health 2000*, Kuala Lumpur: Ministry of Health, pp. 261–77.

Schieber, G.J. and Maeda, A. (1997) 'A curmudgeon's guide to financing health care in developing countries', in G.J. Schieber (ed.) *Innovations in Health Care Financing*, Washington, DC: World Bank.

Sethi, R.C. and Fronstin, P. (2004) 'National health spending rose 9.3 per cent in 2002; sixth consecutive year of faster growth', *EBRI Notes Executive Summary* 25(3). Online. Available at <http://www.ebri.org/notesx/0304note.htm> (accessed 6 June 2005).

The Star, 2 July 2004, 'Nine hospital projects shelved'.

The Star, 13 May 2004, 'Chua: RM2.6m given to needy'.

United Nations (2001) 'Malaysia', in *World Population Ageing 1950–2050*, New York: Population Division, Department of Economic and Social Affairs. Online. Available at <http://www.un.org/esa/population/publications/worldageing19502050/pdf/135malay.pdf> (accessed 6 June 2005).

Wagstaff, A. (2001) 'Measuring equity in health care financing', *World Bank Policy Research Working Paper 2550*, Washington, DC: World Bank.

World Bank (2002) *World Development Indicators Database*, Washington, DC: World Bank.

World Health Organization (WHO) (2000) *World Health Report*, Geneva: WHO.

4 Malaysian health policy in comparative perspective

M. Ramesh

The importance of health care in public policy can hardly be exaggerated: the world spends US$3 trillion on it, amounting to more than one-tenth of world gross domestic product (GDP). No less significantly, voters everywhere rate it as one of the most important electoral issues, a reality no elected government can ignore. But how governments go about addressing their society's health care needs varies greatly across nations, as do outcomes. While the relationship between health care and health outcomes is not straightforward, health policy does make a difference to the quality and quantity of health care available to the population and what they pay for it.

Health policy encompasses two related but separate spheres: provision and financing. Both may be accomplished by either the government or the private sector or, as is usually the case, a combination of the two. Thus governments may themselves build health facilities, hire medical personnel and deliver care directly to the public or allow private providers to deliver health care. Correspondingly, the government may either organize for the payment of health care charges through public channels or stay out of financing arrangements, thus making room for people to pay through private insurance or from out-of-pocket.

Government involvement in financing health care takes two main forms: payment from tax revenues or contributory social insurance. Medical savings accounts have recently emerged as a third form, though this mechanism is still more prominent in policy debates than in practice. It is essentially a compulsory savings arrangement to which individuals contribute a set proportion of their income and then draw on as necessary during periods of illness. In contrast to tax and insurance-based financing, which are based on inter-personal sharing of risks, savings accounts are based on inter-temporal sharing of risks. In other words, the former spread risks across individuals and families while the latter allows for the spread of risks between the individuals' own periods of illnesses and good health.

The greatest challenge facing contemporary health care systems is to establish a system that provides quality care at reasonable costs and a financing system that makes it possible for the whole population to secure the health care they need without promoting perverse incentives. However, the barriers to establishing health care systems that are efficient, effective and equitable all at the same time are almost insurmountable. This is not the least due to ideological beliefs that colour interpretations of different provision and financing systems.

There are some who believe that private provision and financing is always preferable, except for the extreme instances of market failures. Against such a view is the belief that collective provision and financing through the state is the preferred solution. No amount of empirical evidence is sufficient to make the hard-core proponents of either side radically change their view: they find and select the evidence they are looking for to bolster their case. Having said this, it would be inaccurate to dismiss all health policy debates as ideological skirmishes. It is possible to establish criteria for assessing health care systems and draw reasonably objective conclusions. In this chapter, adequate access to health care for the entire population at the lowest cost to society as a whole, regardless of whether it is publicly or privately provided or financed, will be the criteria used for commenting on Malaysian health care arrangements. As such, it is national health care expenditures (and not public or private spending) in relation to health care outcomes that will be analysed in this chapter.

As is the case in most countries, Malaysia has a mixed system of providing and financing health care. However, the state plays a more prominent role in both spheres than is usually the case in the developing world. The state's dominant role is partly a legacy of British colonial rule, under which the state had established a number of public hospitals in urban areas which it financed directly from the public coffers. The arrangement persisted and was actually expanded after Independence, although the private sector eventually experienced even greater expansion.

The objective of this chapter is to describe arrangements for providing and financing health care in Malaysia and to discuss outcomes. Comparisons will be made with neighbouring and developed countries. Lessons from the Malaysian experience will be highlighted. It will be argued that the large state involvement in health care in Malaysia has served the country well, but this positive record could be undermined by concerted attempts since the 1980s to expand the role of the private sector. Furthermore, promoting private provision without first placing adequate checks on providers' activities will inevitably raise expenditures and lead to unsatisfactory outcomes. The situation will be aggravated if expanded private provision is accompanied by compulsory insurance.

Provision

At the time of Independence, health services in Malaysia were concentrated in urban areas and it was only after the establishment of the Rural Health Services Scheme (RHS) in 1953 that modern health care became available to the majority of the population. By the mid-1980s, the scheme

Table 4.1 Hospital beds and physicians for selected countries (per 1,000 people)

Countries	Hospital beds		Physicians	
	1970	*Late 1990s*	*1970*	*Late 1990s*
High income (average)	9.6	7.4	1.4	3.8
Middle income (average)	2.1	3.7	—	1.8
Low income (average)	0.8	—	0.7	2.0
Malaysia	3.5	2.0	0.1	0.7
Singapore	3.7	3.6	1.1	1.4
Thailand	1.1	2.0	—	0.3

Source: GDN Data Query. Online. Available at <http://devdata.worldbank.org/wbquery/> (accessed 22 May 2005).

had succeeded in covering 93 per cent of the rural population (Roemer 1991: 399).

The ratio of hospital beds to population is believed to be positively related to income level, but this is only partially confirmed in Table 4.1, which shows the ratio to be unusually low in Malaysia and Singapore compared to their respective country categories (Singapore is in the high income category, and Malaysia in the middle income category). Remarkably, in Malaysia, the ratio of hospital beds to population has declined rather than increased with a rise in income. The decline is possibly a result of urbanization, population growing faster than the number of beds and more intensive use of beds (for example through greater reliance on day procedures).

The ratio of physicians to population has risen somewhat over the years but is still low in Malaysia (and in Singapore and Thailand) in comparison to the averages for high, middle, as well as low, income countries. The low ratio of both hospital beds and physicians on its own may not be a problem, but this is something Malaysian policy-makers need to monitor in order to ensure adequate access.

As in Singapore, hospital care in Malaysia is heavily dominated by the public sector. Approximately 77 per cent of all hospital beds are in the public sector compared to 23 per cent in the private sector (Ministry of Health 2005). Private health care facilities, though still small in number, have been proliferating since the 1980s and are projected to house nearly half of all beds by the year 2020 (Malaysia 1996: 540). More than 86 per cent of the beds in public hospitals are in third class wards, which provide 'no frills' service at little or no charge, compared to 9 per cent in the second class and 5 per cent in the first class wards (Ministry of Health 2005). In terms of physicians, however, only 54 per cent are in the public sector and 46 per cent in the private sector. Again the share of physicians in the private sector is projected to rise as doctors desert public facilities to pursue more lucrative private opportunities. Between 1990 and 2001, nearly 4,000 doctors resigned from the public sector, most of them to go to work in private practice.[1]

Outpatient services, in contrast to inpatient services, are dominated by the private sector, except for the rural areas where government clinics are often the only health facilities available. In 2003, there were nearly 2,000 public health clinics of various kinds in rural areas (Ministry of Health 2005). For the country as a whole, the private clinics are the nearest health facility for the majority of the population and 57 per cent of the population use them as the primary source of outpatient treatment; and this proportion is growing (Public Health Institute 1999).

There is evidence that the public sector carries a disproportionately higher responsibility for health care compared to the resources made available to it. The public sector has 77 per cent of all hospital beds but only 54 per cent of all physicians, while the private sector has only 23 per cent of beds but 46 per cent of physicians. Furthermore, the public sector looks after more complex cases than its private counterpart. According to a 1992 study, 70 per cent of the cases managed by specialists in the public sector were complex, compared to only 25 per cent in the private sector (Mohammed Taha Bin Ariff 2002). Indeed, 60 per cent of private hospitals provide only basic curative services. Yet, according to a 1997 study, private clinics had more experienced doctors, but did not provide emergency services (Aljunid and Zwi 1997). Remarkably, this study found that nearly three-quarters of the users of public facilities had a favourable impression of the facilities compared to only a half of users of private facilities.

Faced with problems of heavy load in the public sector, in the 1980s the government decided to expand the role of the private sector, rather than provide the former with more resources. The government's 1983 *Privatisation Plan* identified health as one of the target areas, confirmed in the 1991 *Privatisation Masterplan* and the Sixth (1991–1995) and Seventh (1996–2000) Malaysia Plans. However, only minor measures towards privatization were undertaken. The government corporatized a number of hospitals,[2] and turned over the management of the drug store, laundry, cleaning services and maintenance of medical equipment at all public hospitals to the private sector (Malaysia 1996: 540–1). More significantly, the government channelled little additional resources to the public sector, which gave the private sector the opportunity to pick up the slack and expand.

The government's reluctance to pursue privatization aggressively and directly in the public health services, despite its stated intention to do so, was due to the political difficulties it encountered in selling the idea and the practical difficulties of devising a workable plan (Barraclough 2000). The government has found it difficult to formulate a plan that the it can convince voters is affordable and equitable.

After years of debate and stalemate, in August 1999, the government shelved its plan to corporatize public hospitals amid an economic recession that had heightened the population's vulnerability. Accordingly, the Eighth Malaysia Plan (2000–2005) does not directly mention privatization of health care as an objective but alludes to it by mentioning that the government would reduce its role in direct provision and expand its role in the regulation of provision. Yet the government continues to indirectly promote privatization by insufficiently supporting the public sector and thus allowing the private sector to expand (Hong 2000).

Financing

Malaysia has, similar to Singapore, a varied health financing system that includes significant government grants, large out-of-pocket expenses, modest user charges in public hospitals, limited insurance and compulsory savings.[3] There is no national health insurance, unlike in Thailand, Korea, Japan and much of Europe, though the government has been considering one for some years. Private health insurance is fragmented, expensive and only covers a small proportion of the population.

Public health facilities in urban areas impose a nominal charge, which may be waived under a variety of conditions. Health care in rural areas is available free of charge and is paid for from the government's general revenues. As in Hong Kong, the government provides free health care to its civil servants.

Public hospitals, which tend to be located in urban centres, levy varying levels of modest user charges according to the class of ward chosen. However, about 85 per cent of all public hospital beds are in third class wards which have no, or negligible, fees. Unsurprisingly, according to statistics published in 1997, 93 per cent of users of government health clinics and 66 per cent of users of public hospitals paid nothing for the service. For hospitalization, 91 per cent of users of public facilities paid less than RM100 and another 5 per cent paid RM101–200. In contrast, in private hospitals only 14 per cent paid less than RM100 while 53 per cent paid over RM1,000 (Public Health Institute 1999: 69). Correspondingly, the median out-of-pocket payment at public hospitals was RM13 compared to RM1,050 in private hospitals, despite the fact that the former deals with a higher proportion of complex cases (Public Health Institute 1999: 69). The government claims that user fees collected at government hospitals constitute only 5 per cent of the Ministry of Health's expenditures (Chua 1996).

There are also compulsory savings and social insurance schemes in Malaysia which play a modest role in financing health care. Following the example of Singapore's Medisave scheme, in 1994 Malaysia established a separate savings account ('Account III') within the Employees' Provident Fund (EPF) into which 10 per cent of a member's funds are diverted to be used only for treatment of serious illness. However, only a tiny proportion of EPF members have sufficient funds in their Account III to pay for major illnesses (Marzolf 1996: 8). The Social Security Organisation, popularly known as SOCSO, has existed since 1969 to provide work-related sickness, employment injury, and invalidity benefits to all employees earning less than RM2,000 per month. The contribution rate for the Employment Injury Scheme is approximately 1.25 per cent of wages and is wholly paid by the

Table 4.2 Health expenditure in Malaysia and selected countries (per capita, total and government)

Countries	Total expenditure on health, per capita, US$			Total expenditure on health, % of GDP			Government expenditure on health, % of TEH	
	1995	1998	2002	1995	1998	2002	1998	2002
High income	—	2,552	3,039	—	9.9	11.1	60.5	59.4
Middle income	—	102	109	—	5.9	6.0	51.0	49.6
Low income	—	21	29	—	5.0	5.5	30.7	27.2
Malaysia	99	99	149	2.2	3.0	3.8	51.6	53.8
Singapore	881	900	898	3.7	4.2	4.3	41.6	30.9
Thailand	97	73	90	3.4	3.9	4.4	56.8	69.7

Sources: WHO (2002 and 2005: Statistical Annex); GDN Data Query. Online. Available at <http://devdata.worldbank.org/wbquery/> (accessed 22 May 2005).

Note
TEH: Total Expenditure on Health

employer. For the Invalidity Pension Scheme, the rate of contribution is 1.0 per cent of wages, shared equally by the employer and the employee.

Health care spending is positively related to income, in that the richer the country, the more it spends on health. In Malaysia, per capita total (that is, both public and private) spending on health is somewhat higher than the average for middle income countries but nearly 95 per cent lower than the average for high income countries (Table 4.2). In terms of percentage of GDP, however, total health expenditure in Malaysia forms less than 4 per cent, which is significantly lower than the averages for both middle and low income countries, and considerably lower than the high income country average (Table 4.2). Indeed the share is lower than the 5 per cent of GDP recommended by the World Health Organization (WHO). Any discussion of the performance of the health care system in Malaysia must bear its modest level of spending in mind.

Government spending on health care as a proportion of total health spending is also positively related to income. Here again, Malaysia is an exception, albeit in the opposite direction. Nearly 54 per cent of total health spending comes from the government, compared to the average of 50 per cent for middle income countries (Table 4.2). The government's per capita spending on health declined in the wake of the Asian economic crisis, from US$67 in 1996 to US$48 in 1998, but then recovered and by 2002 it had reached US$80.

The government's lead role in financing health care does not impose an inordinate burden on its exchequer, as Table 4.3 shows. Public spending on health care formed 5 per cent of total government spending through the 1990s but has risen rapidly in recent years. However, the current share of

Table 4.3 Government expenditure on health, a comparison of Malaysia, Singapore, Thailand, the United Kindom and the USA

	Government expenditure on health, share in total government expenditure, %			Social security spending on health, share in government expenditure on health (%)		
	1995	*1998*	*2002*	*1995*	*1998*	*2002*
Malaysia	5.0	5.1	6.9	0.0	0.9	1.0
Singapore	9.4	8.7	5.9	19.1	17.6	26.1
Thailand	8.1	12.4	17.1	26.5	26.8	21.8
UK	13.1	13.9	15.8	11.3	0	0
USA	16.8	18.4	23.1	32.1	33.4	30.8

Source: WHO (2002 and 2005: Statistical Annex).

7 per cent of total spending is still lower than in Thailand, the United Kingdom or the USA (though higher than in Singapore).

Significantly, social security forms a tiny proportion of government health care spending in Malaysia. This is hardly surprising considering the limited nature of the SOCSO and the medical savings account under the EPF. Of the 46 per cent of total expenditure on health care in Malaysia that is accounted for by private payment, nearly all comes from out-of-pocket, rather than private health plans of any kind (Table 4.4).

Table 4.4 shows that nearly 93 per cent of private payments in Malaysia is paid out-of-pocket, which is more than double the level found in high income countries and is similar to levels found in low income countries. In contrast, only a quarter of private health expenditures in the USA are from out-of-pocket and the vast majority are from some form of insurance. The

Table 4.4 Comparative private expenditures on health, 1995, 1998 and 2002, for selected countries

Countries	Out-of-pocket health expenditure share of private expenditure on health (%)			Private health plans share in private expenditure on health (%)		
	1995	*1998*	*2002*	*1995*	*1998*	*2002*
High income	—	41	37			
Middle income	—	78	83			
Low income	—	96	96			
Malaysia	96	94	93	0	6	7
Singapore	98	97	97	0	0	0
Thailand	88	78	76	8	12	14
USA	—	28	26	62	61	66

Source: WHO (2002 and 2005: Statistical Annex).

point to note here is the negligible role that health insurance, public or private, plays in Malaysia and the heavy reliance on direct payment either by the consumer, or by the government through central treasury funds.

The concerns of the Malaysian government itself are not, however, mollified by the comparatively low costs of its health care system. It has been planning for major reforms since the mid-1980s. It explains its worry on the grounds that total health expenditures will rise to form 7 per cent of GDP by the year 2020 (Malaysia 1996: 542). While this would be significantly higher than the current level, it is worth remembering that this would still be lower than most countries at Malaysia's income level.

The government's concern with health care costs became evident in the mid-1980s, reflected in the commissioning of The National Health Financing Study in 1985 (Chua 1996). The study recommended the establishment of a contributory national health insurance scheme for all inpatient and outpatient services. The government then commissioned a feasibility study, with assistance from the Asian Development Bank, which in 1988 recommended a compulsory scheme funded from contributions from employers and employees, with the government paying the premium for the poor. While the government indicated support for the proposal, no action was taken to implement it. In the mid-1990s, the government broadened the search for alternative financing mechanisms involving larger private payments which eventuated in the establishment of EPF Account III in 1994. However, the government realized the adverse political implications of any major move to increase private health spending and showed restraint in implementing the proposal.

The Sixth Malaysia Plan mooted the idea of establishing a National Health Financing Authority (NHFA) to fund health care. The Seventh Malaysia Plan alluded to it in more definite terms but offered no details, beyond mentioning that it will be compulsory and funded from contributions supplemented by some government financial contribution (Hong 2000). Currently, the Ministry of Health proposal for the establishment of the NHFA is at the Economic Planning Unit, awaiting a decision; while yet another study has been commissioned (Inter Press Service News Agency, 10 May 2006).

While the government is contemplating national health insurance, it has also expressed its wish to raise user charges in public hospitals. It would like to particularly target high income patients in upper class wards for greater cost recovery (Barraclough 1996: 11). The 1997 economic crisis and the ruling party's political interests in rural areas explain its reluctance to push ahead measures that may be perceived as reducing the government's role in financing health care.

Health outcomes

The provision of health care, coupled with public health measures and improvements in medical technology, has a positive impact on health status,

Table 4.5 Life expectancy at birth and infant mortality rates for selected countries

Countries	Life expectancy at birth, years			Infant mortality rate, per 1,000 live births		
	1970	2002	Percentage increase	1970	2000	Percentage increase
High income	71.4	78.3	8.8	20	5	−300
Middle income	61.2	69.6	12.1	42*	34	—
Low income	48.3	58.1	16.8	95*	—	
Malaysia	63.0	72.8	13.4	46	8	−475
Singapore	68.5	78.4	12.5	20	3	−567
Thailand	59.6	69.2	13.9	74	25	−196

Source: GDN Data Query. Online. Available at <http://devdata.worldbank.org/wbquery/> (accessed 22 May 2005).

Note
* Data for 1990

reflected in improvements in life expectancy and infant mortality rates. The general improvement in the health status of the Malaysian population is indicated in Table 4.5.

Table 4.5 shows that life expectancy in Malaysia has improved dramatically over the years and is now at the level prevailing in upper middle income countries. The record is yet better with respect to infant mortality, which in Malaysia has declined rapidly and is now almost at a level prevailing in high income countries. Infant mortality is a particularly useful indicator of health status as it sums up, and reflects, other indicators of economic and human development.

However, Malaysia has still some way to go in improving its population health, as Table 4.6 shows. A Malaysian can expect to enjoy 63 years of healthy life (male: 58, female: 63) which is lower than in high income countries. Expectations of lost healthy years are also higher than in high income countries. A Malaysian woman can expect to spend 13.3 per cent of her life in ill-health compared to 11.4 per cent for men. The difference between men and women with regard to lost healthy years in Malaysia is consistent with its income level, as the difference tends to decline with income.

Malaysia has managed to achieve fine health indicators at a relatively modest cost. Malaysia, as does Singapore, spends less than would be expected of a country at its income level, unlike Korea and Thailand which spend more (Griffin 1992: 60). However, when public spending alone is considered, Malaysia spends more than would be predicted by its income level, whereas Singapore and Thailand spend less (Griffin 1992: 63). In other words, while the burden of health care financing on the government is high in Malaysia, the overall burden on society as a whole is low. Commentators

Table 4.6 Health-adjusted life expectancy, 2002

	Health-adjusted life expectancy (years)					*% of total healthy life expectancy lost between birth and 60 years*	
	Total population at birth	*Males at birth*	*Males at age 60*	*Females at birth*	*Females at age 60*	*Males at birth*	*Females at birth*
Malaysia	63.2	61.6	10.9	64.8	12.0	11.4	13.3
Singapore	70.1	68.8	14.5	71.3	16.3	11.1	12.7
Thailand	60.1	57.7	12.7	62.4	13.2	12.7	14.1
UK	70.6	69.1	15.7	72.1	18.1	8.8	10.4
USA	69.3	67.2	15.3	71.3	17.9	9.9	10.7

Source: WHO (2005: Statistical Annex).

focusing on government expenditure alone often miss this salient feature of the Malaysian health care system.

The Malaysian health care system is not only inexpensive, it is also generally equitable. Although public health spending across regions is positively related to income, the cross-regional differences are small. Less than 7 per cent of the Malaysian population live in areas with no access to a static clinic within a 5 kilometre radius. However, the Bornean states of Sabah and Sarawak offer poorer facilities and less access to health care than the rest of the country (Roziah 2000). Estate workers, who tend to live on remote plantations, have also been poorly served by the health system (Barraclough 1996: 12).

Malaysian government health expenditures are quite egalitarian. Hospital inpatient subsidies show no clear pattern in relation to income groups; they seem to be rather shaped by incidence of catastrophic illness. Outpatient subsidies slightly favour the poor and rural areas, despite the fact that more ill persons in urban areas use health services than their rural counterparts (Chee 1990: 89). The increasing focus of government health expenditure on the poor is not actually government policy but rather the inadvertent result of desertion of public facilities by the wealthy (Hammer *et al.* 1996: 526).

Public expenditure on inpatient services targeted at the poorest quintile increased from 19 per cent in 1974 to 25 per cent in 1984. Correspondingly, the expenditure on the richest quintile decreased from 20 per cent to 16 per cent over the same period. Expenditure on outpatient services, at 22–24 per cent for the poorest quintile and 15–16 per cent for the richest quintile, remained relatively unchanged over the period. The modest decline in the use of public facilities by the richest quintile was more than offset by the increase in their use of private facilities. The richest quintile accounted for 30 per cent of outpatient visits in 1974 and 34 per cent in 1984; the corresponding figures for inpatient visits to private hospitals were 12 and 46 per cent respectively (Hammer *et al.* 1996).

Conclusions

Malaysia's health care system shares some broad similarities with the UK, Hong Kong and Singapore, yet has developed some unique features. As in these countries, in Malaysia, hospital care is provided largely by the public sector while outpatient care is provided mainly by the private sector. And, again, similar to the UK and Hong Kong, but unlike Singapore, hospital care is largely government-funded. Outpatient care, however, is funded largely by private sources, as in Hong Kong and Singapore but unlike in the UK. The much discussed medical savings account (EPF's Account III) in Malaysia forms an even smaller share of total health expenditures than in Singapore. Social insurance, SOCSO notwithstanding, also plays a small role in Malaysia, unlike most countries in continental Europe, South America and East Asia.

As is the case in Singapore and, to a lesser extent, Hong Kong, Malaysia spends a relatively small percentage of GDP on health care compared to both developed and developing countries. A part of the reason for the low health expenditure in Malaysia is certainly its young population: only 7 per cent of the population is over the age of 60 (compared to 11 per cent in Singapore, 9 per cent in Thailand and 16 per cent in the USA) despite an increase in recent years. The emphasis placed on public health, sanitation and rural facilities following Independence improved health care at modest costs.

The large presence of the public sector in the provision of both primary and secondary health care has also played a significant role in keeping the costs down. The direct provision and financing of hospital care, the most expensive component of health care, provides access to all those who need it at modest cost. Indeed, the very presence of the public sector as a cheaper alternative, partly because of government subsidy, serves as a price benchmark for private providers to follow and thus keeps prices down. The economy of scale afforded by population density and centralized administration are also no less vital. As an OECD study has concluded: 'Centralized control on health care budgets seems to result in lower spending levels than otherwise would be expected. The effect of both public finance and public provision of ownership is ambiguous, but the former probably lowers expenditure' (OECD 1990: 36). It is also significant to note that public outpatient facilities tend to be located in rural areas that are not sufficiently attractive to private providers.

As in many countries around the world, Malaysia has been trying to reduce state involvement in health care (Scarpaci 1989; Homedes and Ugalde 2005). Be that as it may, it is unclear what Malaysia hopes to achieve from the privatization of health care. There is no evidence that greater competition among or from private providers will reduce overall health care costs or expenditures. Increased private funding will not necessarily lead to reduction in government expenditures, even if it reduces the government's share, because private funding is often accompanied by increased overall expenditure (OECD 1992). On the downside, increased private provision and/or financing carries the real possibility of reduced access for those unable to afford it or those living in sparsely populated areas with limited profit potential. Expansion of private provision of health care on a fee-for-service basis distorts the incentive structure and creates opportunity for over-servicing. The problem is compounded when governments maintain a hands-off approach towards what medical practitioners charge their patients (World Bank 1993: 123). Paying doctors on a fee-for-service basis may make for better service, but it is expensive.

The Malaysian government's avowed grave concerns about health care costs are puzzling because, as a percentage of total government costs as well as of GDP, they are considerably below countries at similar levels of economic development and will continue to remain so in years to come. It is possible that the real purpose of raising alarms about public sector costs is to prepare the ground for shedding public responsibilities, rather than to restrain costs. Be that as it may, the government is unlikely to be able to explicitly privatize public health facilities due to fear of a political backlash from its constituents and will instead indirectly promote the private sector by making the public sector unattractive for all but the poor.

Notes

1 Data from the Malaysian Medical Association website. Available at <http://www.mma.org.my/current_topic/presidential.htm> (accessed 1 September 2006).
2 These were the National Heart Institute and the teaching hospitals under the Ministry of Education.
3 Nonetheless, Singapore's public hospitals have been corporatized, and user charges are much higher than in Malaysia's public hospitals. The private share in health financing is higher in Singapore, and the use of compulsory savings is also much greater in Singapore than in Malaysia.

References

Aljunid, Syed and Zwi, Anthony (1997) 'Public and private practitioners in a rural district of Malaysia: complements or substitutes?', in S. Bennett, B. McPake and A. Mills (eds) *Private Health Providers in Developing Countries: Serving the Public Interest?*, London: Zed Books.

Barraclough, Simon (1996) 'Health care policy issues in Malaysia's drive for socio-economic development by the year 2020', *Asian Studies Review* 20(1): 5–19.

—— (2000) 'The politics of privatization in the Malaysian health care system', *Contemporary Southeast Asia* 22(2): 340–59.

Chee Heng Leng (1990) *Health and Health Care in Malaysia: Present Trends and Implications for the Future*, Institute for Advanced Studies Monograph Series SM No. 3, Kuala Lumpur: University of Malaya, Institute for Advanced Studies.

Chua Jui Meng (1996) 'Speech by Minister of Health Malaysia at the official launching of the Pacific Insurance's Blue Cross Medi-Care Hospital and Surgical Plan', 16 April, Kuala Lumpur. Online. Available at <http://www.moh.gov.my/SPEECH/menteri/16041996-0930-BI.htm> (accessed 27 May 2005).

Griffin, Charles C. (1992) *Health Care in Asia: A Comparative Study of Cost and Financing*, Washington, DC: World Bank.

Hammer, Jeffrey S. *et al.* (1996) 'Distributional effects of social sector expenditures in Malaysia', in D. van de Walle and Nead Kimberley (eds) *Public Spending and the Poor*, Baltimore: Johns Hopkins University Press.

Homedes, N. and Ugalde, A. (2005) 'Why neoliberal health reforms have failed in Latin America', *Health Policy* 71(1): 83–96.

Hong Szu Fuei (2000) 'Ensuring equitable access to healthcare 30 September 2000', Malaysian Institute of Economic Research paper. Online. Available at <http://www.mier.org.my/mierscan/archives/pdf/szufuei30_9_2000.pdf> (accessed 4 September 2005).

Inter Press Service News Agency, 10 May 2006, 'Malaysia: privatisation by other names'. Online. Available at <http://www.ipsnews.net/print.asp?idnews=31963> (accessed 11 May 2006).

Malaysia (1996) *The Seventh Malaysia Plan 1996–2000*, Kuala Lumpur: Economic Planning Unit, Prime Minister's Department, Malaysia.

Marzolf, James R. (1996) 'Analysis of the EPF medical benefit scheme: experience and options for expansion', unpublished report prepared for the Employees' Provident Fund (EPF), Malaysia.

Ministry of Health, Malaysia (2005) *Health Indicators*. Online. Available at <http://www.moh.gov.my/indicators.HTM> (accessed 22 May 2005).

Mohammed Taha Bin Ariff (2002) Keynote address by the Director General of Health Malaysia, presented at the National Healthcare Financing Conference, Penang, 19–22 June.

OECD (1990) *Health Care Systems in Transition: The Search for Efficiency*, Paris: OECD.

—— (1992) *The Reform of Health Care: A Comparative Analysis of Seven OECD Countries*, Paris: OECD.

Public Health Institute (1999) *National Health and Morbidity Survey 1996*, Volume 3: *Recent Illness/Injury, Health Seeking Behaviour and Out-of-pocket Health Care Expenditure*, Kuala Lumpur: Public Health Institute, MOH Malaysia.

Roemer, Milton I. (1991) *National Health Systems of the World, Vol 1*, New York: Oxford University Press.

Roziah Omar (2000) 'Getting well in Malaysia', in J. Doling (ed.) *Social Welfare East and West: Britain and Malaysia*, Aldershot: Ashgate.

Scarpaci, Joseph L. (ed.) (1989) *Health Services Privatization in Industrial Societies*, New Brunswick, NJ: Rutgers University Press.

World Bank (1993) *World Development Report 1993: Investing in Health*, Oxford: Oxford University Press.

World Health Organization (2002) *The World Health Report 2002*, Geneva: World Health Organization.

—— (2005) *The World Health Report 2005*, Geneva: World Health Organization.

5 The welfarist state under duress

Global influences and local contingencies in Malaysia

Chan Chee Khoon

SAPs: Structural Adjustment Programmes, also Standard And Poor's?

'[I]t would take a lot more improvements to get Malaysia upgraded,' said Standard & Poor's director (sovereign and international public finance ratings) Chew Ping. Malaysia's central government debt levels were still higher than that of comparable states, said Chew, who expects the government to manage a balanced budget only in 2007. S&P ratings specialist for Malaysia, Liew Chih Wai, said that among his concerns for the future were the low levels of private investment during the past few years . . . He said it was crucial the country continued to attract foreign direct investment . . . [which] was also important to ensure that domestic demand was maintained and [would furthermore] help the government reduce its fiscal deficit.

(*The Star*, 11 March 2004)

On 19 March 2004, the Secretary-General of the Health Ministry Datuk Alias Ali circulated a memorandum instructing the ministry's senior officers to institute with immediate effect an austerity budget for 2004 which should as much as possible maintain the ministry's expenditures at the 2003 level, and which, in any case, would not be increased beyond the allocations committed as of that date.[1] An account of this appeared in Malaysia's popular online press:

The Health Ministry has ordered significant cutbacks in its [planned] expenditure after receiving a Treasury directive that there will be no increase in its financial allocation for 2004 . . . As a result, the Health Ministry now finds that it will not be able to meet staff salaries across the country by as much as RM210 million, unless it undertakes cost-cutting measures.

(Malaysiakini.com, 1 June 2004)

Shortly afterwards, Prime Minister Abdullah Ahmad Badawi announced on 6 May 2004, at the opening of a three-day consultation for the 2005 national budget, the government's intention to reduce the budget deficit from 5.4 per cent of gross domestic product (GDP) in 2003 to less than the targeted 4.5 per cent for 2004 (and by the end of 2005, to between 3.25 and 3.5 per cent of GDP).

This would be achieved through 'the necessary fiscal consolidation measures to increase the efficiency of public spending ... and through the encouragement of more open tender opportunities in government procurements' (*The Edge Daily*, 10 May 2004).

Corporate circles are similarly attentive to capital market sentiments in their operational and financial management. In July 2006, Hassan Marican, president and CEO of Petronas (Malaysia) stated that the national oil and gas monopoly could not increase its contributions to Malaysian government coffers to allow for increased social spending, despite posting record profits from the prevailing high oil and gas prices: '*We need the cash for our capital expenditure ... Petronas is a [Fortune 500] global company, it's rated by [credit rating] agencies, it has papers [bonds] out there in the capital market, so you have to maintain that credibility ... you don't want to be at the same level of some of the other national oil companies where very dollar is taken out, so you stifle investments, stifle expansion plus we could lose our investment grade or ratings ...*' (*No additional cash for government coffers. Malaysiakini.com, July 3, 2006*).

Petronas came onstream in 1974, and soon thereafter was producing an exportable surplus, which helped Malaysia avoid the worst of the energy and debt crises of the 1970s and 1980s (and equally important, the neo-liberal policy dictates of the IMF and World Bank). Like any other middle income country however seeking to borrow from the international capital markets, the Malaysian govenment is also under pressure to get its macro-economic indicators 'right' (by BWI criteria), so as to obtain favorable credit ratings from agencies such as Moody's and Standard & Poor's (a market-enforced SaP, so to speak), hence its determination to reduce its fiscal deficits from the pump-priming levels during the Asian financial crises (5.8% of GDP in 1998) to 3.5% by 2006.

The rise to pre-eminence of finance capital

This evident concern over fiscal deficits and for reduced, but more efficient, public spending illustrates an important trend that Indian political economists at Jawaharlal Nehru University have highlighted, that is, the rise to pre-eminence of globally mobile finance capital in the international political economy, and the deflationary (anti-Keynesian) bias that it imparts to national economies.

Several developments following from the postwar capitalist boom undermined the conjuncture which had sustained it. Important among these was the rise of finance capital, in a new incarnation, to a position of dominance. One episode concerns the large US current account deficits of the fifties and the sixties which, together with capital exports, resulted in an outpouring of US dollars, and which were decreed under the Bretton Woods system to be 'as good as gold.' They led to the formation of the Eurodollar market and, eventually, to the collapse of the Bretton Woods system itself. Another episode was the petro-dollar deposits following the oil shocks, which put enormous funds at the disposal of the metropolitan banks, made them the key actors in the 'recycling' process . . . through these episodes, globalized finance capital rose to a position of pre-eminence.

(Patnaik 1999)

In the 1970s, these enormous funds provided the background and the wherewithal for the indiscriminate, indeed reckless lending by metropolitan banks flush with liquidity. In combination with continuing instability in the world energy markets, global recession and weak commodity prices, and skyrocketing interests on foreign loans,[2] it eventually precipitated massive debt crises in the 1980s in countries of the south.

Joining the ranks of countries which were already much indebted to the international financial institutions (IFIs) were Mexico, Brazil, Argentina, Venezuela, the Philippines, Korea, Turkey and Romania, and other countries which had borrowed liberally from commercial banks in the metropolitan centres. With limited options available, many of these countries had to turn to the IFIs for crisis management loans to cope with their onerous debts, and thereby subjected themselves to IFI loan conditionalities such as structural adjustment programmes (SAPs) and other neo-liberal policy dictates.

Utsa Patnaik elaborates on the deflationary bias of finance capital which she distinguishes from the priorities of manufacturing capital:

[Manufacturing capitalists] are engaged in material production for profit on the basis of borrowed money. Financiers are creditors, and creditors above all wish to prevent inflation, which erodes their returns: they wish to maintain high real interest rates and want complete freedom to move their finances in and out of countries in search of the highest returns, which are mainly speculative in nature . . . Deflationary economic policies combined with the removal of all national barriers to its free movement thus form the core of the policy agenda of finance capital . . . The dominance of finance capital over all other types of capital, and the systematic implementation of its deflationary agenda in over 80 countries through conditions attached to external debt from the international lending agencies, has brought about the present global crisis of livelihoods.

(Patnaik 2003)

As the privatization of social insurance and risk management proceeded in parallel with the opening up of financial and currency markets worldwide, the entry of pension funds, mutual funds (unit trusts), hedge funds and other financial instruments added to the existing glut of capital, thereby further exacerbating the crisis of over-accumulation and demand deficit that had been building up since the 1970s.

In its ceaseless search for opportunities for profitable deployment and redeployment, globally mobile capital has undermined the welfarist state through several modalities. First, its search for low-cost labour, competitive tax regimes and tax havens fosters a 'race to the bottom' and thereby reduces the fiscal capacity of states. Besides lower corporate taxes, runaway firms also leave behind unemployed workers and reduced income tax receipts, even as the need for unemployment benefits rises. Second, neo-liberal trade policies reduce custom duties as a source of state revenues. Third, globally mobile finance capital has an overriding concern with inflation and balanced budgets in the countries where it circulates. Wary of activist Keynesianism, it imparts a deflationary bias to national economies, demanding fiscal discipline to reduce public spending and budget deficits through its threat of withdrawal and flight (Patnaik 2004). Finally, there is the widening imbalance between accumulation and consumption, manifested as over-capacity and demand deficit. To cope with the excess accumulation, pressure builds up to extend the circuit of capital into new arenas for accumulation, encroaching into a hitherto non-commercial public sector domain, that is, privatization and dismembering of the welfarist state.

Malaysia: the not-quite client state

Malaysia has not been among the countries of the south most vulnerable to structural adjustment programmes (SAPs), poverty reduction strategy papers (PRSPs) and other such IFI loan conditionalities and instruments of policy leverage. With an exportable surplus of petroleum which came on-stream in the mid-1970s, Malaysia was spared the worst of the oil shocks and the ensuing pressure on foreign exchange reserves.

Up until the end of the 1970s, Malaysia's foreign borrowings were quite modest despite increased public spending and deficit financing for a rapidly expanding public enterprise sector (for the most part, financed by local borrowings from the Employees' Provident Fund, as well as by the national oil monopoly Petronas' 'off-budget' oil and gas revenues).[3] From the mid-1970s, electronic components assembly was furthermore a burgeoning growth industry, which helped Malaysia weather the global economic slowdown.

By the mid-1980s, however, the depth and duration of the global recession was biting into export earnings from commodities (rubber, tin, palm oil), petroleum and even electronics. At the same time, *yen*-denominated loans incurred to finance heavy industry development (iron and steel, automobiles, cement, etc.) became increasingly burdensome as the *yen* rose strongly in the wake of the 1985 Plaza Accords (a twofold appreciation against the *ringgit*).

Shortly thereafter, however, the rapidly appreciating Japanese *yen* led to a massive redeployment of Japanese (and eventually Taiwanese and some Korean) manufacturing capital to Malaysia and other Southeast Asian countries, which helped sustain an economic boom and high rates of export-led growth right up until the Asian financial crisis of 1997.

The mid-1980s were nonetheless a period of debt and fiscal stress in Malaysia which *inter alia* curtailed the role of public sector enterprises in their mission of affirmative action and ethnic redistribution, key objectives of the New Economic Policy (NEP). Throughout this period, there is little evidence of direct influence or leverage of the IFIs in promoting privatization in Malaysia, beyond the continuing 'technical' assistance and policy advice of the International Monetary Fund (IMF) and World Bank (WB), and their ideological hegemony.[4]

Nonetheless, as discussed earlier, Malaysia was hardly immune from the forces pushing for liberalization, deregulation and privatization. Credit rating agencies such as Moody's and Standard & Poor's produce their sovereign credit ratings based on criteria which largely overlap with those used by the IFIs in their periodic country assessments. These of course routinely affect the marketability of government bonds (Horgan 1999) and corporate bonds (Liu and Ferri 2001), the interest rates payable and other terms of borrowing in private capital markets, and therefore constitute an important influence on domestic policy priorities.

Equally important, countries (including Malaysia) which willingly or otherwise went ahead with opening up of capital markets (plus currency convertibility) made themselves vulnerable to the dictates of the financial markets and their potentially disruptive capital flows.[5]

Privatization and its local contingencies: the New Economic Policy

Notwithstanding its relative insulation from IMF/WB arm-twisting, then, the Malaysian government nonetheless implemented one of the most extensive privatization programmes among Third World countries in the last two decades of the twentieth century.[6] It also has the most commitments for the health care sector under the General Agreement on Trade in Services (GATS) among East Asian countries (Public Services International 1999).

Malaysia's receptivity to privatization is therefore intriguing and is not simply a consequence of IFI influence or dictates, not forgetting of course the independent efforts of the multinational companies with or without IMF/ WB or the World Trade Organization (WTO) paving the way with their initiatives and leverage (Hall 2003).

The exposure and vulnerability to the dictates of global capital markets has been mentioned, but no less important was the domestic political-economic context (most importantly the NEP), and how it articulated with globalizing capital.

The NEP entailed, *inter alia*, massive investments in a diverse range of public enterprises which were envisaged as the major vehicles for *Bumiputera* participation in the modern industrial and commercial sectors. At its peak in 1983, public enterprises accounted for 53.4 per cent of total investment (20.5 per cent of GDP) spread over the manufacturing, services, construction and agricultural sectors.

The debt and fiscal crises of the mid-1980s recession effectively brought to an end this massive expansion of the public enterprise sector. In the event, the recession also provided the circumstances for a decisive turn towards privatization, but this was a privatization re-configured to meet local contingencies. First, to capitalize on the imminent redeployment of Japanese (and Taiwanese) manufacturing capital to Southeast Asia, the Malaysian government set aside those aspects of state interventionism embodied in the NEP and the Industrial Co-ordination Act 1975 which foreign investors found most objectionable. In particular, it waived for a designated period (1 October 1986 to 31 December 1990) the NEP requirements on indigenous equity allocation and employment quotas in an effort to attract foreign direct investment (Promotion of Investments Act 1986).

Second, the Malaysian government speeded up the transfer of assets and commercial prerogatives (licences and lucrative concessions) to selected *Bumiputera* private institutions and individuals (the 'Bumiputera Commercial and Industrial Community', BCIC) which had the 'track record' and the 'proven capacity' to carry through the affirmative action objectives of the NEP. Third, the state would continue to be a major economic actor, but on a more selective basis with heavy investments in key strategic industries (such as automobile manufacture), which the private sector was reluctant to undertake or lacked the independent financial and technical wherewithal to take on.

Hence, just as 'redistribution-with-growth' in the 1960s provided a timely slogan, if not ideological cover for the NEP, so the privatization policies promoted by the IFIs from the mid-1980s onwards provided a convenient vehicle and ethos for the divestment of accumulated public assets and lucrative concessions ('held in trust' for the indigenous community) to well-connected private entities and individuals (mostly *Bumiputera*, but not exclusively so).

Free markets where necessary, captive markets where possible

Not surprisingly, privatization under such circumstances was less about competitive, free markets than about transforming the more profitable public enterprises and lucrative concessions into private monopolies and captive markets.

There is a considerable body of writing on the important topic of 'political business' in Malaysia (see Jesudason 1990 and Gomez 1990, 1991, 1995). What emerges very clearly is that the BCIC was not only to be the flag bearer of a resurgent *Bumiputera* community, but its political allegiance and partisanship had to be secured through intimate links between the ruling Malay party, UMNO (United Malays National Organization) and the expanding Malay corporate circles.[7]

In short, the privatization process was structured in such a way as to ensure that UMNO-linked corporate interests (and their individual nominees) would be major *Bumiputera* beneficiaries in the divestment and outsourcing exercises.[8] As these 'public-private partnerships' took shape, it became clear that health care and its ancillary industries had been targeted as a priority growth sector by an emerging nexus of party-family-corporate interests (Chan 2004).

Market-driven health care: bleeding the public sector

In the last two decades, the market for private health care has grown dramatically along with an expanding middle class and their disposable incomes. With increasing affluence, somewhat diminished by the 1997 currency crisis and its aftermath, more and more people have been choosing to use private health care services in preference to underfunded and crowded public facilities. Private hospitals were few in number in the 1970s, but have proliferated in the urban centres since the early 1980s. Most of these are for-profit institutions, in contrast to an earlier tradition of community and philanthropy-supported hospitals (Chan *et al.* 2000).

As the private hospital sector expanded, it siphoned off staff and other resources from the public sector. With longer queues and more heavily burdened staff, public dissatisfaction with government services has grown and complaints have mounted. Those who could afford it turned to the private sector, which responded to the added demand by building more hospitals and increasing its charges. On current trends, we can predict that those who have to depend on government health services can expect further declines in quality of service, while the private health care sector continues to flourish off the local (and regional) clientele with disposable incomes. In times of economic recession when markets shrivel, we witness the twin irrationality of a staggering overload for the public sector, concurrent with under-patronized excess capacity in the private sector (which in turn seeks relief through a larger share of the regional 'health tourism' market).

The Malaysian government continues to proclaim corporatization and privatization[9] of the public sector as the panacea for these interlinked crises, and repeatedly asserts that the financial and administrative burden on government is excessive. In truth, public sector expenditures in health care are very modest.[10] The official policy furthermore is to rely on the market for more 'efficient' allocation of resources, and for cost-conscious and client-responsive service. To date, there has been little systematic evaluation of health care privatization, in particular the outsourcing of the Health Ministry's support services (most notably, hospital support services, pharmaceuticals and other medical supplies), aside from brief mention of quite sharply increased expenditures (Noorul Ainur Mohd Nur 2003).[11]

In addition to the outsourcing of support services, public (teaching) hospitals attached to the medical faculties of Universiti Malaya (Kuala Lumpur), Universiti Sains Malaysia (Kubang Kerian) and Universiti Kebangsaan Malaysia (Cheras) have been corporatized. Among the Health Ministry's facilities, the Institut Jantung Negara (National Heart Institute) was hived off from the Kuala Lumpur Hospital (cardiothoracic and cardiology departments) in 1992 and corporatized as a fully government-owned referral heart centre. All other Health Ministry hospitals were slated to be corporatized[12] beginning 1 January 2000, but the plan was expediently shelved in August 1999 amidst mounting, vocal unease among the public in the run-up to the November 1999 General Elections (*The Star*, 14 August 1999), apprehensions that have resurfaced with the introduction of private wings in the Health Ministry's hospitals (*The Star*, 20 July 2004).

The government has commissioned a number of studies looking into alternative schemes of health care financing to accompany these reforms, but the lack of information and open discussion has engendered much public anxiety and dissatisfaction. Meanwhile, the corporate private sector, including not a few state-linked interests, has forged ahead with ventures in various sub-sectors[13] (Chan 1996).

Few details have been revealed about the institutional re-structuring and the parallel financing scenarios under consideration. No less than six consultant reports have been commissioned in the last two decades to look into national health planning, health care insurance and financing, household health care expenditures and re-structuring of hospitals, but none has been made available to the public for their perusal.

Private enterprise and the social character of insurance

On 18 January 2000, *The Star*'s front-page headlines announced that the Employees' Provident Fund (EPF) had entered into an agreement with the Life Insurers Association of Malaysia (LIAM) which would allow for:

> [T]he estimated five million active EPF members [to] use their savings to sign up for a health insurance scheme [beginning] this June. Under [this] scheme, contributors can authorise EPF to pay the premiums from their Account III (health) annually ... Members can opt for a low-premium scheme covering 13 critical illnesses [or procedures] – major organ transplants, coronary bypass surgery, heart valve replacement, surgery to aorta, stroke, coma, cancer and benign brain tumour, serious injuries due to accidents, congenital heart diseases, congestive cardiac failure, chronic renal failure, meningitis and encephalitis – or for one covering 36 major illnesses [or procedures] at a higher premium.
>
> (*The Star*, 18 January 2000)

The premiums payable, ranging from RM30 annually (RM10,000 pay-out upon diagnosis, age 35 and below) to RM20,034 annually (RM100,000 pay-out upon diagnosis, expanded coverage, age 65–70) were to be charged in accordance with an age-gradient. Female EPF members would be given a 30 per cent discount in premiums to reflect a lower overall incidence of the designated illnesses, relative to males.

Quite apart from the adequacy of the pay-outs (even as supplements) for meeting the treatment costs of these major illnesses, there are serious reservations about such a scheme as a potential major vehicle for health care financing. An insurance scheme is a profoundly social undertaking. Whether in the form of a publicly managed scheme, a co-operative arrangement or a commercially purchased policy, it is in essence a mechanism for pooling the risk of catastrophic events faced by individuals who band together in a collective enterprise. It is necessarily a group undertaking because it is based on the recognition that the unfortunate, random individual, relying just on his or her resources, would be overwhelmed and unable to cope with a catastrophe.

Cross-subsidy is therefore the heart and soul of insurance, the well subsidizing the ill, with the important proviso that there is little prior indication as to who might suffer the catastrophic event. Such is the logic and rationale that drives the system. The logic of private enterprise, however, is to maximize profit. In the field of insurance, this means discriminating between risk categories, fragmenting the market into those considered at higher risk of illness, and those at lower risk.

This is why insurance premiums increase when one crosses the risk threshold at age 40, and skyrocket when one reaches 60 years and beyond (as is the case with the EPF-LIAM scheme). Family history of heritable illness, in time to be replaced by DNA screening (Chan 2002), will attempt even finer discrimination between risk categories, notwithstanding the cautions of molecular geneticists, epidemiologists and ethicists most familiar with the limitations of the emerging technology. Or more simply, just ask anyone with pre-existing chronic illness, or HIV seropositivity, who has attempted to enrol in a typical insurance scheme.

All this is understandable given the imperative of the commercial sector to turn a profit. But what has happened here? An acknowledged and necessarily social undertaking is being subverted by a process of fragmentation and individualization of risk whose logical end-point is its own antithesis: the sick to bear their own cost-burden of illness, the healthy to rejoice in their good fortune (or 'good genes'?).

These are not alarmist fantasies. Other countries have taken heed of these socially corrosive and exclusionary tendencies. In Australia, there are legislated bans on risk rating, in favour of uniform community rating (but now under threat of 'deregulation'). Partial solutions will not work as evidenced by the experience of Blue Cross/Blue Shield in the USA, which saw their younger, healthier subscribers desert to the 'for-profits' such as Aetna when they offered lower premiums to this low-risk group. Blue Cross/Blue Shield was left holding the baby, or more accurately, the elderly, who are intensive users of medical resources. To no one's surprise, the Blues eventually introduced their own risk rating just to remain viable.

The lesson therefore is quite clear – selective opting-out by low-risk individuals, encouraged by profit-oriented underwriting, will thoroughly undermine the implicit compact and cross-subsidy that is the essence and *raison d'être* of social insurance.

It is particularly regrettable that the EPF, as an employee (social) security fund, is being used as a Trojan Horse to institutionalize risk-profiling as a basis for differential, discriminatory premiums for the aged and high-risk subscribers (perfectly normal in for-profit underwriting but completely at odds with principles of uniform risk-rating and solidarity in social insurance).[14]

With less fanfare – a soft launch in November 1999 followed by a nation-wide roadshow – Cuepacs (Congress of Union of Employees in Public and Civil Services) had earlier introduced its own version of health insurance, CuepacsCare, in a joint venture with AMI Insurans Bhd and MediCare Assistance Sdn Bhd. Unlike the EPF-LIAM scheme, CuepacsCare charges uniform premiums, but excludes a larger proportion of the elderly from eligibility (see below).

A further difference is that CuepacsCare re-imbursements are based on specified inpatient services, subject to a ceiling on payments (maximum RM60,000 a year for individual subscribers) and exclusions of congenital abnormalities, disabilities arising from wars or civil disorders, mental illness, eyesight deficiencies and visual aids, artificial limbs and prostheses, sexually transmitted diseases, quarantineable infectious disease, pregnancy and child delivery services, vaccinations, AIDS and related complications, as well as other pre-existing chronic conditions (such as diabetes, high blood pressure, kidney dysfunction, cardiovascular disease, cancer) in the first year of subscription.

There are several salient points to note in this emerging *mélange* of health insurance schemes. First, the EPF-LIAM scheme is a risk-rated scheme, more in line with commercial underwriting than social insurance. The most objectionable consequence is that those who (will) need health care most would least be able to afford it. Undeniably, health care financing for an increasingly aged population is a major challenge, but a risk-rated scheme with exorbitant premiums for the elderly and other high-risk groups (in effect, rationing by the market) is unacceptable as a solution. The CuepacsCare scheme sidesteps this by excluding from coverage a larger group of the elderly.

Second, the elderly are excluded from coverage: the EPF-LIAM scheme is available only to those aged 70 and below, with the annual premiums increasing sharply with age; CuepacsCare subscribers pay a uniform premium regardless of age, but they have to enrol before the age of 60, and coverage ceases at age 65. Given that the life expectancy (at birth) of Malaysians is approaching the mid-seventies, added to the high prevalence of chronic ailments among the elderly, it is clear that health care financing for the aged has become a major issue of social policy.

Third, the CuepacsCare scheme is a voluntary scheme for civil servants and public service retirees. Because the scheme is community-rated with uniform premiums for all subscribers, there is the possibility of selective opting out by eligible, low-risk individuals so that the subscriber pool might end up being disproportionately high-risk, with over-representation of intensive users of health care. It is unclear if the premiums of RM87 for individual plans and RM225 for family plans would be viable in the long term under such a scenario.

And finally, it should also be noted that most national health insurance schemes rely on joint employer/employee contributions. The emerging patchwork of health insurance schemes in Malaysia however appear to be solely the responsibility of employees (EPF contributions were jointly made, but with the clear understanding that these were employee savings and assets, distinct from employment health benefits).

In response to the proliferation of private medical insurance and managed care schemes, health care professionals (Malaysian Medical Association 1999; Malaysian Medical Association 2000; Primary Care Doctors Organisation of Malaysia 2000) and the lay public (Chan 2000) have proposed various alternatives which share some common features: a single-payer community-rated national health insurance fund which would be financed by employer/employee contributions, eventually to be levied on the self-employed as well, with supplementary contributions from progressive taxation to extend its benefits to all citizens and (legal) residents. It would be operated as a non-profit statutory institution with effective and credible citizen participation.

From a lay public's perspective, the consolidated purchasing power of a single-payer publicly operated health care fund has the further appeal that it would be able to lean more effectively on private health care providers (for cost control) while ensuring that mandated standards in clinical care and institutional upkeep are not compromised – in other words, cost-efficient health care which is in line with norms of medical necessity.

Private sector providers, of course, would be ambivalent about this last aspect, but they evidently consider the threat of profit-driven managed care and health maintenance organizations (HMOs) an even more daunting challenge (Chan 2001).

Yet others are wary of these proposals as *de facto* additional taxes in light of the government's much criticized record as steward of (dedicated) public trust funds, demanding instead for better use of existing sources of public monies, coupled with more stringent assurances for transparent and accountable management of public resources (Barisan Alternatif Health Bureau 2001).

On 3 March 2001, the Health Minister finally announced that a National Health Financing Authority (NHFA) would be established over the next five years, to oversee the establishment of a national health financing scheme. No operational details were available, but the Eighth Malaysia Plan (2001–2005) briefly noted that this would not preclude a continuing, complementary role for private health insurance (Malaysia 2001). Most importantly, it was left ambiguous as to whether the national health financing scheme would allow for opting out by those who preferred private health insurance.

Judging by the multitude of private medical insurance schemes which have emerged in the interim, it appears that the Malaysian government has adopted a *de facto* policy in health care financing which will rely heavily on a patchwork of profit-driven health insurance and managed care schemes as a supplement to the NHFA.

The insurance industry, local as well as foreign, has an obvious interest in blocking the establishment of national health insurance (social insurance) to keep the field clear for private initiatives in health insurance and medical underwriting. They have been discreetly but systematically lobbying against the proposals for publicly operated universal health insurance put forth by health care professionals and the lay public (for example, by floating a proposal for medical savings accounts which involve no risk pooling and therefore keeps the field clear for private medical underwriting).

Foreign insurers (for example, Prudential plc, UK) who brought in funds and acquired local equity during the East Asian currency crisis,[15] as a supportive (and profitable?) gesture to help stabilize a volatile financial situation, are reportedly now looking forward to a business-friendly environment to develop markets for health care and other insurance products. For-profit managed care and health maintenance organizations, modern incarnations of the health insurance industry, have also emerged amidst much recrimination from health care providers (*The Sun*, 25 September 2000; *The Star*, 14 April 2000), but for the moment are mostly locally-led initiatives[16] with foreigners waiting in the wings while the market is being tested.

The implications of these developments are profound because there is a crucial difference between social insurance, which embodies an implicit compact of cross-subsidy in social solidarity, and commercial underwriting, which assigns risk-rated premiums determined by the market's valuation of individual risk. The most objectionable consequence of for-profit risk-rated medical insurance is that those people at highest risk of falling ill and requiring treatment will be those least able to afford premiums, and therefore treatment.

Concluding remarks: the privatization of risk management

Nicholas Barr of the London School of Economics and Political Science has argued that among the key responsibilities of the modern welfare state, two in particular stand out:

> (i) [To] provide poverty relief, redistribute income and wealth, and reduce social exclusion (the 'Robin Hood' function), and (ii) provide insurance and offer a mechanism for redistribution over the life cycle (the 'piggy-bank' function) ... Thus the welfare state exists not only

to relieve poverty, but also to provide insurance and consumption smoothing . . . The welfare state is [therefore] here to stay . . . since the reasons for its existence, including risk and uncertainty will continue to apply . . . [even as it] adapts to economic and social change.

(Barr 2001)

In recent years, it has become clear that the privatization of health care and its financing is merely one instance of a broader transformation of risk-pooling arrangements for coping with uncertainty and threats to human welfare.

In parallel with the opening up of financial and currency markets world-wide, the entry of pension funds, mutual funds (unit trusts), investment-linked annuities and other financial instruments marks a major extension of capital's circuits into new arenas for accumulation, that is, risk management services for retirees' welfare which go beyond health security (Orszag 2000).

In the process, the modern welfarist state, in its role as a pooler of risks for coping with the catastrophic and burdensome events which occasionally befall its citizens, is shrinking. Socialized resources (taxes and other publicly managed revenues) have traditionally financed safety nets in health care, in unemployment and social security, and provided relief in instances where neither the individual nor her/his family and social support network could cope with the consequences of catastrophe.

The privatization of health care provision in principle is still compatible with public financing of health care (via a tax-supported national health trust fund, naational health insurance or some such arrangement). The privatization of risk management, however, is the lifeblood of the insurance (and financial services) industry, and this industry would look favourably upon the market opportunities emerging from a reduced role for government in social insurance and social protection, that is, in the management of uncertainty.

Sir Alan Walters, a former professor at the London School of Economics was a guest speaker in 2000 at the Socioeconomic & Environmental Research Institute in Penang. While listening to him, it struck me that it was perhaps not coincidental that he went from being Chief Economic Advisor to the *doyenne* of privatization, Lady Margaret Thatcher, to his present position as Vice-Chairman of the insurance and financial services giant, American International Group, Inc. (AIG).

Notes

1 '. . . Dimaklumkan bahawa Perbendaharaan Malaysia telah meminta semua Kementerian menyemak semula perbelanjaan mengurus yang akan dibuat dalam tahun 2004. Penekanan perlu diberi ke atas kawalan perbelanjaan dengan mengamalkan perbelanjaan (berhemat) dan seberapa boleh perbelanjaan dalam tahun 2004 adalah sama dengan tahun 2003. Perbendaharaan juga telah menegaskan bahawa tiada tambahan peruntukan yang akan diberikan pada tahun

2004. Sehubungan dengan ini, Kementerian telah menyemak dan membuat perkiraan semula perbelanjaan yang komited (locked-in) dalam tahun 2004. Perkiraan dan kedudukan keperluan peruntukan tahun 2004 adalah seperti di Lampiran 1. Secara umum didapati bahawa Kementerian akan menghadapi kekurangan peruntukan bagi bayaran emolumen sebanyak RM210.24 juta bagi tahun 2004. Memandangkan bahawa tiada peruntukan tambahan yang akan diterima pada tahun 2004, kekurangan ini perlu ditampung daripada penjimatan daripada lain-lain Objek Am di bawah Anggaran Belanja Mengurus (ABM) 2004'. . . . KKM-172/09/2004/(62) bertarikh 19 Mac 2004.

2 Following upon US Federal Reserve Chairman Paul Volcker's policy of fighting inflation with tight money supply and high interest rates in 1982.

3 Petronas, the national oil company, was incorporated in 1974. Its cumulative oil and gas revenues in the last 30 years have been conservatively estimated at about RM250 billion at the low end. As an 'off-budget' agency, it reports directly to the Prime Minister's office and is not subject to procedures of accountability and Parliamentary oversight.

4 World Bank loans for Malaysia had been on the decline since the 1980s and were tapering off by the early 1990s: 'Malaysia has had a long and productive relationship with the Bank, with a total of 99 loans approved since 1958, and a total disbursement of US$2.7 billion. The Bank has supported Malaysia predominantly in agriculture and rural development, but also in industry, infrastructure, health and education. Malaysia's successful development efforts over the past three decades, combined with its continued high growth and budget surplus, led to the Bank's slowly phasing out of an active programme in Malaysia from 1993 onward. Four projects totaling US$368 million were approved fiscal years 1992–94; and although there were no commitments in 1995–97, the Bank has provided technical assistance, policy advice, and analytical work over that time period.' (World Bank News Release No. 98/1826/EAP, 18 June 1998). The post-1997 resumption of social sector loans were disbursed notwithstanding Mahathir's capital controls and his vocal broadsides against the IMF's standard therapy for 'stabilization'.

5 'The Malaysian stock market soared again Friday following the announcement by Morgan Stanley Capital International (MSCI) on Thursday evening that it will include Malaysia in its Emerging Market Index. The Kuala Lumpur Stock Exchange (KLSE) Composite Index (CI) leapt 6.02 per cent, ending the day at 772.88 points . . . MSCI announced that it will reinstate Malaysia in its emerging market and all-country indices from February 2000 as long as there is no reversal of the country's financial liberalization. Malaysia was admitted into the MSCI index in 1992 but was de-listed upon the imposition of selective capital controls in September last year' (*Asia Times Online*, 14 August 1999). Large individual funds, such as the California Public Employees' Retirement System (CalPERS), have the same potential for moving the capital markets, [as do the international ratings agencies]. See, for example, *The Star* (18 February 2004). ['CI surges 17.6 points to 846']

6 In the 1980s and 1990s, power generation and distribution, postal services, telecommunications, airlines and railways, seaports and airports, highway construction, toll-operation and maintenance, and water and sewerage services were corporatized or privatized (Jomo 1995).

7 The overriding importance of party over communal considerations was clear from the federal government's strenuous efforts to deprive the Terengganu state government of its statutory royalties from oil and gas exploitation, after the Islamic opposition party, Parti Islam SeMalaysia (PAS), won control of this overwhelmingly Malay and Muslim state in the 1999 General Elections.

8 A remarkably candid statement of this came from the current Deputy Prime Minister Najib Abdul Razak (concurrently Deputy President of UMNO) who declared in 1987, in relation to the controversial award of the RM3.4 billion North–South Highway project to United Engineers Malaysia (a company in which UMNO had a 50 per cent stake), that 'in the case of the North–South Highway Project, it is a means of UMNO solving its problems by repaying loans taken for the new UMNO headquarters building. As big projects are hard to come by now, I feel it is alright in the case of UMNO to be involved in a company's bid for the highway project' (*The Star*, 31 August 1987).

9 Corporatization, in the Malaysian context, refers to a change in status of a governmental department to a free-standing corporate entity with substantial operational and financial autonomy, typically non-profit and fully government-owned (for example, the National Heart Institute). Privatization covers a range of scenarios including contracting out to private sector concessionaires, build-operate-transfer, build and transfer, management buy out, conversion to publicly listed companies in which the government may still be the substantial or majority shareholder (for example, Tenaga Nasional Bhd, Telekom Malaysia Bhd). See also Jomo (1995) for an extended discussion of this. Public anxiety over corporatization derives from fears that corporatization is a way-station along the route to fully privatized social services and utilities.

10 See Phua Kai Lit (this volume) for a discussion of this.

11 In her thesis, Noorul Ainur Mohd Nur cited figures from the Finance Division of the Health Ministry which indicated that expenditures on hospital support services (cleansing services, linen and laundry, clinical waste management, biomedical engineering maintenance and facilities engineering maintenance, accounting for 14 per cent of the Health Ministry budget) increased from RM213 million (US$54 million) in 1996 to RM468.5 million (US$174 million, 1997), a 2.2 fold increase with little evidence of commensurate expansion of services or improvements in quality. They have since steadily increased to RM507.9 million (US$188 million, 1999). Added to these were the costs of monitoring to ensure that the concessionaires complied with the performance standards stipulated in the contractual agreements, amounting to RM60 million over the 5-year period (1997–2001).

12 Indications were that even district hospitals, a crucial part of primary health care in the rural areas and an important link in the referral chain, were slated for corporatization.

13 Including hospitals, clinics and other treatment facilities, nursing homes and long-term care facilities, testing/diagnostic facilities, health professional services, health administration services, pharmaceuticals, medical supplies and disposables, hospital design, construction and equipping, hospital support (maintenance) services, insurance, managed care, HMOs (health maintenance organizations), telemedicine, training, education and research, and medical informatics (including medical registration).

14 It was for this reason that organizations like the Citizens' Health Initiative (CHI) called for a ban on profit-oriented insurers from health insurance, or at the very least a tight regulation of commercial insurers, to set premiums and to disallow discriminatory risk-rating.

15 Prudential plc (UK), hitherto a minority shareholder in Berjaya-Prudential, made major inroads into the financially troubled joint venture during the East Asian currency crisis. In return for raising its equity to 51 per cent in the joint venture, it won major concessions allowing it to market investment-linked insurance products, hitherto a privilege restricted to local insurers. This paved the way for other foreign insurers to negotiate for wide-ranging concessions

as well. The implications of these developments for health care financing and national health insurance bear watching. Prudential has recently entered the market for health care insurance.

16 Telekom Malaysia Bhd, one of the largest private sector employers in Malaysia (25,000 workers, annual health budget RM22 million) signed up with Pantai Medicare Sdn Bhd, a HMO/managed care subsidiary of the Pantai Holdings Bhd health care conglomerate, for management of its health benefits for Telekom staff and their dependants. CEO Mokhzani Mahathir further indicated that the HMO subsidiary was in advanced negotiations with another 10 companies and aimed to enroll 200,000 members by year-end (*The Edge Daily*, 20 October 2000).

References

Asia Times Online, 14 August 1999, 'Index shift gives Malaysia a 12 per cent boost'.

Barisan Alternatif Health Bureau (2001) 'The government's proposed National Health Financing Scheme: healthcare at what cost? More of our money for the cronies', pamphlet, Kuala Lumpur: Barisan Alternatif Health Bureau.

Barr, N. (2001) *The Welfare State as Piggy Bank: Information, Risk, Uncertainty, and the Role of the State*, New York: Oxford University Press.

Chan, Chee Khoon (1996) 'Health care financing', in Jomo K.S. and Ng Suew Kiat (eds) *Malaysia's Economic Development: Policy & Reform*, Kuala Lumpur: Malaysian Institute for Economic Research (MIER).

—— (2000) 'Towards a citizens' proposal for healthcare reforms', *Ekonomika* 12(3): 10–12.

—— (2001) 'The national health financing authority: six questions for the health minister', *Aliran Monthly* 21(2).

—— (2002) 'Genomics, health, and society', *New Solutions* 12(2): 109–19.

—— (2004) 'Market development in healthcare services in Malaysia: a political economic and institutional analysis', paper presented at the UNRISD International Conference on Commercialization of Health Care: Global and Local Dynamics and Policy Responses, Helsinki, 15–17 March.

Chan, Chee Khoon, Noorul Ainur Mohd Nur and Dzulkifli Abd Razak (2000) 'A sunrise industry: the emergence of investor-led, corporate healthcare', paper presented at the National Seminar on Health & Healthcare in Changing Environments: The Malaysian Experience, Kuala Lumpur, 22–23 April.

Gomez, E.T. (1990) *Politics in Business: UMNO's Corporate Investments*, Kuala Lumpur: Forum.

—— (1991) *Money Politics in the Barisan Nasional*, Kuala Lumpur: Forum.

—— (1995) 'Management buy-outs', in Jomo K.S. (ed.) *Privatising Malaysia: Rents, Rhetoric, Realities*, Boulder, CO: Westview Press.

Hall, D. (2003) 'Multinational corporations and the pattern of privatisation in healthcare', in Kasturi Sen (ed.) *Restructuring Health Services*, London: Zed Books.

Horgan, M. (1999) *The 'Building Blocks' of Effective Government Debt Management*, Geneva: United Nations Institute for Training and Research (UNITAR).

Jesudason, J. (1990) *Ethnicity and the Economy: The State, Chinese Business and Multinationals in Malaysia*, Singapore: Oxford University Press.

Jomo K.S. (ed.) (1995) *Privatizing Malaysia: Rents, Rhetoric, Realities*, Boulder, CO: Westview Press.

Liu L. and Ferri, G. (2001) 'How do global credit rating agencies rate firms from developing countries?', ADB Institute Research Paper 26, September, Tokyo: Asian Development Bank Institute.

Malaysia (2001) *The Eighth Malaysia Plan 2001–2005*, Kuala Lumpur: Economic Planning Unit, Prime Minister's Department, Malaysia.

Malaysian Medical Association (1999), *Health for All: Reforming Health Care in Malaysia*, Malaysian Medical Association.

—— (2000) 'MMA national health care plan', paper prepared for the Second National Economic Consultative Council (MAPEN II), Malaysian Medical Association.

Malaysiakini.com, 3 July 2006, 'No additional cash for government coffers'.

Noorul Ainur Mohd Nur (2003) 'Privatisation in Malaysia at the crossroads: politics and efficiency', unpublished PhD thesis, City University of New York.

Orszag, P.R. (2000) *Voluntary Individual Accounts for Social Security: What Are the Costs?*, Washington, DC: Center on Budget and Policy Priorities.

Patnaik, P. (1999) 'Capitalism in Asia at the end of the millennium', *Monthly Review*, July–August.

—— (2004) 'The new imperialism', paper presented at the International Development Economics Associates (IDEAs) International Conference on the Economics of the New Imperialism, Jawaharlal Nehru University, New Delhi, 22–24 January.

Patnaik, U. (2003) 'Global capitalism, deflation and agrarian crisis in developing countries', UNRISD Social Policy & Development Programme paper number 15, Geneva: UNRISD.

Primary Care Doctors Organisation of Malaysia (2000) 'Resolution from the Primary Care Doctors Organisation of Malaysia public forum on Financing for Healthcare: How will it affect you?', Universiti Malaya, 21 May. Online. Available at <http://www2.jaring.my/pcdom/finance.htm> (accessed 3 June 2000).

Promotion of Investments Act 1986, Kuala Lumpur: Government Printers.

Public Services International (1999) *The WTO and the General Agreement on Trade in Services: What is at Stake for Public Health?*, Ferney-Voltaire: Public Services International.

The Edge Daily, 10 May 2004, 'Lower Budget Deficit'. Online. Available at <http://www.theedgedaily.com> (accessed 11 August 2004).

The Star, 14 August 1999, 'Corporatisation plan for hospitals scrapped'.

——, 18 January 2000, 'Health option: EPF members can use Account III for health insurance scheme from June'.

——, 14 April 2000, 'Doctors still unhappy with managed care organizations' (editorial comment).

——, 18 February 2004, 'CI surges 17.6 points to 846'.

——, 11 March 2004 'S&P: Malaysia unlikely to be re-rated anytime soon'.

——, 20 July 2004, 'Pilot project on private wings in hospitals likely to start next year'.

The Sun, 25 September 2000, 'Managed care organizations imposing too many conditions, say medical practitioners'.

World Bank website. Available at <http://www.worldbank.org> (accessed 20 January 2004).

6 Equity in Malaysian health care

An analysis of public health expenditures and health care facilities

Wee Chong Hui and Jomo K.S.

Malaysia has recorded good health indicators among comparable economies. Since the time the nation attained Independence in 1957, the government has been the main provider of health care. The primary means of health care financing has also been through the public sector, that is, by taxation. This chapter examines governmental priorities in health care, in particular aspects of equity in the distribution of government health services. Although governmental spending on health care has increased over the years, we will argue that the priority accorded to health care has decreased relative to other sectors. We will also show that despite favourable statistics for the nation as a whole, inequities exist in the distribution and utilization of health care services, by geographical location, states and social class.

The underlying concept of equity in our chapter encompasses both vertical and horizontal equity. Vertical equity is concerned with unequal status amongst individuals. For example, the richest 20 per cent of households in Malaysia earned 50 per cent of total household income, compared to 36 per cent for the middle 40 per cent and 14 per cent for the poorest 40 per cent in 1999 (calculated with data from the Eighth Malaysia Plan; Malaysia 2001: Table 3-3). If the poor cannot afford health care, subsidized services should then be provided by the government, in the interest of vertical equity. Horizontal equity is concerned with the equal treatment of equals. For example, the federal government is expected to treat communities equally irrespective of their locality, by state or stratum, if these communities are equal in their principal aspects.

This chapter examines the government's prioritization of health expenditure. It shows that the physical distribution of government health services by stratum and state is inequitable, thereby affecting access for and utilization by lower income groups. The priority accorded to health services in general, and to health services for lower income groups in particular, has also declined over the years. Total government development expenditure by state has been found to be inequitable (Wee 2006). However, we do not have sufficient data to evaluate horizontal equity in government health expenditure.

Descriptive statistical methods are used to analyse official government data in the following discussion. These include correlation analysis, whereby the correlation coefficient, 'r', shows the strength of the relationship between the tested variables. The absolute value of r ranges between 0 and 1.00, and the relationship could be positive or negative. The results are considered statistically significant if the 'p' value is less than 5 per cent ($p < 0.05$). The overall scenario and trend can only be drawn from multiple data sets, each for varying time periods. The analysis also draws on empirical studies conducted during the 1970s.

Government expenditure

Government health expenditure has been increasing in absolute terms through the years. Total federal government health expenditure increased from RM80 million in 1960 to RM175 million in 1970, RM778 million in 1980, RM1,777 million in 1990 and RM4,948 million in 2000. Operating expenditure was 80 to 90 per cent of the total government expenditure. Annual per capita operating expenditure increased from RM15 in 1970 to RM50 in 1980, RM80 in 1990 and RM175 in 2000.[1]

Furthermore, government health services in Malaysia have been highly subsidized. In 1973/74, the Ministry of Health (MOH)'s revenue from inpatient, outpatient and birth delivery services contributed only 3.6 per cent of the costs of these services, that is, the subsidization rate was 96.4 per cent (Meerman 1979: 158–61). More than 75 per cent of MOH outpatient treatments were free, while more than 67 per cent of inpatients got free services (Meerman 1979: 145). Moreover, almost all outpatient services provided by government clinics and 65 per cent of outpatient services provided by government hospitals in 1988 were free of charge (Public Health Institute 1988a). In 1996, 96 per cent of clinic patients and 59 per cent of hospital patients received free services (The Second National Health and Mortality Survey, 1996, cited in MOH c.2000: 56). The MOH collected only 5 per cent of the total amount spent, resulting in a subsidization rate of 95 per cent.

Health has been an important social service provided by the government. Nevertheless, if we compare it with other sectors, it can be seen that the government is giving decreasing priority to health services. Over the longer term, the proportions of government expenditure on health, defence and security, as well as economic services, have decreased in comparison to expenditures on other functions (Table 6.1). Except for the late 1980s and early 1990s, the proportional decrease in health expenditure has been faster than for defence and security or economic projects. Since 2000, however, the priority given to social services has increased, with the priority given to health services having increased more than the average for all social services, while government expenditure for defence and security as well as economic services has decreased.

One reason for this reversal may be traced to the privatization of certain services in health care. Health care privatization gained prominence with the MOH subcontracting its hospital support services to the private sector from

Table 6.1 Proportion of federal government expenditure by functional classification, Malaysia (%)

	Defence & security	Economic services	Health	Social services[1]	Administration	Others
Total expenditure						
1963–65	20.7	25.8	6.8	26.7	8.8	17.9
First Malaysia Plan, 1966–1970	21.9	22.1	6.7	28.1	8.8	19.1
Second Malaysia Plan, 1971–1975	22.3	23.7	6.1	29.6	8.4	16.0
Third Malaysia Plan, 1976–1980	20.4	26.2	4.7	28.1	7.5	17.8
Fourth Malaysia Plan, 1981–1985	17.5	27.3	3.8	26.7	6.3	22.2
Fifth Malaysia Plan, 1986–1990	13.7	21.9	4.6	27.0	8.6	28.8
Sixth Malaysia Plan, 1991–1995	16.7	20.0	5.6	29.8	10.0	23.6
Seventh Malaysia Plan, 1996–2000	13.1	21.0	4.5	33.3	11.8	20.8
Eighth Malaysia Plan, 2001–2005, Estimate	13.0	17.7	7.2	37.5	9.7	22.4
Change (%)						
1963–65 to 1MP	5.8	–14.3	–1.5	5.2	0.0	6.7
1MP to 2MP	1.8	7.2	–9.0	5.3	–4.5	–16.2
2MP to 3MP	–8.5	10.5	–23.0	–5.1	–10.7	11.3
3MP to 4MP	–14.2	4.2	–19.1	–5.0	–16.0	24.7
4MP to 5MP	–21.7	–19.8	21.1	1.1	36.5	29.7
5MP to 6MP	21.9	–8.7	21.7	10.4	16.3	–18.1
6MP to 7MP	–21.6	5.0	–19.6	11.7	18.0	–11.9
7MP to 8MP (Estimate)	–0.8	–15.7	60.0	12.6	–17.8	7.7

Sources: Ministry of Finance (various years) Economic Report; the Malaysia Plans, various years.

Note
[1] Includes health.

Table 6.2 Ministry of Health, Malaysia: operating expenditure, 1981–2000

	Support services		Total	
	Expenditure (RM million)	*Change (%)*	*Expenditure (RM million)*	*Change (%)*
Fourth Malaysia Plan, 1981–1985	135	—	4,442	—
Fifth Malaysia Plan, 1986–1990	164	21.5	5,789	30.3
Sixth Malaysia Plan, 1991–1995	263	60.4	9,548	64.9
Seventh Malaysia Plan, 1996–2000	1,956	643.7	16,784	75.8

Source: Ministry of Health (various years) Annual Report.

1994 onwards. Since this expenditure item is one of the largest MOH budget items, this subcontracting has escalated MOH expenditure. For example, the expenditure for support services increased more than sixfold from the Sixth Malaysia Plan period to the Seventh Malaysia Plan period (Table 6.2). An increase in cost resulting from privatization means that the increase in allocation to health largely went to the private companies that received the contract for the privatized services rather than to an improvement in service quality or coverage.

The overall shift in relative expenditure among the different sectors has equity implications. While expenditures on defence and security are largely ignored in equity studies (Meerman 1979), expenditures on economic projects have been shown to be less pro-poor than social services. Recipients of government economic projects usually require various skills or own certain assets before they are able to benefit from such support. For example, benefits from interest-free loans for business ventures may be realized only if the recipients have entrepreneurial skills, and agricultural subsidies benefit those with large farms more than the land-hungry farmers. On the other hand, expenditure on health or education works towards increasing the capacity of the poor and thereby improving equity.

Geographical distribution of health care facilities

The majority of the Malaysian population (83 per cent) are in Peninsular Malaysia. The First National Health and Morbidity Survey (NHMS 1) in 1986–87 (Public Health Institute 1988b) found that 74 per cent of the population of Peninsular Malaysia lived within 3 kilometres of a static health facility and that 89 per cent lived within 5 kilometres of such a facility. By the time of the Second National Health and Morbidity Survey (NHMS 2)

Table 6.3 Average distance from health facilities by income quintile, 1996 (kilometres)

Income quintile (monthly household income)[1]	Government clinic	Government hospital	Private clinic	Private hospital
1 (RM500 or less)	5.7	23.6	14.2	172.3
2 (RM501-1000)	4.7	17.7	7.9	108.3
3 (RM1001-1500)	4.5	14.9	5.8	79.7
4 (RM1501-2500)	4.0	12.8	4.6	56.2
5 (RM2501 or more)	3.7	10.9	2.8	41.3

Source: Rozita Halina Hussein (2000: Table 2).

Note
[1] Estimated from The Eighth Malaysia Plan (Malaysia 2001: Table 3-3).

in 1996, these proportions had increased to 81 per cent and 93 per cent (Public Health Institute 1997).

Health facilities are generally located further from the poor than the rich, who are mainly found in urban areas. For the poorest quintile, the average distance to the nearest government clinic was 5.7 kilometres, and to the nearest government hospital, 23.6 kilometres, compared to 3.7 kilometres and 10.9 kilometres respectively for the richest quintile (Table 6.3). The nearest private clinic for the poorest quintile was 14.2 kilometres away and the nearest private hospital, 172.3 kilometres, compared to 2.8 kilometres and 41.3 kilometres for the richest quintile.

There are also regional disparities. All states had over 80 per cent of their population living within 5 kilometres of a static health facility in 1996, but the largest states of Sarawak, Sabah and Pahang (38, 22 and 11 per cent of national land area respectively, compared to 0.2 to 6 per cent for each of the other states) had lower shares of their population within a 5 kilometre radius of a health facility. Sarawak had only 60 per cent of its population within a 5 kilometre radius, Sabah had 76 per cent and Pahang had 79 per cent (Public Health Institute 1997). These three states are less developed states, with relatively poorer transport and communication facilities as well as higher levels of poverty.

Urban–rural disparities have also been serious. The NHMS 2 (Public Health Institute 1997) found 92 per cent of the urban population living within 3 kilometres of a static health facility, compared to 69 per cent for the rural population. The rural populations in Sabah and Sarawak were even further from static health facilities, with 50 per cent and 62 per cent of the rural population respectively living within 5 kilometres of a facility.

Distance is directly related to transport costs. Utilization rates for health services were found to fall with increases in transport costs. Transport costs have been substantial – much more than the average government medical fees for outpatients – and are believed to be increasing relatively more over

Table 6.4 Cost of seeking outpatient care from government services and gross household income, 1973/74, 1986/87, 1996 (RM per visit)

	Peninsular Malaysia, 1973/74	*1986/87*	*1996*
Transport		2.00–2.30	4.14^2
Health services		0.20	0.25^3
Total	0.41^1	2.20–2.50	4.39
Monthly household income	342	1,074 (1987)	$2,308^4$

Sources: Heller (1976: 13); NHMS 1 (Public Health Institute 1988b: 7); NHMS 2 (MOH c.2000: 13, 14, 20, 202); Mid-Term Review of the Fifth Malaysia Plan, 1986–1990 (Malaysia 1988: Table 3-4); Mid-Term Review of the Seventh Malaysia Plan, 1996–2000 (Malaysia 1999: Table 3-4).

Notes
[1] Total cost of seeking outpatient care, as from Heller (1976: 13). This study did not break down the cost into transport cost and health services cost.
[2] According to NHMS 2 (Public Health Institute 1997), 20 per cent of respondents spent RM1 and 73.5 per cent spent RM1–10. In this study, it is assumed that the average transport cost for the latter is RM5.
[3] This figure was derived in the following way:

	Clinic	*Hospital*
Free because of subsidy/payments by employers	96%	59%
Paying patients @ RM1 per visit	4%	41%
Average cost per visit	RM0.04	RM0.41
Proportion of government service outpatients	44%	56%

Average cost per visit = (RM0.04 × 0.44) + (RMRM0.41 × 0.56).

[4] Average for 1995 and 1997.

time (Table 6.4). The transport costs for seeking government health care and medical fees increased from RM0.41 in 1973/74 to RM2.20–2.50 in 1986/87 and to RM4.39 in 1996.

Even government health services, relatively affordable compared to private services, have become less affordable since 1973/74, partly because of higher transport costs. While transport costs in 1986/87 were 5.4 to 6.1 times that for 1973/74, the average household income for 1986/87 was only 3.1 times that for 1973/74. Both transport costs and medical fees as well as household incomes doubled from 1986/87 to 1996. Hence, the average transport cost and medical fee for 1996 was 10.7 times that for 1973/74, whereas the average household income for 1996 was only 6.8 times that for 1973/74.

Distance, travel and waiting time

Distance tends to increase travel time. Besides time spent waiting for and receiving treatment, travel time increases the opportunity cost and thus reduces the demand for health services. The opportunity cost of spending time to seek treatment would include income foregone for those unable to get paid sick leave or working time for the self-employed who work, for example, on their farms or are responsible for housework.

Heller (1976) found that the average travel, waiting and treatment time for an outpatient visit to a government facility in Peninsular Malaysia was 65 minutes in 1973/74, with 25 minutes spent travelling. He also found that greater travel time reduced demand for public health services. Meerman (1979: 169) noted 'lower (health service) consumption in rural areas, where ... average time and its variance are high' as a corollary to Heller's finding.

In 1986/87, one-third of patients spent 15 minutes or less seeking treatment, while another third spent 16 to 30 minutes. Utilization of services fell with substantial increases in travel time, particularly if travel time took more than two hours (Public Health Institute 1988b). Nonetheless, the average travel time for seeking treatment had increased to 30–50 minutes by 1996 (Public Health Institute 1997).

However, waiting time for treatment has been a greater deterrent than travel time (Heller 1976). Waiting time increases with the lack of personnel such as doctors. Relatively poorer states have fewer doctors (including doctors in both the government and the private sector). State incidences of poverty and their respective population per doctor ratio for 1985, 1990, 1995 and 1997 were positively correlated (positive values of correlation coefficient, r) and statistically significant ($p < 0.05$) (Table 6.5). This implies that there were relatively fewer doctors to serve the populations in states with higher incidences of poverty. Hence longer waiting times render medical care even less accessible to the relatively poor.

Private doctors tend to locate their practices in high household-income states, where clients have more ability to pay. The government should therefore address the relative shortage of private doctors in poor or low household-income states by placing more government doctors in these states. However, this is not evident in our analysis. There was no significant relationship between population per government doctor by state and poverty incidence by state for 1987, 1995, 1997 and 1999. In fact, the reverse is true for 1984 and 1990, with the higher poverty states having higher population–government doctor ratios in these years (for 1984: $r = 0.57$, $p = 0.026$; for 1990: $r = 0.623$, $p = 0.023$). Similarly, there was no significant relationship between population per government doctor by state and state household incomes in 1985, 1995 and 1999, although higher income states in 1990–1991 had higher population–government doctor ratios ($r = 0.583$, $p = 0.036$).

In fact, time 'wasted' is the main reason why poorer rural populations bypass government facilities in favour of private facilities (Public Health Institute 1997). Distance and poor facilities therefore deter the poor from utilizing government health services.

Table 6.5 Population per doctor and poverty incidence by state, 1985, 1990, 1995 and 1997

	1985		1990		1995		1997	
	Poverty[1]	Population/doctor	Poverty	Population/doctor	Poverty	Population/doctor	Poverty	Population/doctor
Selangor	8.6	3334	7.8	2288	2.2	2148	1.3	1636
Johor	12.2	4186	10.1	3130	3.1	2697	1.6	1938
P. Pinang	13.4	1925	8.0	1798	4.0	1554	1.6	1118
Melaka	15.8	3011	12.4	2640	5.3	1768	3.6	1200
Pahang	15.7	4581	10.3	3509	6.8	3509	4.1	2320
N. Sembilan	13.0	3353	9.5	2604	4.9	2284	4.5	1589
Perak	20.3	3544	19.4	2799	9.1	2187	4.5	1556
Sarawak	31.9	6591	21.0	4786	10.0	4134	7.5	2722
Perlis	33.7	3791	17.2	3411	11.8	3029	10.6	2152
Kedah	36.3	5513	30.0	4253	12.2	3201	11.5	2114
Trengganu	28.9	5557	31.2	4249	24.3	4172	17.3	2502
Kelantan	39.2	6898	29.9	3782	22.9	2720	19.5	1917
Sabah	33.1	7024	34.4	5061	22.4	5870	22.1	4195
r	0.780		0.822		0.676		0.706	
p	0.002		0.001		0.011		0.007	

Sources: The Second Outline Perspective Plan (Malaysia 1991b: Table 2-8); Mid-Term Review of the Fifth Malaysia Plan, 1986–1990 (Malaysia 1988: Table 3-4); The Mid-Term Review of the Seventh Malaysia Plan, 1996–2000 (Malaysia 1999: Table 3-4); The Eighth Malaysia Plan (Malaysia 2001: Table 3-3).

Note
[1] For 1984.

Table 6.6 Visits per capita for government health services by income group, 1973/74, 1996

Income group	1973/74[1]			1996
	Clinic	*Hospital*	*Total*	*Government services*
I – poorest	0.80	0.70	1.50	2.5
II	0.78	0.72	1.50	2.1
III	0.90	0.51	1.41	2.2
IV	0.77	0.57	1.34	1.7
V – richest	0.83	0.28	1.11	1.0
Average = Sum $(0.2 \times$ group)	0.82	0.56	1.37	1.9

Sources: Meerman (1979: 80, 158–61); NHMS 2 (MOH c.2000: 56).

Note
[1] Calculated using (visits per household)/(household size of 5.83).

Utilization of health services

Lower income groups appear more likely to use government health services compared to the better-off, and in the last 20 years, this difference has become wider. In 1973/74, the lowest income quintile averaged 1.50 visits per capita, while the richest quintile made 1.11 visits per capita (Table 6.6). In 1996, the lowest income quintile made 2.5 visits while the richest quintile made 1.0 visit per capita.

The proportion of patients categorized as 'low income' and provided with subsidized services by the government-owned National Heart Institute (NHI) exceeded the poverty incidence in 1992–2001 (Table 6.7). Based on patients' ability to pay, such categorization enabled needy patients to receive subsidized services. A lower proportion were categorized as low-income patients for the (presumably) more affordable outpatient services compared to the more costly inpatient services. The fees for government servants and pensioners are borne by the government. The government has employed less than 15 per cent of the labour force since the mid-1980s and has been reducing its share. Yet, government servants and pensioners constituted 44 to 55 per cent of NHI patients in the period 1992–2001. Together with the subsidized patients, government payments covered the bulk of the fees for the majority of patients in the NHI.

However, low-income groups would have poorer access to private services. Private health services have increased tremendously since the 1960s. In 1973/74, per capita outpatient visits to private facilities were lower than visits to government facilities, 0.5 compared to 0.7 (calculated from Meerman 1979: 80, 158). By 1996, per capita outpatient visits to private facilities exceeded those to government facilities, 2.8 compared to 1.9 (Public Health

Table 6.7 Patients of the National Heart Institute, 1992–2001, % distribution by status/type

	1992/93	1993/94	1996/97	1997/98	1998/99	1999/2000	2000/01
Total outpatients	**35611**	**39265**	**5626Z**	**65612**	**74860**	**87015**	**n.a.**
Government servants and pensioners	52	44	49	51	51	52	51
Government servants	*n.a.*	*24*	*22*	*21*	*19*	*18*	*17*
Pensioners	*n.a.*	*20*	*27*	*30*	*32*	*34*	*34*
Students	n.a.	7	–	–	–	–	–
'Low income'[1]	14	9	8	6	6	6	6
Private paying	34	40	43	43	43	42	43
Total inpatients	**4982**	**6125**	**8089**	**8872**	**8757**	**9428**	**n.a.**
Government servants & pensioners	n.a.	44	47	46	46	42	45
Government servants	*n.a.*	*29*	*26*	*24*	*23*	*18*	*23*
Pensioners	*n.a.*	*15*	*21*	*22*	*23*	*24*	*22*
Students	n.a.	9	–	–	–	–	–
'Low income'[1]	29	26	21	16	20	24	25
Private paying	n.a.	21	31	38	34	20	30
Incidence of poverty	13.5% (1993)		6.8% (1997)		7.5% (1999)		5.1% (2002)

Sources: National Heart Institute (various years) Annual Report; the Malaysia Plans (various years); Noriyah (2004).

Notes
[1] Subsidized services. Patients who cannot afford to pay are categorized as 'low income' patients.
n.a. – not available.

Institute 1997). It has also been found that the lower income groups receive lower levels of personal preventive health care. According to the second countrywide NHMS (Public Health Institute 1997), lower proportions of women with low income, less education and from rural areas had regular breast examinations and pap smear examinations compared to those with higher income, more education and from the urban areas.

Distribution by income

In general, subsidies for public outpatient services as a proportion of household income decreased with increasing per capita income quintile in 1973/74 (Table 6.8). However, in terms of absolute amount of subsidy (in *ringgit*), the inverse relationship with income quintiles was not so consistent, particularly for inpatient services.

In 1996, subsidies represented lower proportions of household incomes across all income quintiles when compared to 1973/74 (Table 6.9 compared to Table 6.8).[2] Nevertheless, the rate of subsidization remains higher for the lower income quintiles compared to the higher income quintiles. In terms of absolute *ringgit* amounts of subsidy, lower quintiles generally received higher subsidies, except for inpatient services, which was highest for the richest quintile.

The subsidization rates by income groups for 1973/74 and 1996 (Tables 6.8 and 6.9) suggest that the ability to pay influences the utilization of government health services. The poor use more government services because of their limited ability to pay. As the cost for a service increases, the patient opts for cheaper facilities. Even those who are better-off tend to use more government facilities for the more costly inpatient services than they do for outpatient services.

Table 6.8 Subsidization of various government health services by income quintile, 1973/74

	Subsidization as % of household income (RM per household)					
	I (Poorest)	II	III	IV	V (Richest)	Average
Rural: outpatient	21.3	11.9	5.8	4.0	0.6	4.0
	(28)	(27)	(18)	(19)	(8)	(19)
Hospital:	22.1	11.9	9.5	5.3	1.8	5.5
outpatient	(29)	(27)	(30)	(24)	(22)	(26)
Inpatient	71.0	59.4	15.8	24.9	7.8	20.5
	(92)	(133)	(50)	(115)	(96)	(97)
Childbirth	1.3	1.8	1.5	0.3	0.0	0.6
	(6)	(4)	(5)	(1)	(1)	(3)

Sources: Calculated with data from Meerman (1979: 80, 158–61).

Note
Household income for quintile V is taken as average income less 0.2 × sum (average income for other quintiles).

Table 6.9 Subsidization of various government health services by income quintile, 1996

	Subsidization as % of household income				
	I (Poorest)	*II*	*III*	*IV*	*V (Richest)*
Outpatient clinic	3.1	0.5	0.3	0.2	0.1
Outpatient hospital	16.4	7.3	5.2	3.4	0.4
Inpatient	41.0	17.3	9.2	7.3	4.9

Source: Rozita Halina Hussein (2000: Graph 8).

Distribution by state

There is no definite indication that more financial resources have been allocated to states with low household income or high poverty incidences. Although the estimated development allocation per household decreased with household income and increased with poverty incidence for the Fourth Malaysia Plan (1981–1985) and the Fifth Malaysia Plan (1986–1990), the correlation coefficient was not statistically significant (p = 0.48).

In Table 6.10, we analyse government allocations for MOH operating expenditure by state household income for an indication of governmental priorities. In 1998, the MOH's operating budget by state was inversely related to state household income. The operating budget included allocations for administration, public health and medical care. Allocations for administration are distributed among salaries and training, as well as for the operation and maintenance of buildings and other assets, which are overhead cost commitments influenced by decisions made in previous periods. Public health activities include vector control, water supply, immunisation and dental care programmes, which have direct and immediate social impact. Medical care refers to curative services for both outpatient and inpatient treatments, also with direct and immediate social impact.

Among the three budget items (administration, public health and medical care), only the correlation coefficient between administration and state household income was statistically significant (p < 0.05). This suggests that low-income states were allocated relatively more for administration. Conversely, the correlation coefficient between the public health budget and state household income as well as that between the medical care budget and state household income were not statistically significant. Analysis of the correlation coefficients between the public health budget and state poverty incidence (r = 0.524, p = 0.081) and between the budget for administration and state incidence of poverty (r = 0.567, p = 0.043) also showed no significant relationship.

Correlation analysis between the value of medical items (for example drugs for medical care) issued by the state and state household incomes, as well as

Table 6.10 Ministry of Health operating budget and gross household income by state

	Household income 1997 (RM)	Allocation (RM per household[1]) 1998			
		Total	Public health	Medical care	Administration
Kelantan	1,249	607	236	22	338
Terengganu	1,497	705	289	15	392
Perlis	1,507	1,121	324	314	482
Kedah	1,590	570	246	3	308
Pahang	1,632	605	255	21	323
Perak	1,940	780	382	10	379
Sabah	2,057	619	302	17	293
Sarawak	2,242	383	196	4	179
Melaka	2,276	657	294	17	338
N. Sembilan	2,378	786	349	23	396
Johor	2,772	511	243	3	255
P. Pinang	3,130	650	338	13	289
Selangor	4,006	242	119	9	114
r		-0.56	-0.37	-0.28	-0.70
p		0.046	0.215	0.345	0.008

Sources: Calculated with data from Ministry of Health (1998) Annual Report and Mid-Term Review of the Seventh Malaysia Plan, 1996–2000 (Malaysia 1999: Table 3-4).

Note
[1] No. of households for the year 2000 were used in the computation.

between the value of medical items issued by the state and state poverty incidences for 1985, 1990 and 1997 were also not statistically significant (results of analysis were, respectively, $r = 0.038$, $p = 0.903$ and $r = 0.248$, $p = 0.414$ for 1985; $r = -0.293$, $p = 0.331$ and $r = 0.260$, $p = 0.392$ for 1990; and $r = 0.251$, $p = 0.404$ and $r = 0.418$, $p = 0.156$ for 1997). Our correlation analysis also shows that government allocations in the 1980s were generally not related to health indicators by state such as infant mortality rate, neonatal mortality rate, toddler mortality rate, still-birth rate, maternal mortality rate and the nutritional status of pregnant women.

Conclusions

This country has in the past managed to achieve a high level of availability of public health care services, with a well distributed system of service delivery points. A major portion of the health services utilized in this country has consisted of highly subsidized government services. Subsidized health care utilized by the lower income groups has constituted higher proportions of their incomes. Utilization of government health services by the poor has also increased from the 1970s onwards. Nevertheless, despite this overall success, there have been inequities.

It is unclear, for example, whether the poor have enjoyed absolute values of subsidies that are comparable to those enjoyed by the higher income groups for all government health services. Many among the poor who need treatment may fail to seek it due to travel and opportunity costs. Private travel costs incurred to seek treatment have been high and have increased at a faster rate than household income. The poor live further from both public and private health facilities than the better-off. The rural poor in the large and relatively poorer states of Sabah, Sarawak and Pahang have to spend more on transport to public health facilities, especially to specialized urban hospitals. The opportunity cost of time spent seeking treatment in the government sector may also deter utilization. Delays in treatment in the government sector have been exacerbated by personnel shortages.

Available data show no significant relationship between development allocations and state household income, poverty incidence or health indicators in the Fourth and Fifth Malaysia Plan periods (1981–1985 and 1986–1990). The data also confirm the low priority given to medical care and public health in low-income states in the late 1990s.

Furthermore, the growth of private health services since the 1980s has benefited the better-off more because of their ability to pay. The government has to pay attention to the relative deprivation of the poor since they will seek subsidized government services because of their limited ability to pay. Nevertheless, access of the poor to health care has been threatened by the outflow of skilled medical personnel from the public sector, and increasing user charges incurred by government.

By using revenues from general taxation to subsidize health services, the government will be fulfilling its allocative function of providing essential services, as well as its distributional function to achieve the equity objective. These are functions that have accorded the state much of its legitimacy. Even so, the government has announced plans to withdraw from the provision of health care. It remains to be seen how the government will fulfil its allocative and distributional responsibilities in health care henceforth.

Notes

1 Calculated with data from Department of Statistics (various years), and the Malaysia Plans (various years).
2 However, this could be due to different methods of computation for the different time periods.

References

Department of Statistics (various years) *Yearbook of Statistics*, Kuala Lumpur: Department of Statistics, Malaysia.

Heller, Peter S. (1976) *A Model of the Demand for Medical and Health Services in West Malaysia*, University of Michigan, Centre for Research on Economic Development, Discussion Paper No. 62, Ann Arbor, MI.

Malaysia (1981) *The Fourth Malaysia Plan, 1981–1985*, Kuala Lumpur: Economic Planning Unit, Prime Minister's Department, Malaysia.

—— (1984) *Mid-term Review of the Fourth Malaysia Plan, 1981–1985*, Kuala Lumpur: Economic Planning Unit, Prime Minister's Department, Malaysia.

—— (1986) *The Fifth Malaysia Plan, 1986–1990*, Kuala Lumpur: Economic Planning Unit, Prime Minister's Department, Malaysia.

—— (1988) *The Mid-Term Review of the Fifth Malaysia Plan, 1986–1990*, Kuala Lumpur: Economic Planning Unit, Prime Minister's Department, Malaysia.

—— (1991a) *The Sixth Malaysia Plan, 1991–1995*, Kuala Lumpur: Economic Planning Unit, Prime Minister's Department, Malaysia.

—— (1991b) *The Second Outline Perspective Plan, 1991–2000*, Kuala Lumpur: Economic Planning Unit, Prime Minister's Department, Malaysia.

—— (1999) *The Mid-Term Review of the Seventh Malaysia Plan, 1996–2000*, Kuala Lumpur: Economic Planning Unit, Prime Minister's Department, Malaysia.

—— (2001) *The Eighth Malaysia Plan, 2001–2005*, Kuala Lumpur: Economic Planning Unit, Prime Minister's Department, Malaysia.

Meerman, Jacob (1979) *Public Expenditure in Malaysia: Who Benefits and Why*, New York: Oxford University Press.

Ministry of Finance (various years) *Economic Report*, Kuala Lumpur: Ministry of Finance, Malaysia.

Ministry of Health (various years) *Annual Report*, Kuala Lumpur: Ministry of Health, Malaysia.

Ministry of Health (MOH) (c.2000) *Health in Malaysia: Achievements and Challenges*, Kuala Lumpur: MOH.

National Heart Institute (various years) *Annual Report*, Kuala Lumpur: Ministry of Health, Malaysia.

Noriyah bt Ahmad (2004) 'Poverty in Malaysia – general trends and strategies', paper presented in Seminar Kemiskinan, Yayasan Kemiskinan Sarawak, Holiday Inn Kuching, Sarawak, Malaysia, 25–26 February.

Public Health Institute (1988a) *Annual Report*, Kuala Lumpur: Public Health Institute, Ministry of Health, Malaysia.

—— (1988b) *National Health and Morbidity Survey, 1986–1987*, Volume II: *Morbidity and Utilization of Services: Overview of Findings and Recommendations*, Kuala Lumpur: Public Health Institute, Ministry of Health, Malaysia.

—— (1997) *Report of the Second National Health and Morbidity Survey Conference*, Kuala Lumpur: Public Health Institute, Ministry of Health, Malaysia.

Rozita Halina Hussein (2000) 'Financing health care through general taxation in Malaysia', in *Proceedings of International Conference on Evidence-based Practice: Towards Evidence-based Policy Making in Health and Development*, Kuala Lumpur: Ministry of Health.

Wee Chong Hui (2006) *Fiscal Policy and Inequality in Malaysia*, Kuala Lumpur: University of Malaya.

Part II
People's access to health care

7 Health care for the Orang Asli
Consequences of paternalism and non-recognition

Colin Nicholas and Adela Baer

The Orang Asli are the indigenous minority peoples of Peninsular Malaysia. They are the descendants of Pleistocene-era inhabitants of the peninsula, that is, from long before the establishment of the Malay kingdoms. The Orang Asli population grew from 54,033 in 1969 to 92,529 in 1994, at a rate of almost 2.3 per cent per year (Lim 1997). In 2003, they numbered 147,412, representing a mere 0.6 per cent of the national population (JHEOA 2005).

Like indigenous peoples the world over, the Orang Asli are among the most marginalized communities, faring very low in all the social indicators both in absolute terms and relative to the dominant population. For example, while the national poverty rate has been reduced to 6.5 per cent, the rate for Orang Asli remains at a high 76.9 per cent. The official statistics also classify 35.2 per cent of Orang Asli as hardcore poor (compared to 1.4 per cent nationally) (Zainal Abidin 2003). It is not surprising, therefore, that the Orang Asli lag very far behind in basic infrastructure and in political representation. The same is true for literacy and educational attainment. In 1990, only 14 per cent of Orang Asli villages had a school. The literacy rate for Orang Asli in 1991 was 43 per cent, while the national rate was 86 per cent; however, not all Orang Asli children attend school and in 1995, 68 per cent of the attendees had dropped out at the primary level (Lim 1997). This drop-out rate means that no more than 30 per cent were functionally literate.

In this chapter, we examine the development of health care services for the Orang Asli by the colonial state and its later trajectory under the post-colonial, developmental state. We will argue that the British colonial state had a paternalistic attitude toward the Orang Asli. In conjunction with the exigencies of fighting the communists during the Emergency era (1948–1960), this attitude led to the inception of the Orang Asli health care services. Within this paternalistic framework, medical professionals in the colonial service provided services that improved Orang Asli health. Nevertheless, the paternalistic framework also led the British to establish laws and institutions that treated the Orang Asli as 'wards of the state', not as an indigenous people with particular rights to land and resources. In the post-colonial period, fundamental changes occurred in the nature and the role of the state, and concomitant changes also occurred in state attitudes toward the Orang Asli. In this context, the original structure of the health care system that had been developed with paternal care was retained, but not its substance or spirit. In the hands of a highly ethnicized, post-colonial state with a narrow Malay nationalist agenda, the paternal structures, of which the health care services is one, have worked against the interests of the Orang Asli.

Orang Asli concept of health and illness

Traditionally in Orang Asli settings, when a person suffered an illness that was serious enough to warrant some action, it became a concern of the whole community. Other ailments, such as skin diseases, evoked no general concern as they were considered to be harmless, since the victims could still function normally. Like most traditional communities, the Orang Asli have long perceived disease as being the result of a spirit attack, or of the patient's soul being detached and lost somewhere in this world or in the supernatural world (Gianno 1986: 6). The Orang Asli also believe that both their individual and their communal health are linked to environmental and social health. If there is too much pollution, for example, or too much blood spilt, and taboos governing correct behaviour have not been followed, then disease and even death will strike (Endicott 1979; Howell 1984). The Orang Asli believe that such illnesses are better treated by incantations and ritual, than by modern medical practices. Treatment is usually given through healing ceremonies, coordinated by one or more shamans and invariably involving the whole community.

Thus, as opposed to the biological concept of disease, the Orang Asli concept of illness is culture-specific (Kleinman 1973). Healing is often a community effort. The shaman or healer (who may also be the midwife in some communities) is an important anchor in the traditional Orang Asli health system. As Wolff (1965) noted, the intimate ties created between patient and healer in a traditional framework reinforce a strong sense of socio-medical reciprocity that government officials or western-trained doctors are rarely able to replicate. It is not surprising therefore that the Orang Asli have an intense desire for healing to be integrated within their local socio-cultural context. Traditional healers and their methods are thus unlikely to disappear easily from Orang Asli culture.

Furthermore, rather than being a mish-mash of mumbo-jumbo, the Orang Asli's traditional medical system is an ordered and coherent body of ideas, values and practices embedded in a given cultural and ecological context. Infused in all this is the presumption that health is a communal or kinship responsibility, that taboos and all other practices related to maintaining health and preventing illness are necessary, and that any breach by one individual will have repercussions on others. The Orang Asli are also very clear about the link between maintaining their environment and maintaining their health and sustenance.

Orang Asli health and health care in colonial times

During the British period, most Orang Asli diets were nutritionally satisfactory (Bolton 1972: 799). Noone (1936) contended that Temiar who have less contact with outside society were generally healthier than those with more contact. As Devaraj (1999) and Kuchikura (1988) have observed, when Orang Asli traditional territories are left intact, undiminished and unappropriated, they provide adequate protein and a healthy variety of fruits and green vegetables.

This does not mean that Orang Asli living in the past were devoid of health problems. On the contrary, in the 1930s, for example, the Temiar were known to have malaria and other fevers, bronchitis, boils, scabies, wounds, neuralgia, dental caries, intestinal worms and yaws (Baer 1999).[1] At that time, modern health care was largely unknown. A few Orang Asli who happened to live near a friendly tin mine or rubber estate did receive basic medical assistance from the company's first-aid provider. Also, some European explorers, game hunters, railroad surveyors and even colonial officials, in humanitarian spirit, provided medical supplies to some Orang Asli communities that they visited.

Moreover, during this time, the encroaching outsiders brought new pathogens to Orang Asli areas. Smallpox, cholera, typhoid, flu, syphilis and other life-threatening maladies became all too common (Baer 1999: 156, n. 57). These diseases, against which the Orang Asli had no immunity, killed many Orang Asli, even wiping out whole villages, and contributed to the long-standing Orang Asli fear and distrust of strangers. The Batek, for example, reported that before 1942 their population was much larger than it is now and that many had died in disease epidemics brought into their lands by encroaching Malays (Endicott 1997).

However, most Orang Asli did not see any medical personnel until after the onset of the Emergency in 1948, when British troops invaded interior areas to combat communist insurgents operating from there. As we shall see below, this was the impetus for the authorities to act in a positive manner towards the Orang Asli. In particular, Orang Asli health and health care, which until then had received no attention from the colonial government, began to attract official concern.

The impact of the Emergency and the establishment of Gombak Hospital

Soon after the British reoccupied Malaya at the end of the Second World War, they regained control of the towns and settled areas, and as they harried the communist insurgents, the Malayan Communist Party withdrew its followers to camps in the forests. These roadless, inland areas offered both concealment and the opportunity to sway the forest Orang Asli to the insurgents' cause, whether on the basis of intimidation or past friendship, or by misinforming them about the political situation. Orang Asli were enlisted as messengers, informers and growers of farm produce to feed the camps.

To 'protect' the Orang Asli from this situation and thereby weaken Orang Asli aid to the insurgents, the British herded Orang Asli into hastily built resettlement camps during the early years of the Emergency (1948–1960). As many as 7,000 Orang Asli died in these squalid camps from disease, malnutrition and depression (Polunin 1953; Carey 1976). When it became obvious that this tactic was a failure, the British began to build forts and associated amenities for the Orang Asli in the forest. These amenities were meant to win their loyalty, but while most forts had a functional medical post staffed by a medical orderly, only two medical doctors were available to pay regular visits to the many Orang Asli villages located near these forts or further afield (Bolton 1968).

With the communist insurgency widespread and on-going, the medical posts at the forts had little effect on the overall health of the Orang Asli. For this reason, the government built a special hospital for Orang Asli in 1957.[2] This was a significant historical development for Orang Asli health services. Run by the Department of Aborigines (Jabatan Orang Asli, or JOA), its first medical director Dr J. Malcolm Bolton planned to provide a hospital where the family of an ill person could accompany him or her. It was thought that this would encourage Orang Asli to seek treatment at the hospital, as it was believed that their primary fear was leaving their familiar forest surroundings and their families (Bolton 1973a, 1973b; Harrison 2001). There were two main advantages to this plan: first, it made the patient more comfortable at the hospital and, second, accompanying family members could be given medical examinations, especially for tuberculosis (Bolton 1973a). The idea was to create a hospital that would become integrated into Orang Asli life.

Bolton recognized that western medicine and traditional medicine occupied different niches in the healing spectrum and so had the potential to be complementary rather than contradictory. He realized that the Orang Asli did not tolerate or accept long-term hospitalization as a necessary means to regain health. Such hospitalization not only cut the patients off from their forest environment and their community but also deprived them of access to their traditional healers and treatments (Bolton 1973a).

However, one of the key reasons for the success of this programme to encourage Orang Asli to stay in the Gombak Hospital was the fact that patients there usually had a 'relative' on the staff who spoke their language, understood their wishes and fears, and could explain to them the origin of their disease and the purpose of the treatment given (Bolton 1968). The original staff at the hospital had no medical training, but they were provided with 'practical training' in government hospitals (Bolton 1973a). By 1963, 143 of the 161 medical staff at Gombak were Orang Asli.[3]

By 1972, there were 139 inland medical posts for Orang Asli, all staffed by trained Orang Asli personnel (Bolton 1973b). 'Flying' doctors and nurses periodically visited many interior areas, sometimes travelling onward by boat or foot (Kinzie *et al.* 1966; Sjafiroeddin 1968). Emergency helicopter evacuation to hospital was also provided, as was iodized salt to goitre-prone areas. Furthermore, since neonatal and infant death rates – as well as maternal death rates – were still high in the 1960s, prenatal and obstetric care at Gombak was given great attention (McLeod 1971). Mothers were tested and treated for anaemia, malaria and intestinal helminths. Iron, folate and vitamin supplements plus a good diet were provided. X-rays were used to screen for tuberculosis. Accompanying family members were also tested, treated, housed and fed. Iron and vitamin tablets were provided for newborns. Moreover, in the 1970s, Gombak Hospital was training midwives for in-village deliveries.

In retrospect, while this era in Orang Asli health care delivery was motivated by the desire of the government to win the hearts and minds of the Orang Asli (and so deprive the communist insurgents of valuable help and information), it was the dedication and empathy of individual medical practitioners, notably Dr Bolton and his teams of volunteer doctors and nurses under the programmes of organizations such as CUSO (Canadian University Services Overseas) and CARE (Cooperative for Assistance and Relief Everywhere), that resulted in significant improvements in Orang Asli health services, as well as an increasing willingness of the Orang Asli to accept modern medicine alongside traditional healing. The introduction of western medicine was, after all, the main thrust of the health programme then (Polunin 1953). The Orang Asli's rights to their culture and traditions were respected by Bolton's staff, in order that the health programme would not be jeopardized.

Post-colonial decline

The Emergency ended in 1960 with the retreat of the communist forces, and the nation gained independence from Britain in 1957. Although the Orang Asli health care services were largely continued, by the late 1970s there were signs that they were in decline.[4] This prompted Khoo (1979), an officer working in the JOA, to publish a plan to improve the JOA medical services for Orang Asli as it became more Malaysianized. His first priority was community education.[5] Second was maternal and child health, given the existing high mortality and high under-nutrition, as well as 'maternal depletion'[6] among Orang Asli mothers. Third was control of diseases such as malaria and tuberculosis, fourth, improvement in curative services and, last, the gathering of information on health problems, that is, research.

Unfortunately, these proposals were not put into effect. By the 1980s, several reports were published asserting that the medical services for Orang Asli under the JHEOA (Jabatan Hal-Ehwal Orang Asli, or the Department of Orang Asli Affairs, the new name for the JOA) were inadequate. Veeman (1986/87), for example, wrote about the attitude of the government and the scarcity of medical personnel. She noted that maternal and infant death rates were still high and that Gombak still had no facilities for handling birth complications. Among other problems, primary health care was still not available to all Orang Asli and travelling medical teams were lax in making their scheduled rounds. The inadequate supply of anti-malarial medicines was also reported:

> [Anti-malarial prophylaxis] is infrequent if not nonexistent. Fansidar and chloroquine have not been freely available to the Orang Asli. Medication is only available when they become so sick that they must leave their forest dwellings and travel long distances to seek medical care at a clinic or hospital.
>
> Lambros *et al.* (1989: 6)

These reports correctly identified the gradual slackening in the medical and health care of the Orang Asli in the 1980s. Unfortunately, the situation did not improve in the 1990s. By then, it was reported that only 67 of 774 Orang Asli villages (9 per cent) had clinics (Lim 1997), compared to 139 medical posts active in the early 1970s (Bolton 1973b).

Orang Asli health today

Direct and indirect health effects on the Orang Asli were reviewed in the late 1990s (Baer 1999). Among the findings, the crude death rate for Orang Asli is twice that for all of West Malaysia (Ng *et al.* 1992). In terms of women's health, sex ratios for Orang Asli today, as in the past, favour men; that is, the women die off at earlier ages (Department of Statistics 1997). Indeed, the maternal death rate for Orang Asli in 1995 was much higher than for other Malaysians. The Orang Asli suffered 4.8 per cent of these deaths, although they made up less than 0.6 per cent of the population at that time.[7] As Hema Apparau reported in 2002, Orang Asli women have the highest recorded rates of postpartum haemorrhage and puerperal sepsis, far above the rates for other groups.

In terms of infectious diseases, Orang Asli children in Perak have three times the state average for tuberculosis incidence, and Orang Asli of all ages have 5.5 times the state average (Jeyakumar 1999). Despite their very small population size, Orang Asli had 51.5 per cent of the malaria cases recorded in Peninsular Malaysia in 2001 (JHEOA 2005: 22). In 2003, this proportion had increased to 53.6 per cent. For 1994, the leprosy rate for Orang Asli was 23 times higher than for others in West Malaysia (Fadzillah 1997). The incidence of leprosy is also on the increase among the Orang Asli, from 8.7 reported cases per 100,000 of the population in 1998 to 19.6 in 2002.[8] Also, the 'old' diseases and infections that have plagued the Orang Asli for as long as they can remember still plague them today. These include skin infections such as scabies, worm infestation, diarrhoea (sometimes resulting in fatality) and goitre. In fact, although goitre is easy and cheap to prevent, up to a third of Orang Asli adults are goiterous today, which is about the same proportion that had goitre 50 years ago (Baer 1999). A 'new' disease, HIV/ AIDS, has also been found among the Orang Asli. Data from the JHEOA hospital in Gombak in 2004 revealed that there were 31 cases of HIV/AIDS among the Orang Asli in 2003.

Orang Asli women and children are especially vulnerable to nutritional deficits and attendant intestinal parasitism. Lim and Chee (1998) found that the nutritional status of the 34 Orang Asli women they examined in Pahang was generally not satisfactory. Their mean nutrient intake levels (except for Vitamin C) were below the required minimum, while their mean iron intakes were about one-quarter to one-third of the required level. In Pahang, 35 per cent of the Semai women studied by Osman and Zaleha (1995) had protein-energy malnutrition and 64 per cent were goiterous; even 35 per cent of the men had goitres.[9] In Perak, 73 per cent of the Temiar women and 48 per cent of the Temiar men studied had intestinal worms (Karim *et al.* 1995). Moreover, the vast majority of Orang Asli children are underweight and stunted (Zalilah and Tham 2002). This supports the findings of Osman and Zaleha (1995) who found that 80 per cent of Orang Asli children studied were undernourished and stunted. Many of the children also had intestinal worms and protozoa, anaemia, dental caries and vitamin A deficiency (Karim *et al.* 1995; Norhayati *et al.* 1995, 1998; Ariff *et al.* 1997; Rahmah *et al.* 1997).

It is well to emphasize here that most Orang Asli lack food security (Zalilah and Tham 2002). With the majority of them living below the poverty line, their narrow margin of survival makes the Orang Asli's health situation precarious. They are also vulnerable to natural hazards and the whims of ecosystem destruction by others.

State ideology and policies, and the JHEOA

The British established the Department of Aborigines (JOA) in 1950 during the Emergency period, to 'protect' the Orang Asli. This department, now the Department of Orang Asli Affairs (JHEOA), controls the Orang Asli through Act 134: Aboriginal Peoples Act 1954 (Revised 1974). Under this Act, the JHEOA is empowered to create and regulate Orang Asli settlements, appoint and remove headmen, control entry into Orang Asli abodes and control the crops Orang Asli grow and the usage of their lands, among other powers that seem to have been arbitrarily defined. Since the provisions of the Act effectively destroy the autonomy of the Orang Asli, they directly contradict the concept of indigenous rights (Nicholas 2000). Notably, this is the only piece of legislation that is directed at a particular ethnic community.

There is an obvious fissure between the actual situation of Orang Asli health today and JHEOA goals, stated in the following verbatim extract from its website:

To create an individual, family and community of Orang Asli who are healthy and productive by a health system that is fair, easily accessible, disciplined and adaptive to change in response to environment and customer's expectation with every stratum besides encouraging individual responsibility and social participation towards improving the quality of life.

(JHEOA website, accessed 9 May 2005)

This fissure is an outcome of state ideology and the way the Orang Asli and the Orang Asli 'problem' are perceived and administered. The Orang Asli are regarded as 'wards of the state' and the JHEOA as their godparent. That the relationship is conceptualized as one of parent and child is reflected in various ways. For example, Jimin Idris, JHEOA Director-General from 1986 to 1992, frequently asserts that he had to care for 70,000 'children', 'from the womb to the grave'. That the Orang Asli are to be treated as children is not something new. In a matter involving an application for land by some Orang Asli towards the end of the nineteenth century, the British Resident wrote that, 'They must be provisionally treated as children and protected accordingly, until they are capable of taking care of themselves' (Selangor State Secretariat 2853/1895). McLellan (1985: 91) further maintains that the JHEOA 'has continued the British paternalistic and the Malay feudal patronage role toward the Orang Asli, so it settles claims and decides policy without actively involving or even consulting those concerned'. The Orang Asli, therefore, are not recognized as a people, but rather as individual subjects requiring large doses of governmental support in order to assimilate them into mainstream society. This underlying attitude extends well beyond legal and land matters, and into the realm of health policy and health care for the Orang Asli.

The underlying assumption in state policies is that backwardness among the Orang Asli is a result of their way of life and remote location. Government policy therefore is to introduce strategies and programmes to 'integrate them into the mainstream'. What exactly this 'mainstream' refers to, is not clearly spelt out. But from early policy proclamations and current development programmes, it is apparent that this four decade-old objective of the JHEOA is basically about integrating all of today's Orang Asli into mainstream Malay society. Such an objective has ramifications for the Orang Asli, even in aspects of health care delivery and their general health situation. Its primary effect is in setting the ideological and political basis for subjugating a people (Nicholas 2000).

When Malaya was granted political independence by the British colonialists upon the defeat of the communists, the Malay-based political party, United Malays National Organization (UMNO), rode to power on the crest of Malay nationalism. Subsequently, nation building was based on the historical pact that accorded special privileges to the Malays in exchange for citizenship rights for the non-Malay immigrant population.

The special position of the majority Malay population was premised on the notion of their indigenous status. As such, the historical precedence of the Orang Asli was difficult to acknowledge. Eventually, the way in which the state tried to resolve this incongruity was by policies that attempted to assimilate the Orang Asli into the Malay population.

The Orang Asli were treated differently and separately but never fully recognized as an indigenous people with all the rights that are conventionally accorded to indigenous peoples by international custom. These rights include recognition as an autonomous people, recognition of the right to traditionally occupied lands, recognition of the right to practise, maintain and developtheir culture, language and religion, and recognition of their traditional knowledge and indigenous systems and the right to protect and promote these.

The non-recognition of these rights has directly brought about the fate of the Orang Asli, in terms of their poor socio-economic status and political inconsequence and, as we argue here, the abysmal state of their health.

Dominance, authority and control

The paternalistic institutions inherited from the British accorded to the Orang Asli a unique position that allowed them to be treated differently from other sectors of Malaysian society.[10] In the absence of a willingness to recognize the Orang Asli as an indigenous people with inalienable rights, and in the context of a particular ethnicized politics, the state translated this difference into dominance and authority over the Orang Asli. As will be seen from the examples given below, this dominance and authority were often manifested in discrimination against, and control over, the Orang Asli. Unfortunately this has been as true for Orang Asli health care as for other aspects of Orang Asli living.

Scape-goating

Blaming the victim instead of oneself appears to be quite commonplace in administrative dealings with Orang Asli, especially in matters about health. For example, in October 1985, when 23 FELDA[11] settlers in Trolak, Perak, came down with jaundice, the health authorities were quick to blame the nearby Semai village and to call for its resettlement. This call was made on the 'possibility' and 'feelings' that the Semai were contaminating the water supply by their unhygienic practices. Although another 1,057 people in the district had come down with jaundice in the preceding month, no drastic action like resettlement was suggested for non-Orang Asli communities. As it turned out, the cause of the outbreak was insufficient chlorination at the treatment plant (*The Star*, 18 October 1985, 2 December 1985).

In February 1997, when two Jah Hut children in Kuala Krau, Pahang, died from an overdose of anti-malarials irresponsibly dispensed by a health department team, the authorities denied it was their fault and suggested that the deaths were due to the parents' negligence. A coroner's inquiry, however, ruled that the cause of death was in fact an overdose of anti-malarials (Nicholas 1997; Baer 1999, *The Sun*, 1 April 2000). Notably, this was the fourth fatal incident arising out of the anti-malaria programme in the same state!

Recently, in April 2004, when four Semai children died within five days with symptoms of vomiting and diarrhoea, the authorities were quick to attribute the tragedy to salmonella poisoning – and, consequently, the poor hygiene of the Orang Asli (*The New Straits Times*, 2 May 2004). The government reiterated that it could only provide proper health facilities and infrastructure if the Orang Asli were resettled. The Health Minister who made this comment did not realize that RPS Terisu in the Cameron Highlands, where the tragic deaths occurred, *was* a resettlement scheme and had been so for many years![12] The cause of the deaths was eventually found to be a rota-virus infection.

Even more recently, in July 2004, when a university study in Tasik Chini found high levels of *Escherichia coli* causing rashes and diarrhoea in some Orang Asli living in their five lakeshore villages, the State Executive Councillor in charge of Orang Asli affairs immediately suggested that the Orang Asli be resettled into one place 'so that they can attain proper amenities'. However, as the village *batins* (headmen) there pointed out, the problem only started when the authorities dammed the Chini River to prevent the lake water from flowing into the Pahang River. Moreover, the university study had found that the contamination was due to improper sewage disposal by a local resort and by the Tasik Chini national service camp at the lakeside (*The Star*, 26 July 2004, 27 July 2004, 29 July 2004).

Such blame-shifting on health problems reveals the underclass status of the Orang Asli. No dominant social group would accept such allegations without a counter-challenge, and no politician would dare to pit themselves against a group that could jeopardize their own position. Such attitudes about the Orang Asli also clearly show how those responsible for promoting Orang Asli welfare and health are themselves ill-informed or ignorant of the issues involved. Worse, they wield their authority and dominance by backing measures that would further marginalize the Orang Asli.

Insensitivity

The official stance of authority and dominance, coupled with ignorance of Orang Asli culture, is sometimes reflected in an insensitive technocratic way of handling problems. For example, in 1996, when the President of the Malaysian Association of Maternal and Neonatal Health revealed that 60 per cent of the 42 mothers who died during home births in 1994 were Orang Asli (*The Sunday Star*, 29 September 1996), the Minister responsible for Orang Asli Affairs immediately ordered that the seven existing Orang Asli health-transit centres be turned into Alternative Birthing Centres (ABCs) (*The New Straits Times*, 28 June 1997, 2 May 2004).

This official order may appear to be decisive and prompt, but on the ground, it had drastic repercussions. For one, Orang Asli mothers-to-be were 'warded' for about a month before the delivery date to 'wait out' their time. Not only was this psychologically stressful for the women, it also placed a heavy burden on the rest of the family, especially for those families living near subsistence. Home births were discouraged and in some cases forbidden by local health staff.[13]

Orang Asli mothers still prefer home delivery because institutional delivery not only creates problems for the rest of the family, but is also culturally 'unfriendly'. It may be true that by encouraging institutional deliveries, maternal death rates will decline, but a more sensitive way of implementing this policy would be to create conditions that allow Orang Asli mothers to feel more secure and comfortable, as well as mitigate the problems faced by families. Another way to reduce Orang Asli maternal mortality is to train resident midwives and to make available telephone and transport services in Orang Asli villages.

The myth of development and resettlement: inability to see traditional resources as necessary to health

Development planners and policy-makers commonly assume that Orang Asli health will improve if the Orang Asli accept development programmes designed for them or accede to resettlement elsewhere (usually with cash-crops as the main means of subsistence). The reality is far from this, based on the known regroupment failures, such as at Busut Baru, RPS Banun, Bekok, RPS Kedaik, Kuala Koh and RPS Terisu.[14]

The poor nutritional status of Orang Asli children living in regroupment schemes shows that the schemes' social objectives are not being met. One nutritionist wrote that:

> Some 15 years after relocation, the nutritional status of Orang Asli children in regroupment schemes can be described as poor with a moderate to high prevalence of underweight, acute, and chronic malnutrition. Their dietary intakes are deficient in calories and several major nutrients ... There exists an over-simplified assumption that introduction to cash-cropping will lead to increased income, which will provide more money for food, and in turn result in improvement in nutritional status ... In reality, relocation entails cultural uprooting and lifestyle changes which may not be overcome by the provision of physical facilities and economic incentives only.
>
> (Khor 1994: 123)

Such lamentable conditions in these myriad schemes are due to the narrow subsistence base and psychological disenfranchisement caused by uprooting Orang Asli from their traditional territories. While the authorities argue that Orang Asli regroupment does not necessary entail relocation, the reality is that the local resource base declines because it must be shared with others who have been moved in from their own homelands. This is a major cause of poor nutrition among the Orang Asli.

In reality, resettlement is often not for the purpose of improving Orang Asli health or lifestyles, but for other reasons such as security (resettling Orang Asli during the Emergency), making way for public projects (the Kuala Lumpur International Airport, the Universiti Kebangsaan Malaysia campus, highways, dams or even making way for private projects (housing developments, golf courses, resorts, other settlers). It is made possible because there is no legislation protecting the Orang Asli as an indigenous people with inherent rights to their traditional territories.

The state of Orang Asli health care today

The Orang Asli health care services are now made up of 125 treatment centres (designated locations where a mobile clinic visits periodically), 20 transit centres (centres where patients and accompanying persons are housed while waiting to be transferred to a hospital for treatment) and 10 health clinics (JHEOA 2005). There is an understanding between the Ministry of Health (MOH) and the JHEOA's Department of Health and Medicine, whereby the MOH provides services to the areas that are accessible by land transportation, leaving the interior villages, numbering 323 villages out of a total of 869, to the JHEOA.

Nevertheless, there are major shortfalls in health service provision to the Orang Asli. The JHEOA itself, in its Orang Asli Community Health Action Plan (JHEOA 2005), points to the lack of comprehensive health services in the interior villages.[15] The same document attributes the falling admissions rate in Gombak Hospital, now a 166-bed hospital, to the shunting of Orang Asli patients to MOH facilities. There are, however, other organizational problems that may be related to this.

Since the early 1990s, there has been no governmental recruitment of Orang Asli paramedics or health providers. This is diametrically opposite to the policy adopted by Dr Bolton and his team in the 1960s. There has been no official reason given for this but some past officers of JHEOA have attributed this state of affairs to the prejudices of certain JHEOA decision-makers, while the JHEOA on its part contends that there have not been any qualified Orang Asli applicants for these positions.

This time period was also marked by accusations of corruption in the JHEOA as acknowledged by a former senior officer of the JHEOA (Mohd Tap bin Salleh 1990: 84, 104). Newspapers even reported that hospital staff had turned parts of the Gombak hospital premises into daylight gambling dens (*Berita Harian*, 3 March 1984, 10 March 1984). There were also cases of Orang Asli girls (accompanying their sick relatives) being abused or asked to engage in prostitution; as well as cases of ambulance drivers asking for monetary incentives in order to send recovered patients back to their village.[16]

Orang Asli were often treated condescendingly or berated when some minor error or omission occurred. As such, many Orang Asli said that they did want to go to the hospital because the employees did not treat them with respect (Gianno 2004: 64) or because they were insensitive, discriminatory and unfriendly (Harrison 2001).

This is not to suggest that there are no instances of exemplary dedication and sensitive dispensation of health care to the Orang Asli today. We acknowledge that particular individual health care providers – be they doctors, nurses or paramedics – have displayed the same genuine concern and responsibility so admirably exhibited by the early volunteer doctors and nurses under the still-remembered supervision of Dr Bolton in the 1960s and 1970s. However, these individuals are the exception and are more likely to be attached to medical centres of the Ministry of Health than to the JHEOA medical service. It is not uncommon to hear JHEOA doctors attributing their 'sacrifice' to serve the Orang Asli to their 'pity' for the people. Also, it is no longer a priority in the Orang Asli medical service to have first-line Orang Asli health workers who can support and clarify technical matters for their hospitalized 'relatives'. The introduction of a programme to train village-level Orang Asli Health Volunteers (Sukarelawan Kesihatan), although an excellent idea, has unfortunately yet to achieve its desired goals.

Orang Asli health care has indeed taken a beating in the past two decades, not for lack of resources or knowledge of what needs to be done, but primarily because the political and ideological basis of the Orang Asli 'problem' has not been corrected (or even acknowledged). The Orang Asli have been treated as not-so-deserving beneficiaries of government largesse, rather than the other way round. This situation is further worsened by discrimination and the formal denial of Orang Asli inherent rights, such as their rights to their traditional lands and resources. Those responsible for Orang Asli health (or, for that matter, their overall well-being and advancement) could not or did not want to see the link between Orang Asli well-being and good health on the one hand, and the Orang Asli's need to be in control of their traditional lands and resources on the other.

With increasing pressures to privatize health care in Malaysia, and the unwillingness of the state to accord the political and social recognition that is due to the Orang Asli as the first peoples on this land, it is difficult to see how Orang Asli health care will improve through the initiative of the state and its functionaries. It remains a major project, therefore, for the Orang Asli to assert the recognition of their rights as a people and with it the delivery of a more sensitive and effective health care system.

Notes

1 Although these earlier studies did not mention goitre, it should be noted that lack of goitre was unusual among inland groups.

2 This was first sited in Kuala Lipis, Pahang, and later moved to a forested area in Gombak, Selangor. Thereafter, it has been called the Gombak Hospital. See the JHEOA website at <http://www.jheoa.gov.my/e-hospital.htm> (accessed 16 September 2005).

3 It should be noted that the daily cost for a patient at Gombak Hospital was only 28 per cent that of other government hospitals (Bolton and Snelling 1975). This low cost probably reflected the fact that the budgeted expenditure per patient was far less, rather than that the hospital had found ways to run its services more efficiently.

4 Yet the then Commissioner for Orang Asli Affairs, Iskandar Carey, maintained that the government's aim was to *raise* the standards of health and hygiene for the Orang Asli, an aim he thought had already been fulfilled (Carey 1976). He also wrote that 120 Orang Asli were paid a monthly allowance to distribute medicines in villages. This was a laudable practice but was far from comprehensive since these 120 people could not serve all the 629 Orang Asli villages in the country (1969 census data).

5 The problem with traditional aetiology was that the Orang Asli did not easily accept the need for preventive medicine: 'If the spirit causing malaria had departed, why continue taking tablets?' (Bolton 1973a: 1122). But they were willing to accept anti-malarial tablets (quinine) as it was thought that the bitter taste they gave to the blood kept the evil spirits away.

6 The physiological ill effects of having many pregnancies.

7 Personal communication between Adela Baer and Ravindran Jegasothy of the Department of Obstetrics and Gynaecology, Seremban Hospital, 2002, and author of 'Sudden maternal deaths in Malaysia, a case report', *J. Obst. Gynaecol. Res.* 28(4): 186–93, 2002, which reported that MOH records were analysed by a national committee of six obstetricians and gynaecologists, a physician, an anaesthetist, a health administrator and a nursing matron. After reading this paper, Adela Baer corresponded with Ravindran Jegasothy about the situation for indigenous women.

8 The 2002 and 2003 statistics on diseases presented in this paragraph were given in a slide presentation by the head of the Public Health Unit of the Health and Medical Division of the Gombak Hospital on 7 July 2004 to a group of visiting Fulbright Scholars from the USA.

9 In stark contrast to the 35 per cent Semai rate, only 7.5 per cent of rural Malay women studied had protein energy malnutrition (Osman and Zaleha 1995). In related work, Osman and co-workers (1993) found that the food intake of Semai adults resettled at Betau in Pahang averaged only 1,143 kcal/day.

10 No other ethnic group in the country has a government department assigned specifically to oversee its protection, well-being and advancement, or an act of parliament to legislate every aspect of its society.

11 Federal Land Development Authority schemes.

12 RPS stands for Rancangan Perkumpulan Semula, or 'regroupment scheme'.

13 Threats of refusing to register the birth of refusing aid in the event of a difficult birth and of laying criminal charges in the event of a tragedy have been used. One anecdote of the experience of a Mah Meri woman may be used to reflect the insensitivity with which Orang Asli women are often treated (personal communication with Reita Rahim, April 2004). On the day when the community celebrated their Hari Moyang (Ancestors' Remembrance Day) in February 2004, a nurse from the district hospital, about 15 kilometres away, came to her house and took her away to the ABC without informing any family member. After a frantic search, the family found her, but was only able to bring her home after much insistence and promises to ensure that she complied with the medication prescribed. The nurses said that they were 'following instructions', and they needed

to ward her due to her low iron and red blood cell levels. Be that as it may, the way she was removed was highly questionable.

14 In the 1960s, half of the Semaq Beri in a resettlement centre died from cholera (Morris 1997).

15 In this document, the lack of comprehensive health services in the interior villages was singled out as the reason for the high tuberculosis infection rates.

16 Personal conversations between Colin Nicholas and Orang Asli hospital assistants based in Gombak Hospital, 1993–1994.

References

Apparau, Hema (2002) 'Reproductive health of Orang Asli women who used the antenatal services of the Gombak Hospital', unpublished B. Med. Sci. thesis, Universiti Putra Malaysia, Serdang, Selangor, Malaysia.

Ariff, R.H.T., M.Z. Mohd Nazli, M.Z. Mohd Rizam, M.S. Mohd Shahriman, Y. Zakaria, K. Kamal Nazmir and S. Mohd Farid (1997) 'Health status of Aboriginal children in Post Brooke, Kelantan', *Malaysian Journal Child Health* 9: 60–4.

Baer, A. (1999) *Health, Disease and Survival: A Biomedical and Genetic Analysis of the Orang Asli of Malaysia*, Subang Jaya: Centre for Orang Asli Concerns (COAC).

Berita Harian, 3 March 1984, 'Hospital Orang Asli jadi tempat judi'.

—— 10 March 1984, 'JOA salikan kegiatan judi di Hospital Orang Asli Gombak'.

Bolton, J.M. (1968) 'Medical services to the Aborigines in West Malaysia', *British Medical Journal* 2: 818–23.

—— (1972) 'Food taboos among the Orang Asli in West Malaysia', *American Journal of Clinical Nutrition* 25: 789–99.

—— (1973a) 'Family centered hospital treatment in the Aboriginal people of West Malaysia', *Community Health* 5: 70–4.

—— (1973b) 'A training-oriented medical programme in West Malaysian Aboriginals', *Medical Journal Australia* 2: 1122–5.

Bolton, J.M. and Snelling, M. (1975) 'Review of tuberculosis among the Orang Asli (Aborigines) in West Malaysia from 1951–1970', *Medical Journal Malaysia* 30: 10–29.

Carey, I. (1976) *Orang Asli*, London: Oxford University Press.

Department of Statistics (1997) *Profile of the Orang Asli in Peninsular Malaysia*, Population Census Monograph Series No. 3, Kuala Lumpur: Department of Statistics.

Devaraj, Jeyakumar (1999) 'Between myth and reality: why are Orang Asli more prone to illness?', paper presented at the World Conference of Primary Care Physicians, Kuching, Sarawak, Malaysia.

Endicott, Kirk (1979) *Batek Negrito Religion: The World-View and Rituals of a Hunting and Gathering People of Peninsular Malaysia*, New York: Clarendon/ Oxford University Press.

—— (1997) 'Batek history, interethnic relations, and subgroup dynamics', in R. Winzeler (ed.) *Indigenous People and the State*, New Haven: Yale University Southeast Asian Monograph 46, pp. 30–50.

Fadzillah, K. (1997) 'Strategies to overcome infectious diseases among the Orang Asli – leprosy and tuberculosis', paper presented at the Second National Conference on Infection and Infection Control, Ipoh, Malaysia.

Gianno, R. (1986) 'The exploitation of resinous products in a lowland Malayan forest', *Wallaceana* 43: 3–6.

—— (2004) '"Women are not brave enough": Semelai male midwives in the context of Southeast Asian cultures', *Bijdragen Tot de Taal-Land en Volkerkunde* 160: 31–71.

Harrison, M. (2001) 'Healthcare decisions among Semelai women of Malaysia', unpublished honours thesis, Dartmouth College, Hanover, NH, USA.

Howell, Signe (1984) *Society and Cosmos: Chewong of Peninsular Malaysia*, Singapore: Oxford University Press.

JHEOA (2005) Pelan Tindakan Kesihatan Masyarakat Orang Asli, Kuala Lumpur: Jabatan Hal-Ehwal Orang Asli. Unpublished document.

JHEOA website. Available at http://www.jheoa.gov.my/e-medical.htm (accessed 9 May 2005).

JHEOA website. Available at <http://www.jheoa.gov.my/e-hospital.htm> (accessed 16 September 2005).

Karim, R., Rahmah, N., Khairul Anuar, A., Mehdi, R. and Abdullah, B. (1995) 'Parasitic infections in the Aboriginal community at Temengor, Hulu Perak, Malaysia', *Malayan Nature Journal* 48: 425–32.

Khoo T.E. (1979) 'Health priorities in the resettlement of the Orang Asli', *Federation Museums Journal* 24: 177–84.

Khor Geok Lin (1994) 'Resettlement and nutritional implications: the case of Orang Asli in regroupment schemes', *Pertanika* 2(2): 123–32.

Kinzie, J., Kinzie, K. and Tyas, J. (1966) 'A comparative health survey among two groups of Malayan Aborigines', *Medical Journalof Malaya* 21: 135–9.

Kleinman, A. (1973) 'Medicine's symbolic reality: on a central problem in the philosophy of medicine', *Inquiry* 15: 206–13.

Kuchikura, Y. (1988) 'Food use and nutrition in a hunting and gathering community in transition, Peninsular Malaysia', *Man and Culture in Oceania* 4: 1–30.

Lambros, C., Davis, D. and Lewis, G. (1989) 'Antimalarial drug susceptibility of *Plasmodium falciparum* isolates from forest fringe dwelling Aborigines (Orang Asli) of Peninsular Malaysia', *American Journal of Tropical Medicine Hygiene* 41: 3–8.

Lim Hin Fui (1997) *Orang Asli, Forest and Development*, Kepong: Forest Research Institute Malaysia.

Lim Hwei Hian, and Chee Heng Leng (1998) 'Nutritional status and reproductive health of Orang Asli women in two villages in Kuantan, Pahang', *Malaysian Journal of Nutrition* 4: 31–54.

McLellan, Susan (1985) 'Orang Asli: an analysis of state penetration and development plans on Aboriginal peoples of West Malaysia', *Review of Indonesian and Malaysian Affairs* 19(2): 80–112.

McLeod, F. (1971) 'Midwifery among the Aborigines', *Nursing Mirror News* 132: 28–31.

Mohd Tap bin Salleh (1990) 'An examination of development planning among the rural Orang Asli of West Malaysia', unpublished Ph.D. thesis, University of Bath, UK.

Morris, K. (1997) 'Forest utilization: commodity and subsistence among the Semaq Beri of Peninsular Malaysia', *Civilisations* 44: 194–219.

The New Straits Times, 28 June 1997, 'Zaleha gets assurance from police'.

The New Straits Times, 2 May 2004, 'Spooked by "mysterious" deaths'.

The New Straits Times, 2 May 2004, 'Orang Asli still plagued by age-old ailments'.

Ng, M.S., Van, K. and Pala, J. (1992) 'Demographic situation of the Aborigines in Malaysia, *Quarterly Review of Malaysian Population Statistics* 18: 9–18.

Nicholas, C. (1997) 'Medicines are for curing, not killing', *Aliran Monthly* 17(3): 7–8.

—— (2000) *The Orang Asli and the Contest for Resources: Indigenous Politics, Development and Identity in Peninsular Malaysia*, Copenhagen: IWGIA and Subang Jaya: COAC.

Noone, H.D. (1936) 'Report on the settlements and welfare of the Ple-Temiar Senoi of the Perak-Kelantan watershed', *Journal of the Federated Malay States Museums* 19(1): 1–85.

Norhayati, M., Noor Hayati, M.I., Nor Fariza, N., Rohani, A.K., Halimah, A.S., Sharom, M.Y. and Zainal Abidin, A.H. (1998) 'Health status of Orang Asli (Aborigine) community in Pos Piah, Sungai Siput, Perak, Malaysia', *Southeast Asian Journal of Tropical Medicine Public Health* 29: 58–61.

Norhayati, M., P. Oothuman, M.S. Fatmah, Y. Muzain Minudin and B. Zainuddin (1995) 'Hookworm infection and reinfection following treatment among Orang Asli children', *Medical Journal of Malaysia* 50: 314–19.

Osman, A., Khalid, B.A.K., Tan, T.T., Wu, L.L., Sakinah, S.O. and Wu, M.L. (1993) 'Prevalence of NIDDM and impaired glucose tolerance in Aborigines and Malays and their relationship to sociodemographic, health and nutritional factors', *Diabetes Care* 16(1). 68–75.

Osman, A. and M.I. Zaleha (1995) 'Nutritional status of women and children in Malaysian rural populations', *Asia Pacific Journal of Clinical Nutrition* 4: 319–24.

Polunin, I. (1953) 'The medical natural history of Malayan Aborigines', *Medical Journal of Malaya* 8: 55–174.

Rahmah, N., Ariff, R.H.T., Abdullah, B., Shariman, M.S.M., Mohd Nazli, M.Z. and Rizal, M.Z.M. (1997) 'Parasite infections among Aborigine children at Post Brooke, Kelantan, Malaysia', *Medical Journal of Malaysia* 52: 412–15.

Selangor State Secretariat (2852/1895) 'Request for instructions regarding two documents issued by Raja Laut to Sakais of Perual and Lanjan'. Alternate ref: L444/95.

Sjafiroeddin, M. (1968) 'Nursing among Aborigines in Malaysia's jungles', *Alumnae Magazine, Columbia University Presbyterian Hospital School of Nursing* 63(1): 39–44.

The Star, 18 October 1985, 'Jaundice outbreak: Dept. wants Orang Asli settlement resited'.

The Star, 2 December 1985, 'Why blame the Orang Asli?

The Star, 26 July 2004, 'Danger lake'.

The Star, 26 July 2004, 'Orang Asli exposed to danger'.

The Star, 26 July 2004, 'Pollution killing Tasik Chini'.

The Star, 27 July 2004, 'Scattered Orang Asli to be resettled in one village'.

The Star, 27 July 2004, 'Development blamed for Tasik Chini's woes'.

The Star, 29 July 2004, 'MB wants Tasik Chini cleaned up'.

The Sun, 1 April 2000, 'Charge the guilty ones, A-G urged'.

The Sunday Star, 29 September 1996, 'Orang Asli encouraged to give birth in hospitals'.

Veeman, V. (1986/87) 'The delivery of primary health care: a case study of the Aborigines of Peninsular Malaysia', unpublished thesis, Diploma of the Royal College of Nursing, Institute of Advanced Nursing, London.

Wolff, R.J. (1965) 'Modern medicine and traditional culture: confrontation on the Malay Peninsula', *Human Organisation* 24(4): 339–45.

Zainal Abidin Haji Ali (2003) 'Pentadbiran Orang Asli: ke mana hala tujunya? pengalaman dan cabaran', paper presented at the Seminar Warisan Orang Asli organized by the Department of Museum and Antiquities and the Ministry of Art, Culture and Heritage Malaysia, Muzium Negara, Kuala Lumpur, 10 May.

Zalilah, M.S. and B.I. Tham (2002) 'Food security and child nutritional status among Orang Asli (Temuan) households in Hulu Langat, Selangor', *Medical Journal of Malaysia* 57: 36–50.

8 Women's access to health care services in Malaysia

Chee Heng Leng and Wong Yut Lin

Access to health care may be understood as the ability to obtain necessary health care and is closely related to the concept of equity. Although it is difficult to define and measure health care access, the concept calls for a consideration of the meaning of health needs, the availability of health services, and barriers to obtaining health care. Even though morbidity indicators may be used to reflect the health needs of populations, it is difficult to ascertain whether utilization of services is adequate to meet morbidity levels. Utilization rates are therefore used as indicators of demand rather than need or access.

Access to health care may also be thought of as being linked to availability, affordability and acceptability.[1] The availability of health care is a prerequisite to its accessibility, while affordability highlights the economic requirements for using health care. There is often a fee charged for using health services, but even if services are free, the cost of travelling to the health facility, and forgone income for absence from work must be recognized. Acceptability refers to whether the services available are acceptable to the user, which implies the extent to which they are perceived to be of good quality, convenient and amenable to use, effective in alleviating pain, or in preventing and treating disease, illness and injury, as well as being culturally appropriate.

As health care access is mediated by social, economic and cultural factors, individuals who belong to a particular social group will face similar barriers to access. Health care access for women, as a specific group, poses problems at different levels. At the basic level, women have specific health care needs even when they are not ill. These include fertility control, pregnancy and childbirth. Since health care access is linked to health needs, this implies that women face barriers that are not faced by men. Nevertheless, the *problematique* extends beyond this fundamental level. For instance, women and men of a particular social group, such as the poor, may face similar barriers in health care access; however, insofar as poverty is gendered, there are proportionately more women who are poor, and therefore these barriers have to be understood through a gendered lens. Furthermore, cultural practices and social norms that circumscribe the mobility and behaviour of women may act as barriers to their seeking health care.

Barriers to women's health care access

The literature on developing countries documents women's lack of access to health care as a manifestation of gender inequalities due to women's low status, subordination, and lack of power and control over resources (Ojanuga and Gilbert 1992; Okojie 1994; Lewallen and Courtright 2002). This structural inequality results in poor nutrition, closely spaced childbearing, lack of pre-natal care, infectious diseases and high maternal mortality. In developed countries, lack of access is still an important problem for the poorer social classes, and recent studies point to institutional problems such as those related to health care provision (Adamson *et al.* 2003) and lack of health insurance (Hsia *et al.* 2000; Wyn and Solis 2001; Sambamoorthi and McAlpine 2003).

Recently, attention has been focused on issues of quality, adequacy and gender sensitivity in the delivery of health care. For example, there are sex differences in the diagnosis, treatment and management of ischaemic heart disease, and women are more likely to be misdiagnosed and less aggressively treated. Explanations for this range from sexist attitudes of physicians who are more likely to discount complaints of women, to the higher likelihood of women experiencing atypical symptoms because the disease model is a male one (Wijk *et al.* 1996). Gender bias in health care institutions has also been documented in the developing world. For example, women with tuberculosis are much less likely to go for treatment (Standing 2001), and a recent study in Vietnam also shows that there is a longer delay in tuberculosis diagnosis for women (Thorson and Johansson 2003).

While concerns have been raised that gender bias in health research models leads to inappropriate and inadequate diagnosis and treatment for women (Fitz-James 1998), it also raises questions with regard to the social construction of women's health and health care. The medicalization of natural processes, as exemplified by excessive numbers of caesarian deliveries and the medicalization of menopause, is another way in which women's health and health care are socially constructed.[2]

Indeed, gender bias in the social construction of women's health is reflected in the very manner in which health care and services are delivered in many developing countries, where within medicine, women's health is relegated solely to obstetrics and gynaecology, and within primary health care, all women's health needs are assumed to be met by maternal and child health programmes. This is because women are primarily seen as mothers and wives, part of rigidly defined gender roles, rather than active members of society with holistic health needs (Wong 2000). Such biologically deterministic views of sex/gender[3] differences in health have become a natural and integral part of the teaching curriculum and research agenda in medical and public health practices, perpetuating the institutionalization of gender bias within health systems (Fee and Krieger 1994).

In this chapter, we assess women's access to health care services in Malaysia in relation to women's health needs and in the context of the country's institutional and social constructs of 'women's health'. We first present an overview of the availability of health care services for women, and then their health needs, as reflected in health status and health problems. We then analyse the institutional and social barriers to women's access, and identify social groups excluded by the health care services. We make the case that while maternal and reproductive health care services are well developed, patriarchal constructs of what constitutes 'women's health' form barriers to access, and effectively exclude certain groups of women from easily accessing care.

Health care access can be seen to be affected by three sets of factors: the characteristics of the population seeking care, the structure of the health system and the behaviour of health professionals (Puentes-Markides 1992). These sets of factors interact in a macro-societal context that includes government policies, economic development and the status of women in society. In this framework, characteristics of a population seeking care can encompass a wide range of factors ranging from their own behaviour to the cultural, social and economic constraints acting on them.

In this study we use a variation of this framework. We consider women's access to health care as an outcome that is first of all contextualized in the larger cultural, social, political and economic milieu (structural factors), second, as resulting from the structure of the health care system, health policies, availability of services and behaviour of professionals (institutional factors) and, third, as depending on the individual's position within society, which will include her social class, educational level and employment status, as well as beliefs and attitudes (individual factors). In a patriarchal society where women are the subordinate gender, these factors generally have detrimental consequences for their access to health care. Furthermore, power relations between men and women draw the boundaries of what women may or may not do in seeking health care.

Health care and women's health in Malaysia

The backbone of the public health care system in Peninsular Malaysia is the rural health service that was built up during the 1960s. The rural health unit consisted of three tiers, the most basic being the midwife clinic cum quarters $(MCQ)^4$ (MOH, *c.* 2000). Later, in the early 1970s, the MCQ was upgraded to a *klinik desa* (rural clinic) in a reorganization of the three-tier system to a two-tier one. At the first tier, each rural clinic served 2,000–4,000 people; at the second tier, a health centre would oversee four rural clinics, and this rural health unit served 15,000–20,000 people.

As part of the upgrading, the midwife, who was the basic health personnel in this service, was retrained to act as a community nurse who would be able to treat 'light ailments' and injuries in addition to her primary maternal health duties (MOH, *c.* 2000). In 1960, the MCQ to rural population ratio was 1 : 121,000; by 1965, it had improved to 1 : 7,300.[5] In 1975, when the MCQ was upgraded, the ratio had further improved to 1 : 4,400, approaching the target coverage of 1 : 4,000.

Maternal health care was therefore the cornerstone of Malaysia's public health services in conceptualization, planning and execution from its very beginning, and remains a significant component today. In the urban areas, maternal and child health services were available through private as well as public delivery points, the public points being polyclinics and public hospital outpatient departments. In 1995, all health centres and polyclinics, whether in the rural or urban areas, were redesignated as health clinics. These clinics now provide integrated primary care services, which include maternal and child health care. In public medical schools, the family medicine speciality was initiated to train family medicine specialists to manage health centres.[6]

Other than maternal health care, screening tests are actively promoted for the early detection of breast and cervical cancers. The Ministry of Health (MOH) promotes the practice of monthly breast self-examination (BSE) for women above the age of 20 and annual clinical breast examination by medical or paramedical personnel; however, mammography is provided only for women at special risk (Public Health Institute 1999b). From the early 1990s onwards, breast cancer clinics were set up at all major government hospitals. Pap smear screening is promoted for all women between 20 and 65 years of age (Public Health Institute 1999c). Official health policy therefore promotes maternal and reproductive health care for all women according to current medical conventions. In reality, there are differences in utilization patterns, which will be discussed later in this chapter.

Women's health needs

Mortality indices are generally composite indicators of the state of economic and social development rather than the availability and quality of health care. Nevertheless, the maternal mortality rate, particularly at low levels, can arguably be used as an indicator not only of the situation of women, but also of maternal health care. Since 1991, official documents have reported the maternal mortality rate to be 0.2 per 1,000 live births.[7] The adjusted rate of 41 per 100,000 live births compares favourably with other developing countries (Table 8.1), although geographical disparities exist within the country, with rural states being worse off (MOH, *c.* 2000). Enumeration is also less reliable in the North Bornean states of Sabah and Sarawak.

Sex differentials in conventional health indicators do not reflect that women are worse off compared to men (Table 8.1). The differential between male and female life expectancies is comparable to the developed countries, and does not resemble the situation in South Asian countries, where the lowered

Table 8.1 International comparisons of maternal mortality rate and life expectancy

	Maternal mortality rate[1] (per 100,000 live births)		Life expectancy at birth (years) 2002	
	Reported[2] 1985–2002[4]	Adjusted[3] 2000	Female	Male
Malaysia	30[5]	41	75.6	70.7
Thailand	36	44	73.4	65.2
Singapore	6	30	80.2	75.8
Philippines	170	200	71.9	67.9
Indonesia	380	230	68.6	64.6
United States	8	17	79.8	74.2
United Kingdom	7	13	80.6	75.6
Japan	8	10	85.0	77.8
Australia	—	8	82.0	76.4
India	540	540	64.4	63.1
Pakistan	530	500	60.7	61.0
Bangladesh	380	380	61.5	60.7
China	53	56	73.2	68.8
Cuba	30	33	78.6	74.7
Costa Rica	29	43	80.5	75.7
Sri Lanka	92	92	75.8	69.8

Source: UNDP (2004: 168–71, 217–20).

Notes
[1] Deaths of women from pregnancy-related causes.
[2] Reported by national authorities.
[3] Adjusted by the United Nations Children's Fund (UNICEF), World Health Organization (WHO) and United Nations Population Fund (UNFPA) to account for under-reporting and misclassification.
[4] Data is for the most recent year available in this period.
[5] More recently reported figure is 20 per 100,000.

female life expectancy has been attributed to sex discrimination (Okojie 1994).[8] Community-based nutritional studies have also not demonstrated any inequalities between male and female children. In a national representative study of Malaysian children under 5 years old, for example, rates of undernutrition were slightly higher among boys than girls (MOH 2001a: 17–28).[9] The 1996 National Health and Morbidity Survey (NHMS 2) found that women had slightly higher prevalence of illness (29.1 per cent) than men (28.0 per cent), while men had higher prevalence of injury (3.2 per cent) compared to women (1.9 per cent) (Public Health Institute 1999a).

In Malaysia, therefore, the health situation of women is relatively good, and the gender health gap that has been shown to exist in South Asia is not apparent. Gender inequalities are, however, seen in work, income and political leadership indices (UNDP 2004).

Government death registration and hospital records show that cardio-vascular disease, cerebro-vascular disease and cancers, the primary causes of death in the general population, are also primary causes of death among women. However, issues related to gender differences in diagnosis and treatment of heart disease, and the use of a male disease model to the detriment of women, which are the subject of investigation in developed countries, has yet to receive attention in health research in Malaysia.

The most frequently occurring cancers in women are breast, cervical, colon and lung cancer, as well as leukaemia (National Cancer Registry 2002). Breast cancer is the leading cause of cancer deaths among women, accounting for about 11 per cent of all medically certified deaths in the country (MOH 1999). Nevertheless, when compared to developed countries and other Asian countries, the age-standardized incidence rate of cervical cancer in Malaysia (21.5 per 100,000 compared to 52.8 per 100,000 for breast cancer) is of greater concern (National Cancer Registry 2002).

Obesity is emerging as a widespread nutritional problem, although being underweight is still a problem. In a survey of rural communities, about 40 per cent of adult women were overweight while about 10 per cent were underweight (Khor *et al.* 1999), and anaemia was found to persist as an important undernutrition problem (Tee *et al.* 1998). A similar rate of obesity was found in urban factory women, among whom it was also found that overweight rates were considerably higher in the older age groups when compared to a national sample (Chee *et al.* 2004).

The existence of health problems such as obesity among a disproportionately large percentage imply that women, for whatever reasons, face difficulties in achieving healthy levels of physical activity and types of diet. Even though the problem may be attributed to health behaviour and lifestyles, there are also structural factors such as the lack of opportunities, space, time and resources for practising healthier lifestyles, particularly among women of lower socio-economic status.

The health needs of women are therefore also very obvious in the area of preventive health. This may encompass better and more adequate health education, as well as information dissemination and promotion; but beyond this, there is a greater need to identify structural impediments to living a 'healthy lifestyle'. Other important health problems of women include HIV/AIDS (where the rate of new infection among women is rapidly rising), mental health, domestic violence and occupational health among the various groups of women workers.

Utilization of services

While keeping in mind that utilization of services is not an indicator of access to health care, utilization rates nonetheless provide a general picture of health care-seeking behaviour. Furthermore, if certain services are not well utilized, it behoves us to investigate if there are barriers preventing their utilization and, therefore, access.

Curative and preventive care

Gender differences in health-seeking behaviour with regard to acute illness or injury have not been detected in large-scale surveys. Data from the NHMS 2 (1996) show that 42.0 per cent of women who had recent illness or injury sought care compared to 42.9 per cent men (Public Health Institute 1999a). Hospitalization rates, however, were higher among women (8.8 per cent have been hospitalized within the last one year) than men (5.7 per cent).

From the same study, it was found that male dominance is reflected in decision-making about where to seek health care. Although the majority of adults decide for themselves on which place to seek care, there was a small proportion for whom the decision was made by others; among these, there were more women whose husbands decided for them, than men whose wives decided for them. Furthermore, within the family where parents were 15–55 years of age, the father was more likely than the mother to be the decision-maker for children's health care. There are of course limitations to the interpretation of survey data which do not uncover deeper intra-family relationships, but they do at least show that the explicitly acknowledged 'head of household' is usually the male.

Utilization of preventive health screening for breast and cervical cancers has been assessed at the national level. In the NHMS 2 the rate of ever doing BSE among women above 20 years old was 34.2 per cent, while the rate of doing BSE at least once a month was 26.5 per cent (Public Health Institute 1999b). The rate of ever having had a Pap smear for women aged 20–54 was 29.8 per cent, while that for having had a Pap smear within the last three years was 22.7 per cent (Public Health Institute 1999c). These rates are considered low; furthermore, both types of screening practices were found to increase significantly by educational level and were also higher among urban women, indicating that women with less education and rural women may have difficulties of access to services as well as to knowledge and information.

Maternal health care

The extensive availability of maternal health services has already been described. Utilization rates in government services appear to have improved. For example, the average number of antenatal visits recorded increased from 5.8 visits per pregnancy in 1985, to 8.6 visits per pregnancy in 2001 (MOH 2001b: 61–3). A commonly used indicator for achieving progress in maternal protection and survival, the proportion of births attended by trained personnel, improved from 85 per cent in 1985 to 97 per cent in 2001. In Peninsular Malaysia, the improvement was from 87 per cent (1985) to 99 per cent (2001), while in Sarawak, it was from 84 per cent (1985) to 98 per cent

(2001) and in Sabah, the corresponding increase was from 72 per cent (1985) to 81 per cent (2001). In a 1997 study conducted by the MOH, it was found that pregnant women who avoided hospital deliveries did so because of structural reasons (the need to care for children, lack of transportation, financial problems, absence of house minder) as well as attitudinal factors (fear, not recognizing the importance of hospital delivery and lack of confidence in the health care system) (MOH 2001a: 216).

Contraception and abortion

In 1994, the prevalence of contraceptive use was 55 per cent, and for modern methods it was 30 per cent (ARROW 2005). This rate is lower than in other countries in the region, including Indonesia, Thailand and Vietnam. It should be noted that the statistics available are from surveys of ever-married women only and, furthermore, lack of utilization does not necessarily mean lack of access. A better indicator is the unmet need for contraception, measured by women who do not want additional children but are not using contraception. There are no nationwide statistics on unmet needs, but a 1996 survey in the rural areas found that it was 30.9 per cent for Malays, 14.5 per cent for Chinese and 31.4 per cent for Indians, for any methods, and 42.1 per cent, 27.2 per cent and 37.1 per cent respectively for modern methods (ARROW 2005).

In Peninsular Malaysia, the prevalence of contraceptive use is lower in the rural states of Kelantan, Terengganu and Pahang, which averaged 24 per cent in 1994 compared to about 67 per cent in the other states. There is reason to believe that unmet needs are higher in the rural states. In the urban areas, utilization is higher, and a 2002 survey of squatter areas in five major urban centres found that the contraceptive prevalence rate was on par with the national average.[10]

Data on abortion is scarce, and its prevalence is under-reported. Available data show that the rate of induced abortion was 1 per cent among women aged 15–44 in the 1966 West Malaysia Family Survey, 2.5 per cent in the 1974 Malaysian Fertility and Family Survey, 10.7 per cent in the 1974 Maternal Health and Early Pregnancy Wastage Study in Peninsular Malaysia and 5.8 per cent in the 1984 Malaysian Family Life Survey (ARROW 2005).

The social construction of women's health needs

Health care utilization and access have to be understood in the wider institutional, legal and social context. Just as women's roles are socially constructed, there is also a prescribed norm in describing their health needs and, therefore, in determining access. The overwhelming focus within women's health has traditionally been on maternal health, narrowly defined as family planning and childbirth-related health care. The work of women's health movements to change this focus began in the 1960s and has resulted in two landmark international conferences – the 1994 International Conference for Population and Development (ICPD, Cairo) and the 1995 Fourth World Conference on Women (FWCW, Beijing) – which endorsed a broader definition of women's health and reproductive health, and affirmed that women's rights to health are necessary in order to achieve this.[11]

It has been a struggle to gain acceptance of this broader definition, even though the sexual and reproductive health and rights advocacy network has gained ground internationally (Chee and Huang 2000; Swedish Association for Sexuality Education (RFSU) 2004). The underlying assumption of health care services in many countries, for example, is that only married women need maternal health care; access is therefore dependent upon marital status. Access to contraception and abortion for single women, usually young, is often blocked by societal norms. The social stigma of premarital pregnancy, and the shame associated with it, constitutes a significant barrier. On the other hand, single women's choice to continue a pregnancy is also constrained by the lack of social autonomy and the social stigma of being an unmarried mother.

For the last 20 years, the struggle for sexual and reproductive health and rights has been fraught with challenges arising from religious and political opposition to the recognition of individual freedom and rights to determining one's sexuality and reproduction, particularly for women, young people, single unmarried adults and lesbian, gay, bisexual and transgender (LGBT) persons. In facing such challenges and opposition, negotiations about words and concepts such as 'reproductive health services' versus 'care' and definitions of the 'family' have taken place over the past two decades (The Swedish Association for Sexuality Education (RFSU) 2004).

Legal framework and social boundaries

The Malaysian state believes that it has a progressive stance on the position of women, but it is, at best, ambivalent on many issues, even with regard to its support for gender equality. As recently as 2001, Article 8.2 of the Federal Constitution was amended to include a non-discrimination clause on 'gender'. Yet there are tensions in the state's position on women's reproductive rights. Although the government endorsed the 1994 ICPD Programme of Action and the 1995 Beijing Declaration to show its progressive stance on women's rights, it also maintains reservations, specifically on the rights to abortion, sex outside of marriage and homosexuality.[12] Indeed, public policy explicitly restricts the provision of contraceptives by government health providers to married couples (ARROW 2005).

The Malaysian government also placed several reservations on its endorsement of the Convention for the Elimination of Discrimination Against Women (CEDAW), particularly when it is perceived to contravene the Syariah (Islamic) Family Law:

The Government of Malaysia declares that Malaysia's accession is subject to the understanding that the provisions of the Convention do not conflict with the provisions of the Islamic Syariah law and the Federal Constitution. With regards thereto, further, the Government of Malaysia does not consider itself bound by the provisions of articles 2 (f), 5 (a), 7 (b), 9 and 16 of the aforesaid Convention.

(United Nations Treaty Collection 2002)

On 6 February 1998, the Malaysian government withdrew its reservation in respect of Articles 2(f), 9(1), 16(b), 16(e) and 16 (h) (United Nations Treaty Collection 2002).

Difficulties in broadening the scope of reproductive health

The national commitment to the ICPD and Beijing platforms includes efforts to expand the scope of reproductive health. Within the government, the responsibility for spearheading these has been given to the Ministry of Women and Family Development[13] and the National Population and Family Development Board (NPFDB). The non-governmental Federation of Family Planning Associations of Malaysia (FFPAM) also plays a major role.

A study conducted in 1998 to assess the extent to which the ICPD recommendations have been implemented found that 'the spirit of the Cairo ICPD, with its emphasis on women's rights, sexuality and gender relations, is not part of the change in Malaysia as yet' (Wong 1999: 186). Officers from top and middle management levels of the civil service, as well as field workers in governmental and non-governmental agencies were interviewed. These interviews revealed no major changes in programmes after the 1994 ICPD, and attention was primarily given to family planning, safe motherhood and HIV/AIDS. The principal response from the government agencies was that prior to the ICPD, they were already planning, if not implementing, policies and programmes that were similar to those in the ICPD programme of action.

The same study found that in the MOH, there were 'some adjustments' in accordance with the ICPD programme of action. First, its maternal and child health programme was renamed 'Family Health', and women's health was separated from child health. The services provided, however, remain focused on antenatal care, safe motherhood initiatives, alternative birthing centres, deliveries, post-natal care, maternal mortality investigation and family planning. The incorporation of HIV/AIDS services is often cited as an example of integration, while the provision of health services for menopause and screening for gynaecological cancers are often used as evidence of a broadening of programmes.

Nevertheless, it is precisely the exercise of trying to broaden the scope of the national cervical cancer screening programme that shows the difficulties involved. Prior to 1995, the official policy was to provide cervical cancer screening for married women only. Current policy is to include all sexually active women, but in practice, unmarried women encounter more barriers to access. Studies show that women who never married almost never have pap smears. In the 1996 NHMS 2, only 2.7 per cent of single women had ever had a pap smear, compared to 33.4 per cent of married women (Public Health Institute 1999c). The close connection between cervical cancer screening and marital status reflects, in part, the governmental strategy to popularize screening through post-natal and family planning service outlets,[14] and, in part, the lack of success in widening its availability to all women.

The FFPAM is, by and large, a conventional organization, although its non-governmental status allows it to go further in embracing the reproductive health and rights framework. The agency abides by governmental policies, even though there are strong pressures from within the organization, particularly from some of its volunteers, to liberalize its reproductive health services. As such, compromises have to be made. For example, its official position with regard to the provision of reproductive services to young, adolescent and unmarried women is that it will provide only counselling and educational services, and not any direct services that are not endorsed by national policy (Wong 1999). Since 2002, however, there have also been efforts within the organization to integrate the rights-based approach, particularly in the educational programmes for adolescents and youths, to provide gender awareness training for staff and volunteers, and to work towards male responsibility in reproductive health.[15]

State and cultural constructions of women's health and reproductive health have long been conflated with maternal health, and are difficult to dislodge. Even though they are seen as 'government-friendly', neither the FFPAM nor the Malaysian AIDS Council have succeeded in arguing for extending and broadening the reach of state reproductive health services, including the provision of contraceptive services, to young, adolescent and unmarried women.

In the post Cairo study referred to earlier in this chapter (Wong 1999), it was also found that officers and field workers from government agencies, across the board, were highly conscious of the country's official position with regard to the institution of marriage and the family, and that the promotion of reproductive health has to be carried out within the context of 'our social, cultural and religious framework'. Whenever contrary views were offered, it was emphasized that these were 'personal' views. The 'official voice' supported 'gender equity' rather than 'gender equality' because the latter was interpreted to be contradictory to the mainstream Islamic precept of male leadership and dominance.[16]

Abortion

The right of access to abortion often provides an arena where one may observe the interplay between state and society in defining social boundaries. The

Malaysian state has placed reservations on its endorsements of various international documents with regard to the right to abortion. Nevertheless, the current laws on abortion permit a liberal interpretation, as it is considered permissible for a medical practitioner registered under the Medical Act 1971 to undertake the procedure, with the proviso that 'such practitioner is of the opinion, formed in good faith, that the continuance of the pregnancy would involve risk to the life of the pregnant woman, or injury to the mental or physical health of the pregnant woman, greater than if the pregnancy were terminated'.[17]

In fact, menstrual regulation and dilatation and curettage are abortion-inducing procedures that have been easily available in government hospitals and the larger family planning clinics of the NPFDB since the mid-1970s (Wong 1999). However, in 1984, the New Population Policy (NPP, which aimed at achieving a 70 million population size by 2100) was implemented, accompanied by various incentives that encouraged childbearing.[18] Although the NPP did not explicitly curtail family planning services, there was confusion following its implementation, and there were reports that women were denied access to the pill or the intra-uterine device (IUD) at government clinics if they were younger than 40, and did not have many children. Another impact was that the abortion-inducing procedures that were previously easily available, at least to married women, were no longer so, and were restricted to cases that can be legally justified. This restricted access in public hospitals remained even after the 1989 amendment that liberalized the Penal Code pertaining to abortion.

There are current initiatives to seek further liberalization of the laws on abortion.[19] This may not entirely be to the benefit of women, or even be ethically sound, and should be monitored by feminists and women's health activists. For example, a proposal specifying 'where the pregnant woman is mentally, emotionally or physically incapable of giving consent, or is below the legal age of valid consent, the opinion of two medical practitioners registered under the Medical Act 1971, based on considerations as provided for in the exceptions stated in Section 312, and acting in good faith, shall be accepted as consent in lieu' (ARROW 2005: 247) could remove the decision-making power from individual women in favour of professionals.

Conclusions

Maternal health care is widely available in Malaysia. It has been the cornerstone of Malaysia's primary health care network. Women's access to reproductive health care, within the context of the conventional marriage and family, is generally high. Women who fall outside of this ambit, however, have greater difficulties in gaining access to reproductive health care.

International pressure together with internal pressures from non-governmental organizations has led the state to endorse international conventions and documents on reproductive health and women's rights.

The Malaysian state supports women's rights pertaining to education and employment. It is progressive on gender issues because this is seen as a means to facilitate women's involvement in the nation's economic and developmental strategies. Pressure from women's groups has resulted in the Malaysian state supporting the ICPD's framework of reproductive health, but it maintains reservations that uphold the traditional institutions of heterosexual marriage and family.

As a result, unmarried women, in particular young adolescent women, are denied access to reproductive health services. In this narrow construct, other groups of women who are not part of the mainstream, such as foreign migrants, drug users and commercial sex workers, will also face discrimination. As long as women's health remains conflated with maternal health, women continue to lack access to health care for their non-reproductive health needs. The discrimination and bias may be reflected in the judgmental attitudes and insensitivities of service providers, but in this chapter, we have shown that it is also built into the policies and programmes of health care, that is, the barriers to women's health care access are at the institutional and structural levels.

Notes

1 These dimensions have also been presented as three sets of factors: (i) availability, (ii) ability, which is determined by economic factors enabling women to meet health care costs, and (iii) permission, which is the result of social factors determining whether women can seek health care outside the home (WHO 2000).

2 While some advocates of 'natural childbirth' criticize hospital deliveries as the medicalization of childbirth, we do not necessarily share this view. Access to quality obstetric care should include delivery by trained personnel and adequate medical facilities during birth complications, but not preclude sensitivity and allowing women greater control in decision-making.

3 'Sex' is used to denote biological differences between men and women, while 'gender' is used to mean that many of the differences between men and women are socially constructed.

4 At the second tier, a health subcentre will oversee four MCQs, and together would serve a total of 10,000 people. At the third tier, a main health centre will oversee four health subcentres. These, together with attached MCQs, would be equivalent to one rural health unit serving 50,000 people.

5 These figures are for Peninsular Malaysia. The states of Sabah and Sarawak joined the federation in 1963. The development of health services in these two states followed a different course, and their organizational set-ups are also different. Although both states have a two-tier system, the dependence on paramedical personnel is greater, and the availability of maternal and child health services relatively more limited. The geographical terrain in these states is less accessible compared to Peninsular Malaysia.

6 The family medicine specialist is a new specialization category. It is significant to have specialists head and run the primary health centres as a strategy to ensure quality care at this level.

7 In 1991, however, a system of confidential enquiry into maternal deaths was initiated (Ministry of Health 1996: 142), following which the number of maternal deaths reported increased more than twofold. Based on this system, the maternal

mortality rate was 44 per 100,000 live births in 1991, 48 in 1992 and 46 in 1993. The same report shows that the adjusted rates compare favourably with Indonesia (420 per 100,000) and the Philippines (80 per 100,000), but not so favourably with Thailand (44 per 100,000) and Korea (15 per 100,000). In the United Kingdom, it was about 10 per 100,000 total births in 1988–1990.

8 In Malaysia, women outlive men by about five years, a pattern that is consonant with that of western countries in the late twentieth century (Arber and Thomas 2001). The pattern is a product of women's biological advantage and men's higher mortality risks due to greater occupational hazards and behavioural risk factors.

9 A similar pattern is found in rural communities (Khor and Tee 1997; Chee *et al.* 2002).

10 Personal communication with the researchers, Tey Nai Peng and Ang Eng Suan.

11 Reproductive health was defined broadly to include not only matters of reproduction, but also sexuality and sexual health: 'Reproductive health therefore implies that people are able to have a satisfying and safe sex life and that they have the capability to reproduce and the freedom to decide if, when and how often to do so.' Women's health was defined as: 'involving their emotional, social and physical well-being and determined by the social, political and economic context of their lives, as well as by biology', and their rights were affirmed as 'the right to the enjoyment of the highest standard of physical and mental health. The enjoyment of this right is vital to their life and well-being and their ability to participate in all areas of private and public life' (United Nations Division for the Advancement of Women, Fourth World Conference on Women, Beijing, 1994, *Platform for Action*, Agenda Item 9, paragraphs 89 and 96).

12 At the Beijing Conference, the Malaysian representative made clear that reproductive rights should be applicable only to married couples formed of the union between a man and a woman (personal communication with Cecilia Ng and beng hui, who were present at the conference).

13 The Ministry was established in 2001. Prior to this, it was the Department of Women's Affairs, placed at various times within the Prime Minister's Department and the Ministry of National Unity.

14 In fact, it is provided as part of the routine in these services, and often the women are not given the information first and then asked to make a choice. In this sense, it is not based on the ICPD concept of reproductive rights.

15 The FFPAM's Women Development Subcommittee has been conducting gender awareness and sensitization programmes for policy-makers (executive board members), volunteers and staff throughout the organization. Integration of rights-based sexual reproductive health as well as gender indicators into the assessment and evaluation of programmes and services has begun (FFPAM 2002: 19–21).

16 Other religions may also endorse male primacy, but an Islamic endorsement is significant because since Islam is the official religion of the country, it may be used to justify official policy.

17 Penal Code (Amendment) Act 1989 (Act 727). Section 312 governs abortion, and was amended in 1989 following advocacy by women's groups to include 'injury to mental health' as one of the conditions.

18 For a more detailed discussion, see Wong (1999). The incentives included further income tax rebates and maternity leave benefits, and in the state of Terengganu, mothers delivering their sixth and subsequent children were given one-off incentive payments. The policy is largely perceived as pro-natalist, even though, officially, it is stated that it seeks to decelerate the rate of fertility decline, not to increase fertility.

19 In 2002, the Ministry of Health convened a number of meetings to review the parts of the Penal Code that are related to termination of pregnancy (ARROW

2005). The review is intended to decriminalize the procedure and reduce the restrictions on access. The initiative is led by the Malaysian Medical Association and has the involvement of other NGOs like the FFPAM and the Obstetrical and Gynaecological Society of Malaysia, and the proposed amendments are currently being reviewed by the Attorney-General's office.

References

Adamson, Joy, Ben-Shlomo, Yoav, Chaturvedi Nish and Donovan, Jenny (2003) 'Ethnicity, socio-economic position and gender – do they affect reported health-care seeking behaviour?', *Social Science and Medicine* 57: 895–904.

Arber, Sara and Thomas, Hilary (2001) 'From women's health to a gender analysis of health', in W.C. Cockerham (ed.) *The Blackwell Companion to Medical Sociology*, Oxford: Blackwell.

Asian-Pacific Resource and Research Centre for Women (ARROW) (2005) *Monitoring Ten Years of ICPD Implementation: The Way Forward to 2015: Asian Country Reports*, Chapter 7 'Country Study: Malaysia', Kuala Lumpur: ARROW.

Bennett, Linda Rae (2001) 'Single women's experiences of premarital pregnancy and induced abortion in Lombok, Eastern Indonesia', *Reproductive Health Matters* 9(17): 37–43.

Chee Heng Leng and Huang Mary Soo Lee (2000) 'Reproductive health and reproductive rights: a brief review of the achievements and shortfalls since the ICPD 1994', in *Reproductive Rights and Reproductive Health: Challenges in the New Millennium* (Seminar proceedings of the Malaysian NGO National Seminar on Reproductive Health: Challenges in the New Millennium, organized by Malaysian NGO Coordinating Committee for Reproductive Health, Summit Hotel, Subang Jaya, Selangor, 20–22 April), Subang Jaya, Malaysia: Federation of Family Planning Association, Malaysia.

Chee Heng Leng, Mirnalini Kandiah, Maimunah Khalid, Khadijah Shamsuddin, Jamilah Jamaluddin, Nor Anita Megat Mohd Nordin, Rashidah Shuib and Intan Osman (2004) 'Body mass index and factors related to overweight among women workers in electronics factories', *Asia-Pacific Journal of Clinical Nutrition* 13(3): 248–54.

Chee Heng Leng, Khor Geok Lin, Fatimah Arshad, Wan Abdul Manan Wan Muda, Poh Bee Koon, Nik Shanita Safii, Norimah Abdul Karim, Normah Hashim, Mohd Nasir Mohd Taib, Rokiah Talib and Norlela Md Husin (2002) 'Nutritional assessment of pre-school children in rural villages of the Family Dynamics, Lifestyles and Nutrition Study (1997–2001): II. Prevalence of undernutrition and relationship to household socio-economic indicators', *Malaysian Journal of Nutrition* 8(1): 33–53.

Federation of Family Planning Associations Malaysia (FFPAM) (2002) *Annual Report 2002*, Kuala Lumpur: FFPAM.

Fee, E. and Krieger, N. (eds) (1994) *Women's Health, Power and Politics: Essays on Sex/Gender, Medicine and Public Health*, Amityville, NY: Baywood Publishing.

Fitz-James, Michael (1998) 'The gap: even though 65 per cent of drugs are taken by women, most are tested primarily in men', *Canadian Healthcare Manager* 5(5): 29.

Hsia, Judith, Kemper, Elizabeth, Kiefe, Catarina, Zapka, Jane, Sofaer, Shoshanna, Pettinger, Mary, Bowen, Deborah, Limacher, Marian, Lillington, Linda and

Mason, Ellen (2000) 'The importance of health insurance as a determinant of cancer screening: evidence from the Women's Health Initiative', *Preventive Medicine* 31: 261–70.

Khor Geok Lin, Azmi M.Y., Tee E.S., Kandiah M. and Huang M.S.L. (1999) 'Prevalence of overweight among Malaysian adults from rural communities', *Asia Pacific Journal of Clinical Nutrition* 8: 272–9.

Khor Geok Lin and Tee E. Siong (1997) 'Nutritional assessment of rural villages and estates in Peninsular Malaysia: II. Nutritional status of children aged 18 years and below', *Malaysian Journal of Nutrition* 3(1): 21–47.

Lewallen, Susan and Courtright, Paul (2002) 'Gender and use of cataract surgical services in developing countries', *Bulletin of the World Health Organization* 80(4): 300–3.

Ministry of Health (MOH) (1996) *Malaysia's Health 1996: Technical Report of the Director-General of Health, Malaysia*, Kuala Lumpur: Ministry of Health Malaysia.

—— (1999) *Annual Report 1999*, Kuala Lumpur: Ministry of Health Malaysia.

—— (c. 2000) *Health in Malaysia: Achievements and Challenges*, Kuala Lumpur: Ministry of Health Malaysia, Planning and Development Division.

—— (2001a) *Malaysia's Health 2001: Technical Report of the Director-General of Health*, Kuala Lumpur: Ministry of Health Malaysia.

—— (2001b) *Annual Report 2001*, Kuala Lumpur: Ministry of Health Malaysia.

National Cancer Registry (2002) *The First Report of the National Cancer Registry: Cancer Incidence in Malaysia 2002*, Kuala Lumpur: Ministry of Health Malaysia.

Ojanuga, Durrenda Nash and Gilbert, Cathy (1992) 'Women's access to health care in developing countries', *Social Science and Medicine* 35(4): 613–17.

Okojie, Christina E.E. (1994) 'Gender inequalities of health in the Third World', *Social Science and Medicine* 39(9): 1237–47.

Public Health Institute (1999a) *National Health and Morbidity Survey 1996*, Volume 3: *Recent Illness/Injury, Health Seeking Behaviour and Out-of-pocket Health Care Expenditure*, Kuala Lumpur: Public Health Institute, MOH Malaysia.

—— (1999b) *National Health and Morbidity Survey 1996*, Volume 20: *Breast Examination*, Kuala Lumpur: Public Health Institute, MOH Malaysia.

—— (1999c) *National Health and Morbidity Survey 1996*, Volume 19: *Cervical Cancer Screening*, Kuala Lumpur: Public Health Institute, MOH Malaysia.

Puentes-Markides, Christina (1992) 'Women and access to health care', *Social Science and Medicine* 35(4): 619–26.

Sambamoorthi, Usha and McAlpine, Donna D. (2003) 'Racial, ethnic, socio-economic, and access disparities in the use of preventive services among women', *Preventive Medicine* 37: 475–84.

Standing, H. (2001) 'Gender equity and health sector reform', in *How Does Being a Woman or a Man Affect Your Health? Gender and Health Training Materials*, London: Commonwealth Secretariat.

Swedish Association for Sexuality Education (RFSU) (2004) *Passion for rights: Ten Years of Fighting for Sexual and Reproductive Health*, ed. Ylva Bergman, Stockholm: Norra Skane Offset.

Tee E. Siong, Khor Geok Lin, Tony Ng Kock Wai, Zaitun Yassin, Chee Heng Leng and Safiah Md Yusof (1998) 'Nutritional assessment of rural villages and estates in Peninsular Malaysia: prevalence of anaemia', *Malaysian Journal of Nutrition* 4: 1–29.

Thorson, A. and Johansson, E. (2003) 'Equality or equity in health care access: a qualitative study of doctors' explanations to a longer doctor's delay among female TB patients in Vietnam', *Health Policy* 68: 37–46.

United Nations Development Programme (UNDP) (2004) *Cultural liberty in Today's Diverse World, Human Development Report 2004*. Online. Available at <http://hdr.undp.org/reports/global/2004/> (accessed 6 August 2004).

United Nations Division for the Advancement of Women (UN-DAW) (1994) *Beijing Declaration and Platform for Action, Fourth World Conference on Women, Beijing, 1994*. Online. Available at <http://www.un.org/womenwatch/daw/beijing/platform> (accessed 6 August 2004).

United Nations Population Fund (UNFPA) (1994) *International Conference on Population and Development (ICPD), Programme of Action, Cairo, 1994*. Online. Available at <http://www.unfpa.org/icpd/icpd.htm> (accessed 6 August 2004).

United Nations Treaty Collection [As of 5 February 2002] Declarations and Reservations. Online. Available at <http://www.unhchr.ch/html/menu3/b/treaty9asp.htm> (accessed 6 August 2004).

Wijk, Cecile, van Gijsbers, M.T., van Vliet, Katja P. and Kolk, Annemarie M. (1996) 'Gender perspectives and quality of care: towards appropriate and adequate health care for women' *Social Science and Medicine* 43(5): 707–20.

Wong Yut Lin (1999) 'Country study of Malaysia', in *Taking up the Cairo Challenge: Country Studies in Asia-Pacific*, Kuala Lumpur: Asian-Pacific Resource and Research Centre for Women (ARROW).

—— (2000) 'Gender issues in medical and public health education', *Asia-Pacific Journal of Public Health* 12(Supp): S74–7.

World Health Organization (WHO) (2000) *Women of South-East Asia: A Health Profile*, Regional Publications, Southeast Asia Regional Office (SEARO) No. 34. Online. Available at <http://w3.whosea.org/women2/wdeterminants.htm> (accessed 6 August 2004).

Wyn Roberta and Solis, Beatriz (2001) 'Women's health issues across the lifespan', *Women's Health Issues* 11(3): 148–59.

9 HIV/AIDS health care policy and practice in Malaysia

Huang Mary S.L. and Mohd Nasir Mohd Taib

Since the beginning of the HIV/AIDS (human immunodeficiency virus/ acquired immune deficiency syndrome) epidemic more than two decades ago, HIV/AIDS has become a major disease of the developing world, decimating the continent of Africa and rapidly spreading through Asia where it is contracted primarily through heterosexual transmission and drug use. In Thailand, for example, the large sex industry, as well as proximity to the Golden Triangle with its supplies of heroin, fuelled the epidemic throughout the 1990s.

It became clear from early on in the epidemic that public education has to be the cornerstone of any successful containment strategy. It also became obvious that educational strategies, to have any chance of success, have to be grounded in an understanding of human behaviour and how that behaviour can be changed. Furthermore, educational messages have to be truthful and accurate, and transmitted in honesty and seriousness of purpose, with compassion for the human condition.

Thailand, one of the earliest Asian countries to face the full brunt of the disease, is also among the few where the rate of new infections has been curtailed through effective action taken as early as the early 1990s. Employing a pragmatic and multi-pronged approach, the country embarked on a campaign to promote 100 per cent condom use. This contrasted with some other countries, where the rhetoric was dominated by moralistic preaching of abstinence from extra-marital sex. Thailand also quickly undertook programmes aimed at educating, as well as making available sexually transmitted disease (STD) services to sex workers rather than continuing to deny, or to condemn, their existence. In this way, education, treatment of STDs and testing strategies could be carried out among this social group, thereby stemming one of the principal routes of infection.

It has also been shown that a harm reduction approach in educating drug users on the dangers of sharing needles, teaching them how to sterilize needles, and exchanging clean needles for used ones has greater success in stemming the spread of HIV than approaches that stubbornly take the moral high ground in telling drug users to stop drug abuse, or try to scare them with threats of disease and death. Although adopted with great success by

Australia and much of Europe, Asian countries, with the exception of Vietnam and Indonesia, have been slow to adopt this approach (Wodak *et al.* 2004).

In Malaysia, there is general agreement that HIV/AIDS requires the attention of all developmental agencies of the government, because political commitment is essential for stemming the epidemic, as well as for mitigating its effects. The spread of HIV/AIDS involves dealing with sensitive issues related to sexuality, including the sexual orientation of individuals, gender power inequality within a marriage and sexual activity of unmarried young adults, as well as sex work issues. Political leaders are therefore often faced with the dilemma of either taking pragmatic approaches or agreeing to the demands of religious leaders who not only advocate abstinence before marriage and faithfulness of all married couples but require that all programmes in the country subscribe to the same approach. Other approaches (especially harm reduction) are seen by this group as condoning 'sinful practices' and being promoted by westerners.

This chapter discusses state policies and practices with regard to HIV/AIDS prevention and treatment in Malaysia where the epidemic has been slower in taking off than in neighbouring Thailand. However, the rate of new infections is now increasing exponentially, and has become a major health problem. In this chapter, we will survey what has been done. Although there have been efforts in the right direction, we contend that progress is limited by the overriding moralistic agenda of the state. The state promotes moralistic messages related to sexual abstinence and zero tolerance of drug abuse. We argue that such an approach is unrealistic and non-pragmatic, and is a barrier to an effective strategy for stemming the disease.

The HIV/AIDS epidemic in Malaysia

By the classification of the World Health Organization (WHO) and UNAIDS (Joint United Nations Programme on HIV/AIDS), Malaysia is considered a country with an epidemic concentrated mainly among intravenous drug users. In 2002, 76.3 per cent of cumulative HIV cases and 61.8 per cent of AIDS cases resulted from infection through injecting drug use (MOH 2004). This reflects the country's long-standing drug problem, generally attributed to its geographical proximity and accessibility to the Golden Triangle, which makes it an easy transit point for drug distribution despite the mandatory death sentence for drug pushers.

It is estimated that HIV prevalence among the general public is around 0.03 to 0.4 per cent (MOH 2004). HIV prevalence is also very low among antenatal mothers who were tested (0.04 per cent in 2002). Nevertheless, the 2001 Consensus Meeting (of government, non-governmental organizations (NGOs) as well as university personnel involved in HIV/AIDS work) estimated that the overall prevalence of around 5 per cent among female sex workers and STD patients in selected urban centres was slowly increasing

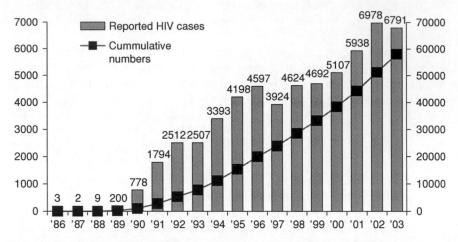

Figure 9.1 Reported and cumulative HIV cases by year, Malaysia
Source: Ministry of Health HIV/AIDS statistics for various years.

(WHO 2003). Indeed, it has become apparent in the last few years that heterosexual transmission has risen (from 59.3 per cent of all women infected in 2001 to 63.9 per cent of all women infected in 2002), confirming the suspicion that the infection has indeed permeated the community at large (MOH 2004).

The first case of HIV was detected in Malaysia in 1986, and since then, yearly reports of confirmed cases of HIV as well as AIDS have been increasing (Figure 9.1). By the end of 1990, the cumulative total of HIV infections had increased to 992 (778 reported in 1990 alone), while the cumulative number of AIDS cases was 18. By the end of 1995, the number of detected HIV cases in that year (4,198) was almost six times the number five years previously, while those infected with AIDS swelled to 233. The year 2000 saw 5,107 new infections, averaging almost 14 per day; in 2002, it was reported that each day saw an average of 17.4 new infections. In the same period, AIDS cases numbered 1,168 in 2000 and 1,193 in 2002 (MOH 2002, 2003, 2004).

It should be noted, however, that these figures reflect, in large part, the introduction of testing programmes. Drug users who are rounded up by the police, those who go to government rehabilitation centres, and prisoners are routinely tested. Part of the increase in the statistics may also be due to the introduction of new testing programmes such as the testing of antenatal mothers (which began in 1998) and compulsory testing of Muslim couples before marriage in the southern state of Johor in 2001.

More than 90 per cent of the total infected with HIV (93.8 per cent) and AIDS (91.8 per cent), and of total deaths from HIV/AIDS (93.3 per cent)

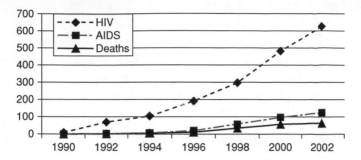

Figure 9.2 Number of women infected with HIV and AIDS, and number of deaths by year, Malaysia

Source: Ministry of Health HIV/AIDS statistics for various years.

are males. Even so, what has been most alarming is that the number of women tested positive each year has increased from 2.6 per cent of total HIV infections in 1993 to 5.0 per cent in 1997 (prior to the introduction of the testing for antenatal mothers), and to 9.0 per cent in 2002 (Figure 9.2).

By ethnicity, the majority of those infected are Malays (72.6 per cent), due in part to the fact that Malays make up the majority of the total population (in 2000, Malays and other *Bumiputeras* constituted 65 per cent of the population), as well as the fact that most people who go for drug rehabilitation in government-sponsored rehabilitation institutions (and therefore undergo mandatory testing) are Malays. Up to the end of 2002, infected Chinese made up 15.1 per cent of total infected, and Indians 8.6 per cent (MOH 2004). There seems to be a pattern in the mode of HIV/AIDS transmission by ethnicity, with Malays and Indians mainly infected through drug use, and the Chinese (who are more likely to have visited sex workers) mainly through heterosexual transmission.

One of the most worrisome aspects about this epidemic is the fact that 80.2 per cent of those living with the virus and 65.9 per cent of those who have AIDS are in the 20 to 39 age group. Analysis of the cumulative HIV cases up to 2002 by occupation indicates that in 32.8 per cent of the cases, there was no record of occupation, while 14.5 per cent were unemployed. Among the rest, the major occupational groups included factory workers who made up 4.8 per cent, fishermen 3.7 per cent, long distance drivers 2.5 per cent and government staff 2.2 per cent.

In summary then, the epidemic grows at an alarming rate, with the rate of growth over 2002 and 2003 averaging 18.3 newly detected cases per day, for a small country with a total population of 25 million (Department of Statistics 2003). Furthermore, the accelerated increase of the infection among women in recent years signals that the epidemic has permeated the general population. The challenges that confront the country are therefore very urgent.

National commitment and action

Inter-ministerial Committee on AIDS

In Malaysia, the Ministry of Health (MOH) has been entrusted to take action on HIV/AIDS. In 1992, the Inter-ministerial Committee on AIDS was formed under the chairmanship of this ministry to advise the Cabinet on policies and strategies to address the epidemic. This committee is made up of various relevant ministries, with the Malaysian AIDS Council (MAC) representing the non-governmental sector.

Under this ministerial level committee are two sub-committees: the National Coordination Committee on AIDS, which is the forum for governmental and non-governmental agencies to discuss social, economic, cultural, religious, legislative and all other issues related to the prevention, control and management of HIV/AIDS in Malaysia; and the National Technical Committee on AIDS, which is responsible for the formulation, evaluation and review of all technical aspects of the national HIV/AIDS Prevention and Control Programmes. The National Technical Committee directs two other sub-committees, namely the Committee on HIV/AIDS Prevention and the Committee on Patient Management. In addition, in each state there is a State Action Committee on AIDS chaired by the Chief Minister with the State Health Department as its secretariat. These committees are responsible for planning and coordination of activities at the state level. A district action committee on AIDS under the chairmanship of the District Officer is responsible for action at the district level.

It is important to look at HIV/AIDS as a development issue, and therefore the formation of the high-level inter-ministerial committee was a step in the right direction. However, placing this committee under the MOH rather than the Prime Minister's Department does not allow the committee to act with sufficient authority. Perhaps this is part of the reason why the meetings held are few and far between. Furthermore the MOH is also responsible for many other infectious diseases, including avian flu and SARS (severe acute respiratory syndrome), both of which require immediate and urgent action. Treating HIV/AIDS as a health issue serves to downplay the wider reaching socio-economic consequences of the epidemic.

National Strategic Plan

The National Strategic Plan, formulated in 1988 and reviewed in 2001, has input from both governmental and non-governmental bodies. The vision of the plan is 'to ensure that our community lives in an environment that is at least risk for HIV infection and to minimize the personal and socio-economic impact of the HIV infection and AIDS' (MOH 2001: 5) The objectives of the plan are set out in broad terms, encompassing the mobilization of resources and the promotion of inter-agency collaboration, while

the strategies envisioned include education and communication, early detection and surveillance, as well as the provision of appropriate medical/health services and supportive care at the institutional and community levels.

Despite the formulation of the National Strategic Plan, efforts to promote and disseminate the plan have been hampered by a lack of resources. No extra funding was earmarked for the implementation of the plan. It was assumed that the various ministries would incorporate the HIV/AIDS-related programmes within existing programmes using existing allocations. In Malaysia, official HIV/AIDS activities are overseen by the AIDS/STD Section under the Disease Control Division of the Department of Public Health. In contrast, Thailand, recognizing that HIV/AIDS could become a threat to the nation, moved the control of the HIV/AIDS programme from the Ministry of Public Health to the office of the Prime Minister; with this move came the recognition that it was on the national agenda, and the budget increased from US$1 million in 1988 to US$44 million in 1993 (Punpanich *et al.* 2004).

Governmental policies and programmes

Educational programmes

In the absence of a cure or vaccine, prevention is the main priority. The MOH does this through the 'promotion of good moral values and healthy lifestyle practices, early detection and prevention of spread through effective counselling as well as mobilizing community support and participation through special programmes and collaborative efforts' (MOH 2001). Part of the HIV/AIDS education has been incorporated into various existing programmes such as the school health education programmes and healthy lifestyle programmes.

However, the single most extensive programme in the area of HIV/AIDS prevention is the 'Keep healthy without AIDS programme for adolescents' (Program Sihat Tanpa AIDS untuk Remaja or PROSTAR). PROSTAR trains peer educators who are then expected to train, plan and conduct suitable activities for other young people. As of December 2002, there were 833 PROSTAR clubs in schools and districts, as well as in special clubhouses throughout the country. Some 928 activities were held, reaching 72,001 young people (MOH 2004). In addition to education for the community, the Ministry also conducts training programmes for its own staff to promote safety and reduce stigma in relation to HIV/AIDS.

The role of the Ministry of Education in the area of HIV/AIDS mainly revolves around the incorporation of information into the school curriculum. Training modules incorporating the skills approach are also being developed for teacher training.[1] These modules cover physical and social development, gender roles, sexually transmitted diseases and HIV/AIDS as well as some aspects of sexuality and preventive education.

Screening and compulsory testing

At present, anonymous testing (rapid test), with pre and post-test counselling, is available free of charge at all government health clinics throughout the country.[2] At the same time, compulsory screening is aimed at specific groups. One such group are prisoners, who are tested in correctional centres at entry, at six months and pre-release. Compulsory testing is also directed at all inmates of the 28 drug rehabilitation centres run by the National Narcotics Agency of the Ministry of Home Affairs, as well as drug users rounded up in police raids.

Compulsory testing is an infringement of individual rights, and in the absence of proper counselling creates more harm than good. Public health experience has demonstrated that programmes that do not respect the rights and dignity of individuals are not effective. Furthermore because of the stigmatization and discrimination of people living with HIV/AIDS (PLWHA), individuals who may be infected tend to go 'underground' to escape mandatory testing.[3]

Since 1998, women attending government antenatal clinics have also been screened. This is a voluntary screening programme (see later section on NGO efforts). However, the work burden at governmental antenatal clinics is so high that pre and post-test counselling is often not carried out properly. When knowledge and understanding of HIV/AIDS testing is generally low, and there is little pre-test counselling, this may result in *de facto* compulsory testing.

Since the first year, when 49.7 per cent of attendees were tested, this programme has expanded, and in 2002, 92.8 per cent, numbering 387,208, were screened. The aim of this programme is to detect and treat positive mothers in order to reduce the rate of transmission to the unborn child. Zidvudin (AZT) is given to mothers to reduce the possibility of infection in their children, and all mothers and babies detected in this programme qualify for free highly active antiretroviral therapy (HAART).

Testing is expensive. For example, in 2002, the MOH tested 359,411 mothers to identify 139 positive cases (0.039 per cent) (MOH 2003). If proper counselling was carried out, and mothers were give a choice, there may not be a need to carry out so many tests and the pick-up rate could be almost the same. The question is whether the money could be used more not wisely in other ways, such as for educational purposes.

Furthermore, in the state of Johor, the Religious Department carries out compulsory testing before allowing couples to marry. As this stipulation may only be applied to a Johorean, the other partner who is not from the state does not need to be tested, rendering the test irrelevant in such cases.

Foreign workers are also screened for HIV/AIDS, in addition to other diseases, before the Ministry of Human Resources will approve or renew their work permits.[4] However, this can only be enforced for documented migrant workers, whilst there is a large group of undocumented workers

who do not fall under such surveillance. At the end of 2002, foreign workers made up 2.6 per cent of the total HIV infections in Malaysia but in 2003, this increased to 4.8 per cent (MOH 2004). Again, such statistics are only available for documented workers.

Other than these testing programmes, the MOH carries out routine surveillance through collecting data from private and public health facilities. HIV/AIDS is an infectious disease subjected to notification procedures, that is, medical practitioners are required by law to notify the authorities of all cases that come to their attention, and upon notification, the MOH will carry out epidemiological investigations and partner notification. The MOH also monitors the situation through research and evaluation, including sentinel studies, carried out from time to time in conjunction with universities and NGOs.

Treatment and management

The main objective of the MOH in the area of treatment and management of HIV/AIDS cases is to provide comprehensive health and medical care, including counselling, for those infected with and affected by HIV and AIDS, as well as to reduce morbidity and suffering among them. In Malaysia, all treatment of secondary infections is free and available at all government health centres. However if PLWHA need antiretroviral drugs, two antiretrovirals (AVR) in the HAART regime (generally consisting of three AVRs) are given free of charge and clients are expected to purchase the third. With the Health Ministry's amendments to the Patent Act, the much needed drugs can now be procured at a cheaper rate from India. What would have cost RM1,200 per month will be reduced to RM350 (*The New Straits Times*, 12 August 2004). Nonetheless many PLWHA still cannot afford this because once treatment has started it becomes a monthly expense. In addition to this they will also have to pay for various other tests from time to time to monitor the viral load in the blood. The final objective of the Ministry is to incorporate diagnosis and management of HIV into the primary health services, but the challenge of training all relevant staff would be enormous.

The Malaysian Code of Practice and Management of HIV/AIDS

A study by the Department of Occupational Safety and Health (DOSH) led to a national seminar in 2001, during which the 'Malaysian Code of Practice and Management of HIV/AIDS' was developed. The code calls for companies to have a written policy which clearly states the employer's commitment to preventing the spread of the virus, as well as protecting HIV-positive employees from discrimination and stigmatization at the workplace. This includes protection against discrimination such as requiring HIV-testing as a precondition for employment, as well as protection of the rights of HIV-positive persons to confidentiality and privacy. Furthermore, the code stipulates that disciplinary action be taken against employees who discriminate against, or stigmatize, co-workers who are HIV-positive or perceived to be HIV-positive (Selvaretnam and Marina Mahathir 2001: 3).

Since 2001, the MOH, together with DOSH, have conducted several activities aimed at encouraging the private sector to adopt this code. Despite these efforts, which included roadshows throughout the country, very few companies actually adopted the code. At any rate, it is a code of practice and, even if adopted, there is no compulsion for companies to implement it.

Non-governmental efforts: the MAC

In 1992, some MOH officers, together with people from a few NGOs, initiated the formation of the Malaysian AIDS Council (MAC) for better collaboration among the NGOs in addressing issues pertaining to community-based responses to HIV/AIDS. Since then, the MAC has played a major role in the channelling of government funds to NGOs for HIV/AIDS work.[5] To date, the Council has 37 affiliated members all of whom are NGOs directly or indirectly involved in HIV/AIDS work. The MAC coordinates NGO efforts in order to reduce unnecessary duplication and programme overlap as well as to ensure programme effectiveness.

Although the MAC channels funds to NGO affiliates which mainly conduct programmes focused on education and to a smaller degree on care and support, it also conducts its own public education activities, which are focused on where needs are highest. For example, in 2003, the MAC, together with the Malaysian Chinese Association (MCA),[6] initiated the 'Iceberg II' project aimed at bringing the message to the Mandarin-speaking community. They also conducted 'youth to youth' theatre drama workshops as a demonstration of an effective way to reach young people.

The MAC Resource Centre acts as a clearing house as well as a library for professionals and young people who need HIV/AIDS information, and the Council is also involved in providing care, support and treatment. When the government was not able to provide medication for PLWHA, the MAC fought for generic drugs to be brought in, and initiated a special 'drug assistance fund' to help PLWHA pay for medication. It also has a Paediatric AIDS fund which supports infected and affected children, and a special loan scheme which provides financing for infected and affected women to expand or start a small business.

Perhaps the most important role that the MAC has taken is in the area of advocacy. In its capacity of advocating for the rights of PLWHA, it published the Malaysian AIDS Charter in 1995, and it also played an active part in the development of the Malaysian code of practice for the workplace, mentioned earlier. For many years, the MAC, through its 'Law, Ethics, and Human Rights' division, has fought for the rights of PLWHA and aided in many cases of PLWHA who have lost their jobs.

When the state of Johor introduced compulsory testing for all Muslim couples wanting to get married, the MAC advocated a voluntary alternative. When the MOH initiated antenatal testing of all mothers who attend government antenatal clinics, it was the MAC that fought for the rights of women to voluntary testing. The provision of free life-long medication to women whose statuses were detected at these clinics also resulted directly from the advocacy efforts of the MAC.

The MAC has also played an important advocacy role in pressing for sex education to be introduced in schools, and for harm reduction for intravenous drug users to be officially adopted. It must be recognized that there have been several attempts made by political leaders to introduce sex education into the curriculum but these have invariably produced negative reactions from parents, as well as religious leaders.[7]

Two major challenges: sex and drugs

The primary problems surrounding work on HIV/AIDS prevention revolve around two major taboo subjects: sex and drugs. There is an element of denial that these two major subjects have to be confronted in order to deal effectively with the HIV/AIDS epidemic. The reluctance has to do with official quarters not wanting to be seen or to run the risk of being construed in any way to be condoning drug abuse, or encouraging sexual activity among unmarried persons. This results in non-realistic prevention strategies that do not deal with the facts: that unmarried persons, most of them young, have sex; that intravenous drug users will continue injecting with shared needles even while cognizant of the risk; and that drug users have sex, and will spread the infection to their partners.

Youth and sex

The youth population (15–24 years) of Malaysia is expected to grow from 4.03 million in 1995 to 4.98 million in 2005. This growing number of young people presents a challenge because they are reaching maturity earlier, getting married later and, therefore, exposed to more years of sexual health risk than ever before. At the same time, social norms remain conservative, and state and cultural institutions continue to work on a premise that appears to deny the existence of sexual activity among young people.

Studies in schools have found that young people do have knowledge about the etiology, effects and causes of HIV/AIDS. Nevertheless, there are glaring omissions. For example, using the condom as a means of prevention is not often taught, for fear of being seen to be promoting sexual promiscuity among the young. An evaluation of the 'PROSTAR' programme pointed out that 13 per cent of peer educators were not able to give accurate answers on condom use, which the evaluators attributed to the lack of emphasis given to the messages on sex and the use of condoms (Samsuddin and Latiffah 2001).

Another important omission is the lack of emphasis on helping young people to develop the skills that enable them to make wise choices. It is only in the last two years that the Ministry of Education embarked on a skills approach to the teaching of HIV/AIDS. The demands made on teachers to impart skills to young people call for innovative approaches in sensitive areas, where most teachers may be embarrassed or which they may feel uncomfortable dealing with. Therefore, even if curriculum and guidelines are made available, it is still a big challenge to change mindsets and approaches among teachers so that young people are reached in an effective manner.

Another challenge that the Ministry of Education has to address is to provide sexual and reproductive health, including HIV/AIDS, education early enough to reach those children who will drop out before completing their high school education. There is a tendency for boys to drop out from formal education earlier than girls. For example, in 2001, the sex ratio of children attending primary schools was 105 : 100, in lower secondary school it was 102 : 100, but in upper secondary school the sex ratio was only 92 : 100 (Department of Statistics 2003). Thus although there were more boys than girls in primary and lower secondary schools, the reverse is true in the upper secondary schools, because more boys would have dropped out before completing high school. This sex difference coincides with another, which is that boys are more likely than girls to have been involved in premarital sexual intercourse (Siti Norazah and Low 2002), leading to a high risk for this group.

Many of the educational programmes aimed at youths have only managed to engage with the 'easy to reach', those who already have a certain level of education or who are part of an organization. Data of drug users provided by the National Narcotics Agency (2002) show that 98 per cent of drug users in Malaysia are males and almost one-third of them did not complete their basic education. Young people with low educational achievement who migrate from rural to urban areas in search of jobs are also exposed to activities that may increase their risk of infection. Therefore, this 'vulnerable group' is also not reachable. There is an urgent need to reach them through appropriate ways, so as to provide them with the education and skills to protect themselves.

Drugs and AIDS: the twin epidemic

It is not possible for Malaysia to fight HIV/AIDS without addressing the problem of drug use. In 2002, while HIV/AIDS increased by 19 new cases per day, drug users increased by 50 persons per day. The National Narcotics Agency estimated that the cumulative number of drug users in the country up to 2004 was 274,420 (National Narcotics Agency 2004), while the con-sensus meeting convened by WHO and the MOH estimated that there could be 170,000 to 240,000 *injecting* drug users (WHO 2003).[8]

At a conference on harm reduction in Australia in 2004, the Malaysian MOH speaker informed the audience that harm reduction efforts in Malaysia include sending drug users to rehabilitation centres by court order, counselling, HIV screening and treatment. Voluntary drug substitution treatment (DST) with buprenorphine was being piloted at one centre; at the same time, more than 200 general practitioners have been trained in administering DST. A methadone study was ongoing in one of the public universities; while two community NGOs have safe injecting programme[9] for drug users and programmes promoting condom use among sex workers (Mohd Khairi 2004).

These harm reduction efforts are at a very early stage, and far from proven to be effective. Despite a drug problem that has transcended a generation, Malaysia is only beginning to pilot-test the effectiveness of drug substitution.[10] The present official policy of zero tolerance for drugs is interpreted, even in the drug rehabilitation centres, to mean that people should not be on drugs at all, and hence harm reduction education is not necessary and is therefore out of question.

Furthermore, it is a well-known fact that for harm reduction to work, as in the case of Thailand and Cambodia, it must be carried out nationwide. Leaving harm reduction to NGOs cannot solve the problem because the coverage of NGOs tends to be very limited. At the same time there are only one or two NGOs which promote harm reduction among marginalized groups and even these NGOs do not have a needle exchange programme. At best they teach drug users how to sterilize the needles. In the absence of countrywide harm reduction programmes among drug users, the battle cannot be won.

The denial syndrome comes to a head when the twin taboos of drugs and sex intersect, and this is reflected in the official reluctance not only to make clean needles available, but also to make condoms available to drug users. Only married inmates of rehabilitation centres who tested positive receive some education on condom use. In fact, a 1998 study on 1,950 male drug users in 16 rehabilitation centres found that 82 per cent of the intravenous drug users reported ever having had sexual partners (MOH 2003). Sometimes, drug users are driven by their addiction into sex work, thereby exposing themselves as well as their clients and partners to the risk of infection. Therefore, to be effective, harm reduction efforts have to make available clean needles, as well as condoms.

Stigma and discrimination

Stigma and discrimination against HIV/AIDS in Malaysia are so prevalent that not many PLWHA dare to reveal themselves to the public. The few who have had the courage to do so tend to be from the rehabilitation centres. While it is important to 'put a face to the epidemic', publicizing the plight of ex-drug users reinforces the false notion that we only get infected through drug use, and gives people who do not use drugs the impression that they are not vulnerable. At the same time, any infected person is often construed to have been infected through the use of drugs or through 'illicit sex', or sex with multiple partners. The average person who has no personal acquaintance with PLWHA tends to be afraid of them, and is not convinced that it is the PLWHA who should be afraid because of their compromised immune systems. Knowledge and attitude studies have shown that while there is widespread knowledge about how we can be infected, and that most will advocate equal rights for PLWHA, not many are willing to work with PLWHA, let alone share food or utensils with them (Lokman *et al.* 1998; Zulkifli 2002).

Stigma and discrimination prevent people who may have been involved in high risk behaviour from going for testing, and those who are positive tend to seek treatment from hospitals far from home. In fact many flood the general hospital in Kuala Lumpur in an effort to avoid meeting friends and relatives. Some PLWHA are rejected by their families who fear that having a positive son or daughter at home will bring shame to the whole family. In some instances the PLWHA themselves do not want to go home to their families for the same reason.

Care and support for the infected and the affected

As more and more people living with HIV develop AIDS, there is a need to move towards care and support for them. Often marginalized, not just by society but by their own families as well, PLWHA need a place to go to. A few NGOs run homes for PLWHA, but these are mainly found in and around the capital city. The other PLWHA who are spread throughout the length and breadth of the country have no access, because the institutional homes in the Klang Valley are always overcrowded, and also because they often do not know that such homes exist.

Malaysia is fortunate to have a publicly funded health care system that is still intact. PLWHA in the country have access to free medical treatment for all secondary infections. Fee charges for hospitalization are not high at government hospitals, and if individuals can prove to the medical social workers that they are not able to pay for hospitalization, fees can be waived. Privatization of the health care system is therefore a threat, and it is the recognition of this that led Marina Mahathir, then President of the MAC, as well as several other AIDS NGOs, to endorse the Citizens' Health Manifesto, calling for a moratorium on the privatization of health care, pending a thorough review.[11] The challenge ahead for state health care services would be the increasing cost of providing adequate medical care to the increasing number of PLWHA.

Among the children who are made orphans by the epidemic, those who are HIV-positive find themselves without a home, because staff of orphanages are afraid of being infected, and therefore reject them. The only three NGOs running homes for orphans are over-subscribed. UNAIDS (2003) estimated in 2003 that Malaysia had 18,000 AIDS orphans (children who have lost one or both parents to HIV/AIDS).

One of the indicators recommended by the United Nations in the evaluation of the degree of adherence to the UNGASS declaration[12] is the presence of laws ensuring that children living with HIV/AIDS are not discriminated against. To date, Malaysia has not passed such a law. It is perversely argued that there is no practice of such discrimination in Malaysia and therefore having such a law would be discriminatory by singling out HIV-positive children for protection.[13] As a result, even though there are vacancies in public orphanages, positive children are often refused entry. At the same time not many extended family members would adopt these children upon the death of parents. Children whose parents were drug users or sex workers face the most discrimination.

Conclusions

The fact that there is no cure for HIV/AIDS despite the millions spent on research has made it one of the most feared diseases. Prevention is the mainstay, but in Malaysia, efforts to prevent HIV/AIDS have been hampered by moralistic attitudes. To deal with the problem realistically, state agencies have to work with those at highest risk, that is, the drug users and the sex workers, in ways that are not judgmental. The moralistic stance that providing them with the means to prevent infection, that is, condoms and clean needles, is tantamount to condoning their practices has to be transcended. Despite warnings by NGOs and international organizations, and despite Thailand's example of showing that the effective way of confronting the epidemic is to be realistic and not moralistic, HIV/AIDS has been allowed to permeate the community in Malaysia. HIV/AIDS now has the potential to escalate into a major and costly epidemic that will affect the social and economic development of the country. The only way to beat the epidemic is to recognize that we must be realistic rather than moralistic. Being realistic means that after 20 years of being moralistic in our approach perhaps we should be trying new approaches before it is too late.

Notes

1 One of them, the 'Training of teachers manual on preventive education against HIV/AIDS in the school setting', prepared by UNESCO, the Principal Regional Office for Asia and the Pacific (PROAP) and the Southeast Asian Members on Education Organization & Regional Centre for Tropical Medicine Network (SEAMEO-TROPMED) is currently being pilot-tested in selected schools (Sharifah Maimunah 2003).
2 Donated blood is also screened, and there are educational programmes for donors.
3 See Mercey (1998) on compulsory antenatal testing, and Haerry *et al.* (2004) on compulsory testing and human rights.
4 In 2004 the number of foreign workers employed in Malaysia was estimated to be 1.16 million (Kanapathy 2004).

5 All funding from the government for work in HIV/AIDS is generally channelled through the MAC.
6 This is a political party in the ruling coalition, Barisan Nasional.
7 See, for example, Taylor (2002).
8 These estimates vary from study to study. For example, Navaratnam and Foong (1989) estimated that there were already 119,001 drug-dependent persons in Malaysia in 1986, but almost 20 years later, the estimates have only doubled, despite the National Narcotics Agency reporting that a total of 177,817 new users were detected between 1988 and 2001.
9 In these programmes, injecting drug users are taught to flush their syringes twice with water, twice with an easily available bleach, and another two times with water (two by two by two).
10 It was reported that the government deferred to the following year an RM150 million plan to issue free needles and condoms. Instead, a pilot programme to use methadone, a synthetic drug, to treat addicts will be launched, as it is more acceptable to Muslim religious leaders (*The Straits Times*, 4 September 2005).
11 Website of the Citizens' Health Initiative, list of endorsers, available at <http://www.prn.usm.my/chi/endorsers.html> (accessed 8 August 2005).
12 The Declaration of Commitment on HIV/AIDS entitled 'Global Crisis – Global Action' passed by the United Nations General Assembly Special Session on HIV/AIDS in June 2001. Online. Available at <http://www.un.org/ga/aids/coverage/FinalDeclarationHIVAIDS.html> (accessed 8 August 2005).
13 Related to the authors by caregivers of homes run by NGOs, and also from discussions with welfare officers.

References

Department of Statistics (2003) *Vital Statistics of Malaysia 2003*, Kuala Lumpur: Department of Statistics Malaysia.

Haerry, D., Wasserfallen, F. and Wiessner, P. (2004) 'Compulsory HIV testing from a public health and human rights perspective', *PWHA-NET Forum*. Online. Available at <http://archives.hst.org.za/pwha-net/msg00589.html> (accessed 10 October 2005).

Kanapathy, V. (2004) 'International migration and labour market developments in Asia: economic recovery, the labour market and migrant workers in Malaysia', paper presented at the Workshop on International Migration and Labour Markets in Asia, Tokyo, Japan, 5–6 February.

Lokman, A.R., A. Osman and K. Kasmini (1996) 'Knowledge, attitude and behavioral tendency about AIDS in lower secondary schools in the district of Petaling, Selangor', *Medical Journal of Malaysia* 51(3): 372–9.

Mercey, D. (1998) 'Antenatal HIV testing', *British Medical Journal* 316: 241–2.

Ministry of Health (MOH) (2001) *National Strategic Plan: Prevention and Control of HIV Infection, Malaysia*, Kuala Lumpur: Ministry of Health.

—— (2002) *Number of HIV-infected Cases Reported in Malaysia 1986–2001*, Kuala Lumpur: Ministry of Health.

—— (2003) *HIV/AIDS in Malaysia 2002*, Kuala Lumpur: Ministry of Health.

—— (2004) *Annual Report 2002, AIDS/STD Section*, Kuala Lumpur: Ministry of Health.

Mohd Khairi Yakub (2004) 'Drug users and HIV/AIDS in Malaysia', paper presented at the 15th International Conference on the Reduction of Drug Related Harm (15th ICRDRH), Melbourne, Australia, 20–24 April.

—— (2002) *Buletin Statistik Dadah 2001*, Putrajaya: Ministry of Home Affairs, National Narcotics Agency.

National Narcotics Agency (2004) *Laporan Dadah 2004*, Putrajaya: Ministry of Home Affairs, Division for Prevention, Planning and Research, National Narcotics Agency.

Navaratnam, V. and Foong, K. (1989) *Development and Application of a System for Monitoring Drug Abuse: The Malaysian Experience*, United Nations Office on Drugs and Crime.

The New Straits Times, 12 August 2004, 'Healing touch'.

Punpanich, W., Ungchusak, K. and Detels, R. (2004) 'Thailand's response to the HIV/AIDS epidemic: yesterday, today and tomorrow', in R. Detels (ed.) *HIV Surveillance, Prevention, Intervention and Treatment in Asia*, a special supplement to *AIDS Education and Prevention*, 16 (Supplement A): 119–36.

Samsuddin, A. Rahim and Latiffah Pawanteh (2001) *Penilaian Intervensi Sosial PROSTAR Terhadap Kesedaran AIDS Di Kalangan Remaja*, Kuala Lumpur: Ministry of Health and Universiti Kebangsaan Malaysia.

Selvaretnam, J. and Marina Mahathir (2001) 'The Malaysian workplace code of practice: insights on its development', *Sexual Health Exchange 2001 4*, Royal Tropical Institute (KIT) in collaboration with SAfAIDS (Southern Africa AIDS Information Dissemination Service), Zimbabwe.

Sharifah Maimunah Syed Zain (2003) 'Family life education in Malaysian schools', paper presented at National Youth Seminar on Youth-Friendly Sexual and Reproductive Health Programme, Federation of Family Planning Associations Malaysia, Subang Jaya, Selangor, 9–11 August.

Siti Norazah Zulkifli and Low, W.Y. (2000) 'Sexual practices in Malaysia: determinants of sexual intercourse among unmarried youths', *Journal of Adolescent Health* 27(4): 276–80.

The Straits Times, 4 September 2005, 'KL puts needle and condom plan on hold'.

Taylor, Rachel (2002) 'The spread of AIDS in Asia', an interview with Marina Mahathir, President of the Malaysian AIDS Council, *World Press Review*, 25 November. Online. Available at <http://www.worldpress.org/Asia/824.cfm#down> (accessed 10 October 2005).

UNAIDS (2003) *Report on the Global AIDS Epidemic*, Geneva: UNAIDS.

Wodak, A., Ali, R. and Farrell, M. (2004) 'Future of HIV/AIDS in Asia depends on harm-reduction policy for injection drug users', *British Medical Journal* 329: 697–8.

World Health Organization (2003) *Consensus Report on STI, HIV and AIDS Epidemiology: Malaysia – 1999*, Manila: World Health Organization.

Zulkifli, S.N. (2002) 'Knowledge, attitudes and beliefs related to HIV/AIDS among adolescents in Malaysia', *Medical Journal of Malaysia* 57(1): 3–23.

10 Health care and long-term care issues for the elderly

Ong Fon Sim

A country is said to be ageing when at least 7 per cent of the population is composed of the elderly, defined as people aged 60 or older (United Nations 1993). Technological advancement in the medical field has resulted in a 'two-way pull', that is, lower death rates and longer lives on the one hand, and lower infant mortality rates, as well as lower fertility rates on the other. In the second half of the twentieth century, 20 years were added to the average lifespan, bringing global life expectancy to its current level of 66 years (United Nations 2002). If the predicted trends in global ageing continue, a revolutionary demographic transition, where record numbers of people live into old-old ages (defined as 75 years and over), will occur in just three generations (United Nations 2002).

Ageing is a phenomenon that was once associated with the developed nations. Today, ageing is occurring in developing countries at a pace faster than that previously experienced by developed nations. It has been argued that this will mean that developing economies will have less time than the developed nations had to respond to the consequences of population ageing. However, we believe that developing countries do have sufficient time to prepare and be ready to face the challenges of ageing, provided that individuals, families, communities, institutions and policy-makers have a shared vision, interest and goals. In addition, lessons can be learned from the experiences and the successes of developed nations in managing population ageing.

For Malaysia, life expectancy is currently 70.9 years for males and 75.5 years for females, and the old age dependency ratio (measured by the number of persons aged 60 years and over per 100 persons aged 15–59) is projected to increase from 10 in 2000 to 15.7 in 2020 (Malaysia 2003). In addition, the older population itself is ageing, with an increasingly larger proportion of old-old. This remarkable demographic change poses challenges to Malaysian society.

The challenge for any aged society is the issue of successful ageing, which according to Rowe and Kahn (1998) consists of three aspects: (i) decreasing the risk of diseases or disease-related disability, (ii) increasing physical and mental functioning, and (iii) being actively engaged in life. Of particular interest is the broader issue of active ageing, adopted as a policy framework by the World Health Organization (WHO 2002), which emphasizes the social, cultural and environmental aspects that enable older persons to participate fully in all areas of life. Clearly, health and the maintenance of physical and mental functioning are two determinants for successful ageing. Even when disability sets in, successful ageing will still be relevant if the elderly can have options to choose among the various types of long-term care.

Long-term care

Long-term care (LTC) is a broad term, variously defined and interpreted in different countries and even within individual health and social care systems (Phillips 2000). Generally, it is care delivered to individuals who are dependent on others for assistance with the basic tasks necessary for physical, mental and social functioning over sustained periods of time (Kane and Kane 1989). It may also be defined as the service provided to those suffering from chronic physical or mental illnesses, mental retardation or other severe disabling conditions (Estes and Lee 1985). The help may be for moving about, dressing, bathing, eating, using the toilet, taking medication and so on.

The World Health Organization (2002) defines LTC as the system of activities undertaken by informal caregivers (family, friends and/or neighbours) and professionals (health, social and others) to ensure that a person who is not fully capable of self-care can maintain the highest possible quality of life. This should be according to his or her individual preferences, with the greatest level of independence, autonomy, participation, personal fulfilment and human dignity. The goal of such care is to allow the recipients to function at the highest level of autonomy possible.

The term 'LTC services' is often synonymous with the concept of institutional services (Harrington and Swan 1985; Cheah 1995). Institutional LTC services are provided primarily by nursing homes, although some general hospitals and chronic disease hospitals do provide LTC services. Besides institutional care, informal sources of support (family and friends) and paid helpers in the community are other sources of care for the elderly.

For a long time, the family has been the main institution providing support to the elderly (emotionally, physically and financially) in both developed and developing countries (Gibson *et al.* 2003). Family members are the caregivers preferred by the elderly themselves (Ong and Wong 2002). According to Jacobzone, Camblis and Robine (2000/1) most international data on LTC show that informal care could account for up to 80 per cent of total care. The differential rates of institutionalization may reflect the extent of informal care, as they vary from 5 to 8 per cent in most developed countries, to about 2 per cent in developing countries (United Nations Secretariat 1994).

In recent years, however, average household size has declined, which has affected the potential of family members to be caregivers. Since women are generally the main care providers, with greater participation of women in the formal sector, the pressure to provide institutional support to the elderly has intensified, pushing upwards the potential growth of institutional care.

In addition, LTC needs will become more prevalent with the ageing of the older population and as degenerative pathologies set in accompanied by an increase in the level of functional disability. Widowhood in old age may give rise to further pressure for LTC.

It has been widely acknowledged that there has been a steep increase in the need for institutional LTC in developing countries due to the increase in disability and a change in the capacity of informal support systems to address these needs. Demographic shifts and epidemiological changes are major forces that impact on the ability of informal support systems to provide care. In 2005, female labour force participation as a percentage of total population was 48.7 per cent increasing at an average rate of 2.5 per cent per year (Malaysia 2006). Therefore, the need to share the responsibilities of care among the different stakeholders is more pressing now than before. A major problem in developing countries is an absence of data on LTC needs and services, which are usually home-based and mainly performed by informal caregivers, especially family members. Therefore, close estimates of LTC needs among the elderly population in developing countries such as Malaysia have to be derived from the records of people requiring health care for chronic illnesses or disability.

Profile of the elderly in Malaysia

Malaysia has adopted the age demarcation of 60 years and older as the cut-off classification for the elderly, based on the United Nations World Assembly on Ageing, Vienna, 1982. By 2010, Malaysia will be transformed into an ageing society with the elderly constituting 7.4 per cent of the total population (Table 10.1). The rate of growth of the elderly population is increasing faster than that of the total population, leading to a shift from a young population to an ageing one. The elderly proportion of population

Table 10.1 Past, present and future elderly population trends, Malaysia, 1970–2030

Year	Citizens aged 60 years and older		Growth rate (per cent)	
	Number ('000)	Percent of total population	Elderly population	Total population
1970	546.1	5.2	3.5	2.6
1980	745.2	5.7	3.1	2.3
1991	1032.3	5.9	3.0	2.6
2000	1398.5	6.3	3.4	2.6
2010	2134.9	7.4	4.2	2.2
2020	3439.6	9.9	4.8	1.9
2030	4933.4	12.0	3.6	1.7

Source: Rabieyah Mat and Hajar Md Taha (2003: 4).

Table 10.2 Age distribution of the Malaysian population, 1970, 1980, 1991 and 2000

Age group (years)	Percentage of the total population by age groups			
	1970	1980	1991	2000
0–14	44.9	39.6	36.7	33.5
15–44	40.7	45.6	47.6	48.8
45–59	9.2	9.2	9.9	11.6
60–74	4.4	4.6	4.6	5.0
75+	0.8	1.1	1.2	1.3

Source: Rabieyah Mat and Hajar Md Taha (2003: 5).

will grow from 6.3 per cent in 2000 to 12.0 per cent in 2030, doubling in proportion to the total population and three times more in numbers (Rabieyah Mat and Hajar Md Taha 2003).[1] By 2100, the elderly will constitute 29.6 per cent of the total population (World Bank 1994).

From 1970 to 2000, the proportion of those in the age group 0–14 dropped by as much as 11 percentage points while those in the age groups 15–44 and 45–59 increased steadily, indicating that the nation will continue to progress towards ageing (Table 10.2). The old-old population is expected to grow in numbers from 277,000 in 2000 to 1.3 million in 2030. The continuous technological advancements in the medical field that add years to life will add further pressure on health care and LTC needs as the number of elderly continues to increase, and as they progress into the old-old category.

Table 10.3 presents the ageing phenomenon by ethnic groups. Ageing is a more serious phenomenon among the Chinese compared to the Indians or

Table 10.3 Percentage of elderly by ethnicity, 1991 and 2000

	Percentage of elderly (60+ years)		Percentage of old-old (75+ years) within the elderly group	
	1991	2000	1991	2000
Malaysian citizens				
Bumiputera[1]	5.4	5.7	18.5	20.0
Chinese	7.6	8.8	26.1	19.1
Indians	5.4	5.6	17.7	17.0
Others	6.9	4.8	22.2	23.2
Non-Malaysian citizens	2.7	3.1	21.7	30.3
Total	5.9	6.3	21.2	19.8

Source: Rabieyah Mat and Hajar Md Taha (2003: 8).

Note
[1] Incudes the majority ethnic group 'Malays' and 'Other *Bumiputera*' groups.

Table 10.4 Percentage distribution of elderly by marital status, sex and age group, Malaysia, 2000

Marital status	Male			Female			Total		
	60–74 years	75+	Total	60–74 years	75+	Total	60–74 years	75+	Total
Never married	2.2	1.9	2.2	2.0	1.4	1.9	2.1	1.7	2.0
Currently married	88.3	73.0	85.5	56.0	27.3	49.9	71.7	47.4	66.9
Widowed	8.6	23.4	11.3	39.3	68.0	45.5	24.4	48.4	29.2
Divorced	0.9	1.6	1.0	2.6	3.2	2.7	1.8	2.5	1.9
Total	100.0	100.0	100.0	100.0	100.0	100.0	100.0	100.0	100.0

Source: Rabieyah Mat and Hajar Md Taha (2003: 10).

Bumiputeras. Although in 2000, the proportion of elderly *Bumiputeras* was lower than the elderly Chinese, the absolute numbers are larger. Among the Malays and Chinese, the percentage of old-old is similar, with about 20 per cent of the elderly falling in the old-old category, while the corresponding percentage for the Indians is higher at 23 per cent. Ageing within the elderly category has significant implications since the demand for health care and other care facilities tends to increase with age.

Widowhood is more prevalent among females than males. In 2000, more than two-thirds of females aged 75 years or older were widowed, compared to only 23.4 per cent among males (Table 10.4). Longer life expectancy among women could explain the prevalence of widowhood among females, as they tend to out-live their partners. Additionally, males are more likely to remarry than females.

Health status and health care for the elderly

Although ageing may not necessarily be accompanied by disability and poor health, it would not be inaccurate to expect a significant increase in a whole range of diseases and disabilities that are associated with old age. Biological ageing is frequently associated with a diminished functioning of the body that leads to a reduced level of ability to care for oneself. In order to understand the health status of the elderly in Malaysia, several studies that were conducted on health status and health related issues are reviewed here.

The World Health Organization sponsored a survey of the elderly in Peninsular Malaysia in 1984/85 (Chen *et al.* 1986). Purposive sampling was used to obtain a sample of 1,000 persons that was an approximate cross-section of Malaysian society drawn from five geographical areas, the three dominant ethnic groups (55 per cent Malays, 36 per cent Chinese, 9 per cent Indians), and both rural (66 per cent) and urban (34 per cent) areas.

A majority were married (65 per cent) and had no formal education (56 per cent). It was reported that although 72 per cent felt they were healthy, all the respondents reported specific health problems and half of them took prescribed medication. The use of over-the-counter medication was reported by 29 per cent while 21 per cent relied on traditional medication. Common problems included poor eye-sight and problems with chewing and hearing. This study concluded that the elderly in Malaysia were still a neglected group in that little priority was given to the important issues associated with them.

Chia (1996) conducted a survey of 1,414 respondents aged 55 and above (53.5 per cent men, the rest women) in the Kuala Langat District of Selangor. About 70 per cent of those aged 65 and below rated themselves as healthy while about 62 per cent of those older than 75 years had a similar response. In Tan *et al.* (1999), a lower age limit of 50 years was used to select the sample of older persons with the aim of capturing the next cohort of elderly. Geographical areas in four districts in Peninsular Malaysia were selected to provide adequate representation of rural and urban areas, as well as different ethnic and socio-economic groups. In-depth interviews conducted with the sample of 802 older persons (342 males, 460 females), who were majority Malays (81 per cent), married (68 per cent) and had no schooling or had only received primary education, found that about one-third of the respondents reported good health while 17.7 per cent reported poor health and 39 per cent reported having some chronic health problems.

In general, common health problems found were eyesight problems (with women over 75 years being the worst affected), cataracts, difficulty chewing and dental problems, that is, needing prosthesis (Chen *et al.* 1986; Chen and Jones 1989; Tan *et al.* 1999). Eyesight problems were more serious among the elderly than were hearing problems. Although there were no changes in hearing-ability among women with increasing age, there was marked decrease in age among the men who indicated they could hear well. According to Tan *et al.* (1999), about 40 per cent of the elderly people indicated that they had specific health problems, with a higher percentage of women indicating this. High blood pressure seemed to be the most common problem affecting them. While rheumatism was a problem for women, it hardly affected the males. Joint problems also seemed to affect the females more than the males (Chia 1996). A higher proportion of the old-old reported heart problems, compared to the young-old, but there was not much of a sex difference. In the second countrywide representative national health and morbidity survey carried out in 1996 (NHMS 2) (Public Health Institute 1997), it was found that about 23 per cent of the elderly aged 60 or above were diabetic. Among those aged 55–64, the rate of psychiatric morbidity was 150 per 1,000 while for those aged 65 or above, it was 315 per 1,000.

Most of the elderly surveyed were found to be functionally able, as measured by the ability to carry out activities in the activities of daily living index (ADL). Chen *et al.* (1986) found that more than 90 per cent of the elderly could perform all the activities in the ADL. Similarly, in a separate study of a semi-rural district, it was found that 80 per cent of men between 65–74 and 64 per cent of men over 75 could do all the activities in the ADL (Chia 1996). For the females, the percentages were 71 per cent and 68 per cent respectively. The ability to perform activities in the ADL deteriorated with age. The main difficulties encountered were walking and shopping, and activities that are related to the ability to walk. Another activity that the elderly had trouble performing was 'getting to the toilet on time'. 'Getting in/out of bed' was a problem only for the old-old group, more so for the females than the males. Only about one-fifth of the elderly could perform heavy work such as lifting goods (Tan *et al.* 1999). Generally, males had better physical health than females, particularly at the older age groups of more than 70 years.

Recent studies

Recent studies on health and health care of the elderly include Ong and Wong (2002) and Ong (2003), as well as an on-going project.[2] These studies have common features in being surveys based on quota sampling, which was used to ensure adequate representations from the three major ethnic groups and both males and females. The study by Ong and Wong (2002) was carried out in the Kuala Lumpur/Petaling Jaya area, and involved those aged 60 or older. It was found that the majority (95 per cent) could still function well in activities of daily living. However, the number of elderly who could perform instrumental activities of daily living (IADL)[3] diminished.

In terms of self-assessment of health status, 35.6 per cent rated their health as good or very good, 52.9 per cent rated it average, and only 11.6 per cent reported poor health. The findings were consistent with the past studies discussed above. When comparing themselves with others of their age, a positive outlook could be observed as 42.1 per cent rated their health as better than their peers. About 40 per cent reported their health as about the same as their peers whereas 18.2 per cent said they felt that they were worse than their peers. About 60 per cent reported having chronic health problems, with the most common being high blood pressure and arthritis.

One year later, Ong (2003) interviewed respondents aged 50 or older from five major cities in Peninsular Malaysia. Those aged 60 or older totalled 377 of the 645 respondents and among them it was found that 150 (39.8 per cent) did not take any prescription drugs while slightly over 60 per cent took at least one prescription drug a day, and a small percentage (5.3 per cent) had to take more than five types of medication daily. The respondents were asked to indicate the types of health problems (from a list of 12 types provided) for which they have sought treatment. About 20 per cent reported that they did not have any health problems while the rest had at least one type of illness (Table 10.5). Consistent with the findings of Ong and Wong (2002), it was found that high blood pressure was the most common problem followed by arthritis or rheumatism (Table 10.6). Diabetes was also a common problem.

Table 10.5 Frequency of health problems among one group of urban elderly in Peninsular Malaysia, 2002

Number of illnesses[1]	Urban elderly (60 years and older) (N=377)	
	Number	Percentage
None	75	19.9
1	72	19.1
2	121	32.1
3	52	13.8
4	31	8.2
5 or more	26	7.0

Source: Ong (2003).

Note
[1] Respondents were asked to tick from a list of 12 illnesses (for which treatment had been received) all the problems that apply.

Table 10.6 Health problems reported among one group of urban elderly in Peninsular Malaysia, 2002

Types of problem[1]	Urban elderly (60 years and older) (N=377)	
	Number	Percentage
High blood pressure	154	40.8
Arthritis/Rheumatism	120	31.8
Diabetes	102	27.1
Chronic orthopedic/Back/Spine	70	18.6
Hearing problem	66	17.5
Heart/Circulatory disorder	60	15.9
Vision Problem	58	15.4
Respiratory disorder	34	9.0
Stroke	27	7.2
Urinary disorder	23	6.1
Nervous system	20	5.3
Mental disorder	5	1.3

Source: Ong (2003).

Note
[1] Respondents were asked to tick all the problems that apply.

In an on-going project, 149 respondents were interviewed on patronage of health care services.[4] Notwithstanding the types of illnesses or the purpose of medical check-ups, the elderly tended to seek service from government clinics and hospitals. For minor illnesses, about 34 per cent of the elderly sought treatment from private clinics or hospitals (Table 10.7). About 17 per cent chose self-treatment, relying on over-the-counter medication.

Table 10.7 Patronage behaviour among the elderly for health services by location, 2004

	Urban		Rural		Total	
	Frequency $(N=98)$	$\%^1$	Frequency $(N=51)$	$\%^1$	Frequency $(N=149)$	$\%^1$
Minor illnesses						
Government clinic/hospital	54	55.1	29	56.9	83	55.7
Private clinic/ hospital	29	29.6	21	41.2	50	33.6
Alternative healer	1	1.0	2	3.9	3	2.0
Self-medication	22	22.4	3	5.9	25	16.8
Chronic illnesses						
Government clinic/hospital	56	57.1	33	64.7	89	59.7
Private clinic/ hospital	30	30.6	14	27.5	44	29.5
Alternative healer	0	0.0	0	0.0	0	0.0
Self-medication	0	0.0	2	3.9	2	1.3
Medical check-up						
Government clinic/hospital	55	56.1	34	66.7	89	59.7
Private clinic/ hospital	29	29.6	15	29.4	44	29.5
Alternative healer	1	1.0	0	0.0	1	0.7
Self-medication	1	1.0	0	0.0	1	0.7

Source: '*Consumption behaviours of older people in Malaysia*', on-going research project funded under the Intensification of Research Priority Areas Programme of the Ministry of Science, Technology, and Innovation, Malaysia. The author of this chapter is the principal investigator.

Note
1 Percentages do not add up to 100% due to multiple responses.

A negligible percentage used traditional or alternative healers. For treating chronic illnesses, more of the elderly relied on public, rather than private, health care services. Similar patronage behaviour could also be observed for medical check-up services. The patronage pattern of health care services clearly indicates that public health care remains an important service provider for the elderly. At least one earlier study had shown similar trends in terms of purchasing behaviour for health care (Tan *et al.* 1999).

A comparison of the behaviour of the rural and urban elderly shows that more rural respondents relied on government clinics and hospitals for minor illnesses and chronic illnesses as well as for medical check-ups (Table 10.7). There are far more choices of health care service providers for the urban elderly compared to their rural counterparts, because private clinics and hospitals are mainly located in urban areas.

Table 10.8 Reasons for patronizing health service providers, 2004 (N=149)

	Minor illnesses		*Chronic illnesses*		*Medical check-up*	
	Frequency	*%*	*Frequency*	*%*	*Frequency*	*%*
Confidence in doctor	57	38.3	48	32.2	55	36.9
Recommended	27	18.1	44	29.5	36	24.2
Cheap	39	26.2	22	14.8	20	13.4
Distance	26	17.4	22	14.8	25	16.8
Location	7	4.7	7	4.7	5	3.4
Others	18[1]	12.1	5	3.4[2]	3	2.0

Source: 'Consumption behaviours of older people in Malaysia', on-going research project funded under the Intensification of Research Priority Areas Programme of the Ministry of Science, Technology, and Innovation, Malaysia. The author of this chapter is the principal investigator.

Note
[1] Easy, fast.
[2] Fast, no long queue.

Identifying the reasons for the patronage behaviour reveals that cost is a major consideration, with 'cheap' being cited as a major reason for choosing government clinics and hospitals (Table 10.8). 'Confidence in doctor' emerged as the second most important reason why government clinics and hospitals were popular. The implications that can be drawn from these findings are that the costs of health care will be a strain to the government as the ageing of the Malaysian population intensifies and facilities for the elderly need to be upgraded as a matter of urgency.

In light of rising costs of health care, many of the concerns and much of the panic over the ageing population relate to the burden said to be placed on the health care system. In spite of the government-initiated health care programme for the elderly started in 1995, the question of availability and issues of equitable access to health care still remain. Many of the services such as geriatric care and psycho-geriatric care, therapy and patient education are still not available in the rural areas.

Health care and LTC needs and facilities

In assessing LTC needs, it is essential to examine two important issues: first, the living arrangements of the elderly and, second, their health care needs. Understanding the present living arrangements of the elderly is important since co-residence indicates the availability of care within the family. On the other hand, a nuclear family system points towards a greater need for institutional care if and when disability sets in.

The elderly in Malaysia, as in other non-western countries, tend to reside with their adult children. The population censuses show that this trend has been slowly giving way to a nuclear type of family living arrangement. Over the years, the proportion of nuclear family showed an increase, while the extended family type declined, albeit very gradually. A higher percentage of households in the rural areas had the nuclear type of family compared to the urban families (Department of Statistics 1998).

Da Vanzo and Chan (1994) hypothesized that co-residence of older people with their adult children is influenced by the costs and benefits of co-residence, such as companionship and emotional support, as well as fulfilment of physical and financial needs. Other determinants of co-residence could be the presence of opportunities for co-residence and the preference of seniors and their children. In addition, reciprocity of support is mutually beneficial to the elderly and their children. Ability to provide support for daily living activities to their family members, in particular their grandchildren, adds to the self-worth of elderly people. Ong and Phillips (2003) found that support is always reciprocal, but this tends to decline with age, with the elderly increasingly receiving, rather than giving, support. Ong and Wong (2002) found that 30 per cent of the elderly who did not co-reside with their adult children lived within a radius of less than 60 kilometres from the elderly. This suggests that the adult children are 'near' enough to provide help when the need arises. Only 10 (8.3 per cent) out of the 121 surveyed lived in nursing homes.

If co-residence remains the norm, as suggested by Da Vanzo and Chan (1994), homes for the aged would not be widely used. However, the likelihood of co-residence may change in the future with more socio-economic development, higher gross domestic product (GDP) per capita, and changes in lifestyles and preferences. A two-way pull may result in reduced incidence of co-residence. First, co-residence may decline because adult children can afford separate dwellings. Second, the availability of foreign domestic helpers relieves female members from household chores and allows them to join the formal labour force. Third, the future cohort of elderly would be different from the present cohort as they would be better educated, financially secure, living their own lifestyle and would perhaps cherish their privacy. The convergence in the desire for privacy among the elderly and their adult children would therefore result in a preference for a nuclear family form in the future.

In a study of the health care needs of the elderly conducted by the Ministry of Health (MOH 1995), the elderly were asked to express their needs as well as their assessment of the medical services in Malaysia. Quota sampling of four villages in different parts of the country yielded 528 respondents who were balanced ethnically (one-third each Malays, Chinese and Indians) and by gender, with a predominance of those who had never attended school (61.6 per cent). It was found that the elderly felt that during episodes of acute care, hospital and family should be the major caregivers while about 50 per cent felt that the community should also be responsible for some part of the care process. For example, community members can provide services such as assisting them during hospitalization, looking after their homes and poultry, and visiting them in their homes after their discharge, as well as providing home help services and transportation for their next visit to the doctor. Included in the 'wish list' of the elderly were home visits by doctors, clinic sessions exclusively for the elderly, 'elderly only' counters and the privilege to receive treatment, and health education on matters that relate to quality of life and well-being.

Hospital care facilities[5]

Since the inception of the Health Care Programme for the Elderly, 1995, considerable progress has been made in the area of primary care. Throughout Malaysia, 522 clinics provide health care for the rural elderly. Among the services provided are health promotion and education, health screening and assessment, medical examination and treatment, home visits and home nursing, counselling, physiotherapy and occupational therapy. The government is in the process of formulating a policy for home-care nursing which, when implemented, will represent significant progress for elderly care.

Nevertheless, Malaysia still lags behind in terms of facilities and expertise for LTC. Only four government hospitals provide geriatric services to the elderly; they are the Kuala Lumpur Hospital, Seremban Hospital, Klang Hospital and Universiti Malaya Medical Centre. The other hospitals integrate medical care of the elderly within other disciplines. In Seremban Hospital, the types of LTC services provided are home nursing, home visits by doctors, follow-up at the geriatric clinic, nursing home assessment (although the hospital has no control over the running of private nursing homes), rehabilitation and training of domestic helpers, usually conducted at the ward or rehabilitation centre. There is one private hospital known as Hospital Geriatrik located in Shah Alam, Selangor, which also provides LTC facilities such as doctors' visits and nursing care.

There are only six geriatricians in Malaysia: two are serving in government hospitals, two at Universiti Malaya Medical Centre, one in the private sector and another at Universiti Putra Malaysia. Malaysia has only five psycho-geriatricians of whom three are in government hospitals and one each at the University of Malaya and the National University of Malaysia. To date, a total of 13,000 health care workers have received training and re-training in the care of the elderly. From these statistics, it is obvious that there is a disparity between the demand for health care and the number of physicians trained to provide care.

Infrastructure support for the care of the elderly has been progressing slowly, with the announcement of another hospital with geriatric services to be built and operational during the Eighth Malaysia Plan (Malaysia 2001). The ultimate aim is to introduce geriatric care to all district hospitals by the year 2020. Although training for caregivers is also being conducted, greater publicity about this could help to create greater awareness and participation.

Public sector programmes for LTC

Policy on LTC *per se* does not exist in Malaysia. The most obvious effort by the government in the provision of LTC is the setting up of homes for the chronically ill. At present there are two centres, one in Kuala Kubu Baru, Selangor and the other in Dungun, Terengganu.[6] The total capacity for the two homes is about 150. These homes provide care, treatment and protection to the elderly (60 years and above only) who are chronically ill. The range of services and facilities include care and protection, medical treatment, guidance and counselling, and physiotherapy, as well as religious and recreational activities. Usually, the residents of these homes have no family support and will remain there until they die.

Nursing homes

The first private nursing home in the country was established in 1983. It is estimated that there are about 40 to 50 larger (40 beds or more) nursing homes concentrated in the Klang Valley and Penang, and hundreds more smaller operations (usually fewer than 10 beds) located in bungalows and in other private residences (*The Edge*, 19 February 2001). These nursing homes offer 24-hour nursing care and provide care for people with different needs – from the elderly to the disabled. Other services include day care, home help and catering services (meals on wheels).

The nursing home could be regarded as a facility for LTC (Cheah 1995). Generally, there are no recreational activities, apart from televisions. Nevertheless, this is slowly changing. For example, Hospital Geriatrik in Shah Alam provides many types of recreational activities such as chess, games and bowling. The costs of nursing home care range from RM1,200 per month to RM3,000 per month (or RM14,400 to 36,000 annually)[7] depending on the stage of disability as well as the choice of room arrangement. The elderly in Malaysia tend to perceive the nursing home as a place to wait till life ends; because of that, they prefer to remain in their own home environment. Embedded in a culture that stresses filial piety, adult children have expressed their reluctance to send their ageing elderly to nursing homes unless it is the last resort (Ong and Wong 2002).

Due to the lack of regulation and supervision by the authorities, the quality of care provided by nursing homes is inconsistent. Of the hundreds of nursing homes that are estimated to be in operation throughout Malaysia, only 188 are licensed by the Social Welfare Department. Of these, only 29 are elder nursing homes,[8] of which seven are run by NGOs, while the rest are private businesses. The 29 elder nursing homes collectively have 1,046 residents (*The Edge*, 19 February 2001). From the regulatory perspective, the Day Care Centre Act 1993 and Care Centre Regulations 1994 are in force to govern the minimum standards to protect the interests of the elderly (Cheah 1995). It is anticipated that the Private Healthcare Facilities and

Services Act 1998 will eventually have regulations specifically for nursing homes.

Community care

Family support has been crucial in providing care, but community care can help to alleviate the pressure of providing care on a long-term basis. Domiciliary care is the most common aspect of community-based services to older people. It includes basic care (help with daily living, mobility, self-care), home nursing and home visiting. In Malaysia, home nursing service is provided by the public and private sectors, as well as by voluntary bodies. Under the Central Welfare Council of Peninsular Malaysia (MPKSM), a voluntary home-visiting service, known as the Home Help Service, is offered to elderly people. Services include home visits, hospital visits, occupational therapy, simple medical tests and counselling. This is an out-reach programme that brings care to the elderly. For year 2000, a total of 66 caregivers offered their services to 491 elderly persons, 260 female and 231 male. Those aged 70 and above are the largest group that will benefit from this programme. For the states of Sabah and Sarawak, Home Help Service is comparatively recent, having been introduced in the year 2000. For the state of Sabah, there is a total of 159 registered elderly, and 275 home visits have been made.[9]

Currently, MPKSM is in the initial stages of planning and building day care centres for the elderly. A total of 17 centres have been planned for the period 2000–2002. A day care centre is a place for the provision of care to elderly people who are not capable of performing some of the activities of daily living. These centres provide the basic essentials in accordance with the Care Centre Act 1993 and Care Centre Regulations 1994. The first centre is located in Kuala Lumpur. The services provided by these centres enable families to keep their elderly folk at home, even if there are no caregivers available during the day. The completion of these centres represents a step forward for Malaysia in LTC.

Conclusions

Responding to the challenges set forth by ageing requires a coordinated strategy that involves the sharing of responsibility by different stakeholders: the individual, the family, the community and the government. Currently, the government is continuing with healthy lifestyle campaigns, emphasizing healthy behaviour, as well as prevention of diseases. Creating greater awareness about the benefits of healthy living is not difficult, but eliciting co-operation from the people for the adoption of a healthy lifestyle is a major challenge. Although infrastructural development plans are in place, there is a wide gap in human resource requirements. Geriatricians, psycho-geriatricians, nurses and other health care personnel are urgently needed before the provision of quality care can be achieved, whether in health care or LTC.

As community and home-based care are encouraged, the question of funding programmes that would facilitate the delivery and quality of care arises. Although home and community care can be more cost-effective than institutional care, heavy reliance on informal care carries its own costs. Several decades of research on family caregiving in many countries have shown that the caregivers themselves need more support (Gibson *et al.* 2003). In view of the rapidly increasing number of elderly, the magnitude of the problems faced by informal caregivers warrants either a policy or a programme on support for caregivers. In Malaysia, the Ministry of Women and Family Development, with the collaboration of the MOH, would be the appropriate ministry to formulate and implement policies and programmes related to support for caregivers.

Access to health care is an important aspect for the elderly, as enshrined in the National Policy for the Elderly, introduced in 1995. The Policy is aimed at upgrading the dignity and self-worth of senior citizens within the family, society and nation, and improving the potential of the elderly so that they can continue to be productive in national development. While the National Policy for the Elderly marks a major step forward in providing care and protection to the elderly, a national policy on LTC may take some time to realize.

Even in the developed nations, there has been a shift from institutional care towards community-based care. If Malaysia takes this as an indication of the way that LTC should develop, then we should work to retain the present arrangement where the provision of care largely relies on family care. It is not difficult to speculate that the government will not introduce any programme or policy that has an over-dependence on public funding. However, the government has to come up with a strategy and a scheme for health care financing that would ensure that the elderly are protected. It should consider more funding for community-based care and a programme supporting informal caregivers. Until ageing produces profound social and economic impact, the Malaysian Government is likely to continue with the existing arrangement for LTC, but with a deepening and broadening of the present level of services.

Notes

1 Data provided in Rabieyah Mat and Hajar Md Taha (2003) are based on the population census of Malaysia and demographic statistics derived from vital registration data.
2 The project, entitled 'Consumption behaviours of older people in Malaysia', is funded under the Intensification of Research Priority Areas (IRPA) Programme of the Ministry of Science, Technology, and Innovation, Malaysia. The author of this chapter is the principal investigator.
3 The IADL is a common scale used in assessing physical health of the elderly. Activities included in this scale are ability to use the telephone, get to places beyond walking distance, go shopping for groceries, prepare own meal, do own housework/ handy work, do own laundry, take own medicine and manage own money.

4 This is part of the IRPA-funded study 'Consumption behaviours of older people in Malaysia', which is a larger study comprising 1,500 respondents aged 55 or older.
5 Statistics on facilities and staff strength reported in this section were all obtained through an interview with an officer in the Family Health Development Division of the MOH, in September 2004.
6 Information obtained from Central Welfare Council of Peninsular Malaysia (Majlis Pusat Kebajikan Semenanjung Malaysia, MPKSM).
7 Information obtained by primary search through telephone calls in 2001/2002. At that time, the exchange rate was fixed at RM1.00 to US$3.80.
8 Catering to the elderly only.
9 Statistics obtained directly from MPKSM records.

References

Cheah, M. (1995) 'Health care for the aged – critical issues and new opportunities in retirement and nursing homes', paper presented at the National Conference on the Private Healthcare Industry: Shaping the Future of Malaysian Healthcare towards the Twenty-first Century, Petaling Jaya, March.

Chen A.J. and Jones, G. (1989) *Ageing in ASEAN – its Socio-economic Consequences*, Singapore: Institute of Southeast Asian Studies.

Chen C.Y.P., Andrews, G.R., Josef, R., Chan K.E. and Arokiasamy, J.T. (1986) *Health and Ageing in Malaysia*, Kuala Lumpur: Faculty of Medicine, University of Malaya.

Chia, Y.C. (1996) 'Primary care in the elderly', in *Proceedings of the First National Symposium on Gerontology: Issues and Challenges of Ageing, Multidiscipline Perspective*, Kuala Lumpur: Gerontology Association of Malaysia.

Da Vanzo, J. and Chan, A. (1994) 'Living arrangements of older Malaysians: who co-resides with their adult children?', *Demography* 31(1): 95–113.

Department of Statistics, Malaysia (1998) *Senior Citizens and Population Ageing in Malaysia*, Kuala Lumpur: Department of Statistics.

—— (2000) *Labour Force Survey Report, Malaysia 2000*, Kuala Lumpur: Department of Statistics.

Estes, C.L. and Lee, P.R. (1985) 'Social, political and economic background of long term care policy', in C. Harrington, R.J. Newcomer, C.L. Estes *et al.* (eds) *Long Term Care for the Elderly: Public Policy Issues*, California: Sage.

Gibson, M.J., Gregory, S.R. and Pandya, S.M. (2003) *Long-Term Care in Developed Nations*, Washington, DC: AARP.

Harrington, C. and Swan, J.H. (1985) 'Institutional long term care services', in C. Harrington, R.J. Newcomer, C.L. Estes *et al.* (eds) *Long Term Care for the Elderly: Public Policy Issues*, California: Sage.

Jacobzone, S., Camblis, E. and Robine, J.M. (2000/1) 'Is the health of older persons in OECD countries improving fast enough to compensate for population ageing?', OECD Economic Studies No. 30, p. 170.

Kane, R.L. and Kane, R.A. (1989) 'Transition in long term care', in M.G. Ory and H. Bond (eds) *Ageing and Health Care: Social Science and Policy Perspectives*, London: Routledge.

Malaysia (2001) *Eighth Malaysia Plan 2001–2005*, Kuala Lumpur: Economic Planning Unit, Prime Minister's Department, Malaysia.

—— (2003) *Mid-term Review of the Eighth Malaysia Plan 2001–2005*, Kuala Lumpur: Economic Planning Unit, Prime Minister's Department, Malaysia.

—— (2006) *Ninth Malaysia Plan 2006–2010*, Kuala Lumpur: Economic Planning Unit, Prime Minister's Department, Malaysia.

Ministry of Health (MOH) (1995) *A Study of the Health Care Needs of Elderly in Malaysia*, Kuala Lumpur: MOH Malaysia.

Ong Fon Sim (2003) 'Life events, stress and consumer behaviour: an analysis of consumption-related lifestyles, brand and patronage preferences among older adults in Malaysia', unpublished PhD thesis, Faculty of Business and Accountancy, University of Malaya, Kuala Lumpur.

Ong Fon Sim and Phillips, D.R. (2003) 'Stress, resources, and life satisfaction among older adults in Malaysia', *Hallym International Journal of Ageing* 5(2): 111–29.

Ong Fon Sim and Wong Lee Heong (2002) 'Living arrangement and long-term care of elderly in Malaysia', unpublished research report, Faculty of Business and Accountancy, University of Malaya, Kuala Lumpur.

Phillips, D.R. (2000) 'Long-term care', in E.F. Borgatta and R.J.V. Montgomery (eds) *Encyclopedia of Sociology*, 2nd edn, New York: Macmillan Reference, pp. 1652–63.

Public Health Institute (1997) *Report of the Second National Health and Morbidity Survey Conference*, Kuala Lumpur: Public Health Institute, Ministry of Health, Malaysia.

Rabieyah Mat and Hajar Md Taha (2003) 'Socio-economic characteristics of the elderly in Malaysia', paper presented at the 21st Population Census Conference, Kyoto, Japan, 19–21 November.

Rowe, J.W. and Kahn, R.L. (1998) *Successful Ageing*, New York: Pantheon.

Tan Poo Chang, Ng So Tnor, Tey Nai Peng and Halimah Awang (1999) *Evaluating Programme Needs of Older Persons in Malaysia*, Kuala Lumpur: Faculty of Economics and Administration, University of Malaya.

The Edge, 19 February 2001, ' "Golden oldies" in "Survey and Guide" '.

United Nations (1993) *World Population Prospects: The 1992 Revision*, New York: United Nations.

—— (2002) 'Implications of an ageing society', Division for Social Policy and Development, United Nations, 28 November.

United Nations Secretariat (1994) 'Overview of recent research findings on population ageing and the family', in *Ageing and the Family*, New York: United Nations Publications.

World Bank (1994) 'Averting the old age crisis: policies to protect the old and promote growth', *A World Bank Policy Research Report*, New York: Oxford University Press.

World Health Organization (2002) 'Long-term care in developing countries: ten case studies', ed. Jenny Brodsky, Jack Habib and Miriam Hirschfeld. Online. Available at <http://www.who.int/ncd/long_term_care/index.htm> (accessed 24 August 2004).

World Health Report (2002) *Core Health Indicators: Malaysia*. Online. Available at <http://www3.who.int/whosis/country/indicators.cfm> (accessed 24 August 2004).

11 Health care in Sarawak

Model of a public system

Khoo Khay Jin

Sarawak is a model of how a publicly financed health care system can achieve near-universal coverage for basic health care and preventive services – with hugely positive outcomes – at relatively low cost, albeit with some inevitable inefficiencies. Many of the inefficiencies in the system derive from the special characteristics of Sarawak – a relatively prosperous state with a significant proportion of the population having irregular or low *monetary* incomes,[1] a large physical area with a small and unevenly distributed population about half of whom live in regions difficult to access through ordinary land transport, and a corresponding low population density in most parts of the state.

When thinking about how the state health care system has been able to achieve a relatively high level of coverage despite demographic and geographic impediments, one is led to two key considerations. First, the quality of human resources in health care provision at the lower levels is crucial, because this level is the front line in preventive work – extension services and public health control services. This was demonstrated by the recent outbreak of a hugely damaging measles epidemic in a cluster of Penan longhouses in the interior (more on this later in this chapter). Second, it is important to have system adaptability and flexibility in the face of a changing population and a society with changing demands; unfortunately, there is increasing centralization in a system that, to date, has offered significant flexibility to health care management and administration in the East Malaysian states of Sarawak and Sabah.

Considering that the majority of Sarawak's population is indigenous, one may also argue that it is ultimately more useful to view indigenous peoples' health care needs as essentially similar to that of other, non-indigenous peoples; and that health care needs and health care provision need to be understood in socio-cultural terms. This implies that there is a need for information provision and exchange and some degree of community participation in the design and implementation of health care systems, in order to reduce to the greatest extent possible the inevitable information asymmetries – on both sides of the service divide.

This chapter aims to describe the health care delivery system as it exists, and has existed, in Sarawak over the last three decades and more, and population health outcomes as measured by conventional indicators. Following that, the chapter will discuss some areas of concern and highlight issues for the future of the health care system. Contrary to some facile arguments for privatizing health care services, the special characteristics of Sarawak make it an illustration of the likely market failures in virtually any conceivable system that is dominated by privatized health care provision and/or health care financing. Moreover, it is important to recognize that health care access in Sarawak is determined to a greater extent than usual by out-of-pocket payments pre- and post-actual care or treatment: briefly, although public health care services incur a low nominal payment in Sarawak, transport costs to and from the site of such services are high in most regions of the state, and this does not yet take into account that accessing such care often means having to stay at least overnight at the location of the care provider, thus incurring additional costs.[2]

Sarawak: an overview

Sarawak has a land area of 124.5 thousand square kilometres. This makes it about the same size as Peninsular Malaysia and about half the size of England, Scotland and Wales combined. However, this relatively large land area has a population of about 2.1 million persons (2000), compared to Peninsular Malaysia's 18.5 million (2000).

Not only does Sarawak have a small population in a relatively large land area, but that population is very unevenly distributed. About 39 per cent of the population is found in and around the four major coastal towns of Kuching, Sibu, Bintulu and Miri, with another 9 per cent in smaller towns.[3] The remaining 52 per cent are dispersed throughout the rural and interior areas of the state. The net result is that while the mean density is 17 persons per square kilometre, it in fact ranges from about 1 person per square kilometre in the remote district of Belaga, to over 273 persons per square kilometre in the state capital of Kuching.

There are 27 officially categorized ethnic groups in Sarawak.[4] The 2000 Census publications list 12 named indigenous groups[5] and a residual 'Other *Bumiputera*[6] (Sarawak)' indigenous category, Chinese, Indian and a residual 'Others'. However, in its published tabulations, it only has five named categories – Malay, Iban, Bidayuh, Melanau, Chinese and three residual categories of 'Other *Bumiputera*', 'Others' and 'Non-Citizens'.

Popular discourse in Sarawak distinguishes the Malay-Melanau, Iban, Bidayuh, Orang Ulu and Chinese.[7] The linkage of Malay and Melanau is both a political and a religious grouping in so far as all Malays are, by definition, Muslims, as are about three-quarters of Melanau; together, they are perceived as politically dominant. Iban, Bidayuh and Orang Ulu are increasingly grouped as 'Dayak', and see themselves as subordinate in political and economic power, even if they are '*Bumiputera*' or 'indigenous' in the socio-political hierarchy of the country. Chinese are viewed as economically

Table 11.1 Population of Sarawak by ethnicity and urbanization rate, 2000

Ethnicity	Proportion (%)	Urbanization rate (%)
Malay	22.3	54.8
Iban	29.1	28.5
Bidayuh	8.0	25.3
Melanau	5.5	36.4
Other *Bumiputera*	5.7	22.3
Chinese	25.9	78.7
Others	0.4	64.5
Non-citizens	3.0	54.8
Total	100.0	48.1

Source: Department of Statistics, Malaysia (2001a).

dominant and as political 'king-makers', although they see themselves as politically subordinate in the national order.

Table 11.1 shows the relative proportions of these groups, and their respective urbanization rates. The groups classified as '*Bumiputera*' – the first five categories in the table – are distinguished not only by culture and religion, but also by levels of urbanization, by geography/location, by economic activity and by levels of socio-economic well being. The variation in level of urbanization is shown in the table. In terms of geography, Malays are largely concentrated in the coastal zone and Melanau are concentrated in the coastal zone centred on the towns of Sibu and Miri. Iban occupy the middle interior of the state, while Bidayuh are largely concentrated in the western part of the state. Finally, 'Other *Bumiputera*', the bulk of whom – about 80 per cent – are Orang Ulu, are found in the deep interior of the state, mainly in the upper reaches of the Rejang River and in the middle and upper reaches of the Baram River.

Thus, in Sarawak, the 'indigenous population', even on a restrictive definition, amounts to over 40 per cent of the population. Moreover, for the most part, their health-seeking behaviour is not hugely different from others. Indeed, it is becoming increasingly similar, other than for income, class and locational issues. In brief, a discussion about health care provision for indigenous groups in Sarawak translates largely into issues relating to rural health delivery in a context of a large area with a relatively small – and lower income – population and difficult communications.

In terms of economic activity, the broad distinctions are between (i) 'Dayak' groups which remain predominantly agriculturalists, largely swidden, (ii) Malay-Melanau, substantial numbers of whom are agriculturalists and fisherfolk, but who are also well represented in other economic and occupational sectors, in particular the public administrative sector, and (iii) Chinese who are overwhelmingly in the urban commercial, industrial and service economy, but are also prominent in the modern resource extraction sector.

Table 11.2 Income and poverty by ethnicity, Sarawak, 2002

Ethnicity	Mean household income, 2002 (RM) (1)	Poverty rate, 2002 (% of households) (2)
Malay	2,482	5.2
Iban	1,547	10.5
Bidayuh	2,294	n.a.
Melanau	1,957	n.a.
Other *Bumiputera*	1,883	6.8[1]
Chinese	3,773	1.0
Others	2,523	n.a.
Sarawak	2,515	5.8

Sources: (1) Wan Abdul Aziz (2005); (2) Leete (2004).

Note
[1] This refers to 'other indigenous', presumably covering Bidayuh, Melanau and 'Other Bumiputera'.

Sarawak is a relatively prosperous state,[8] with a gross domestic product (GDP) per capita of about 0.88 times the Malaysian average (2000), and a relatively low poverty rate of 5.8 per cent of households (2002).[9] However, there is considerable inter-ethnic differentiation, as shown in Table 11.2.

Statistics on income distribution, other than on the gross national level, are not publicly available. At the national level, income inequality is substantial, as indicated by the 2002 Gini Coefficient of 0.46, by the considerable difference between the mean and median income, and by the more than 2 : 1 ratio of urban to rural mean household incomes.[10] A study based on income statistics from the late 1980s suggests that there is also substantial intra-ethnic inequality in all regions of the country (Shireen 1998). There is no reason to believe that the pattern has changed substantially, and this is supported by the household income figures for indigenous minorities[11] in Sarawak in 2002 showing large gaps between mean and median incomes, with several groups having median incomes within RM100 of the poverty line income.

Without going into detail, these substantial differences in income are reflected in differences in educational attainment and, correspondingly, different levels of information access above and beyond that arising from the differential availability of communications infrastructure in urban and rural contexts.

Summarizing, health care services in Sarawak have to address a population (i) more than half of which is rural and low-income, (ii) living in sparsely populated regions with poor communications infrastructure and correspondingly high transport costs, (iii) with considerable ethnic diversity, (iv) with substantial income inequalities and corresponding differences in demand for services, and (v) with substantial differences in educational levels and correspondingly subject to different degrees of information asymmetry.

As will be seen, health care service provision, especially in preventive care, has met these challenges admirably, at relatively low cost and despite problems in sourcing personnel. This is indicated by Sarawak's standing in the basic health indicators which have often been a source of surprise in the national capital, Kuala Lumpur. Indeed, despite Sarawak's level of income, patterns of disease incidence and health challenges are moving towards those found in higher income countries; and this is happening without, as yet, a corresponding adjustment in the health care system, especially in rural areas. Thus, although communicable diseases must remain an area of concern, the challenges relating to Sarawak health care service provision are (i) how to deliver health services for non-communicable and diseases of lifestyle to a small, relatively low income population in a vast area with a poor communications network, and (ii) how to operate an efficient public and preventive health service, including surveillance for epidemic infectious disease, in such a context.

Sarawak's health care system

Organization[12]

Sarawak's health care system is part of the federal system under the federal Ministry of Health (MOH).[13] However, for various reasons, it enjoys significantly greater autonomy than the states of the Peninsula, and can obtain supplementary funding from the state government. The Malaysian system is a public-private mix, with a substantial private presence in primary care and an increasing private presence in secondary care. However, in Sarawak, the bulk of the system remains largely public, both in finance and service provision.

Administratively, on the public side, the Sarawak Health Department is headed by a state director assisted by five deputy directors overseeing 11 divisional teams, each comprising a health officer, hospital director, dental officer and pharmacist. The divisional teams in turn oversee 33 districts, each with a health officer, hospital director and dental officer.[14] These districts manage district hospitals (not all districts), health clinics, village clinics and maternity and child health (MCH) clinics,[15] village health teams (VHT), mobile clinics[16] and the flying doctor service (FDS)[17] for the most remote and inaccessible areas.

Funding for the Sarawak Health Department comes from the federal ministry. In 2002, this amounted to over RM525 million, or almost 20 per cent of the federal operating budget for Sarawak. This is a substantial increase from the RM120 million operating budget in 1986, which then represented about 13 per cent of the federal operating budget for the state. Half of this operating budget goes to emoluments.[18]

On a per capita basis, this operating budget represents an expenditure of RM240 per capita in 2002, up from about RM80 per capita in 1986. On

Table 11.3 Public/private mix in health service provision, Sarawak

	Public	Private	Total no. (year)
Doctors	65%	35%	801 (2002)
Hospitals	19^1	10^2	29 (1999)
Clinics[3]	50%	50%	450 (1999)
Dentists	41%	59%	88 (2002)

Source: Sarawak Health Dept; Dept of Statistics, Sarawak, Yearbook of Statistics (2001).

Notes
[1] Excluding the two special hospitals.
[2] Including maternity homes which are not, strictly speaking, full hospitals.
[3] Not including mobile clinics.

the user end, the 1998/99 Household Expenditure Survey reported an average household expenditure on health of RM29 per month per household – RM45 per month per urban household and RM17 per month per rural household.[19]

In terms of publicly provided facilities, as of 2002, there was one general hospital, located in the state capital, Kuching, four district hospitals with specialist care, 14 district hospitals without specialist care, two special hospitals, for mental health and leprosy, 200 health clinics, 10 village clinics, 32 MCH and 120 mobile clinics,[20] 26 dental clinics and 128 school dental clinics.

As noted, the health care system in Sarawak is a public-private mix. Table 11.3 shows the relative proportions in terms of doctors, hospitals, clinics and dentists. Note that the relative number of hospitals is not a guide to the relative number of beds – the public system has disproportionately more beds than the private. Moreover, public clinics, especially in rural areas, usually have a small number of beds as well, whereas private clinics almost never do.

Virtually all private facilities and personnel are in urban areas, indeed concentrated in the four major towns of Kuching, Sibu, Bintulu and Miri. However, wealthier rural people do make trips to town expressly for these private facilities, especially to see specialists, or to access services which the public system may be reluctant to provide, for instance tubal ligations for younger women after a second child.[21]

Access and utilization

In the late 1990s, according to the National Health and Morbidity Survey of 1996 (NHMS 2), a majority of people had convenient access only to the public system, and a majority used it, rather than the private system, even when a private facility was the closest to them. Given the coding flaws in the dataset,[22] Table 11.4 provides some simple cross-tabulations by stratum – urban and rural – as a rough approximation to ethnicity,[23] and occasionally by broad ethnicity, as per the coding in the dataset.

Table 11.4 Nearest medical facility by stratum, 1996

	Urban	Rural	Sarawak
By type and stratum (% sample)			
Public hospital	24.3	19.5	21.4
Public clinic	34.2	65.8	55.9
Private hospital	8.5	1.8	4.5
Private clinic	33.0	13.0	21.2
By type, mean distance, and stratum (km)			
Public	5.2	11.9	
Private	3.5	14.7	
Combined	4.5	12.3	

Source: NHMS 2.

Table 11.4 indicates the dearth of private facilities, in particular hospitals, in rural areas. The apparent near parity in access to a public hospital between urban and rural is largely due to the availability of district hospitals which provide generic secondary care. Thus, while 9 per cent of the urban population list a public general hospital as the nearest static health care facility, this is true of only 2 per cent of the rural population, whereas 15 per cent and 17 per cent of the urban and rural population, respectively, list a district hospital as the nearest static health care facility (these figures are not shown in Table 11.4).

Nevertheless, despite the availability of facilities, the rural population has to travel two to three times the distance of their urban counterpart to access a static health facility (Table 11.4). As would be expected, the disparity is greatest – over four times the distance – in the case of the private facility. This inevitably translates into a greater cost to access a health facility.[24]

Whether this additional cost is indeed *the* reason for the differential use of public and private facilities would require additional investigation; but there would appear to be evidence that this is the case (Table 11.5). What is indisputable is the clear and significant difference in the pattern of use.[25]

While the urban population has a tendency to bypass[26] the public facility in favour of the private, the rural population overwhelmingly depends on the public facility. Nevertheless, a substantial proportion – over 40 per cent – of the urban population uses the public facility, while almost one-fifth of the rural population uses a private facility. There are clear ethnic differences in this bypassing behaviour. Thus Chinese overwhelmingly bypass the public facilities, while Malays and other *Bumiputera* do not, or do so marginally (Table 11.5).

User costs

User cost is one probable reason for using the public system. Three indicators are used to assess user costs, namely user fees, transport costs and transport time.

Table 11.5 Pattern of medical facility utilization according to proximity, 1996 (% population distribution)

Nearest facility	Facility consulted			
	Public	*Private*	*Other*	*Total*
Urban				
Public	47.1	46.3	6.7	67.5
Private	36.6	58.5	4.9	32.5
Total	43.7	50.3	6.1	100.0
Rural				
Public	77.5	17.6	4.9	88.7
Private	73.1	25.0	1.9	11.3
Total	77.0	18.4	4.6	100.0
Chinese				
Public	32.4	62.6	5.0	77.2
Private	39.0	51.2	9.8	22.8
Total	33.9	60.0	6.1	100.0
Malay				
Public	73.9	24.4	1.7	71.9
Private	31.1	64.4	4.4	28.1
Total	61.9	35.6	2.5	100.0
Other Bumiputera				
Public	75.5	17.9	6.7	82.5
Private	62.6	36.1	1.2	17.5
Total	73.2	21.1	5.7	100.0

Source: NHMS 2.

Table 11.6 Costs of utilization, and mean transportation time, by facility and stratum, 1996

	Public facility	*Private facility*
Mean user charge (RM)		
Urban	2.00	43.00
Rural	2.00	23.00
Mean transport costs (RM)		
Urban	5.00	3.00
Rural	7.00	11.00
Mean transport time (mins)		
Urban	33	28
Rural	63	125

Source: NHMS 2.

There is a clear and large disparity in user fees between the public and private facilities (Table 11.6), and this applies to both urban and rural.

However, the rural population pays more in transport costs, with the quantum being expectedly larger for transport to private facilities. Added to this is the time taken, with rural people taking as much as two to four times the time taken by urban people.

Practices

In determining health outcomes, however, public health strategies are generally more important than the availability of treatment facilities. In Sarawak's case, it may be argued that it is the innovations in public health and preventive services and practices – often delivered via the public primary services – that have made all the difference.

Amongst these innovations are the issuance and use of home-based medical records – for child health since the 1970s, for antenatal care since the 1980s and for outpatient care since 1992. This has been important in providing some measure of continuity of care and for childhood immunization for a dispersed and mobile rural population.

Iodine deficiency used to be a major rural health problem. However, with the distribution of iodized salt and iodized water, the problem has been eliminated,[27] and it is now extremely rare to see persons with enlarged goitres.

The Health Department has also been responsible for the school nutrition programme. Although such a compensatory scheme comes rather late in the growth cycle, it nevertheless helps to eliminate anaemia and undernutrition amongst those of school age, and its coverage is virtually universal since current rates of attendance at primary school (for ages 7–11) stand at over 90 per cent, with the notable exception of the Penan.

The Penan,[28] who inhabit some of the most remote and inaccessible areas of Sarawak, are covered by the Flying Doctor Service (FDS), introduced in 1973, and now covering some 175 locations and 70,000 persons. In addition, a Village Health Promoter (VHP) programme was introduced in 1981. However, it has not functioned well, especially in more remote areas, as provisioning them is a problem and VHPs are all volunteers without any incentive scheme. Thus, irregular contact and communications has resulted in a decline in their activity after an initial spurt.

Antenatal and perinatal care has been given special attention. All pregnant women accessing the public health services – in Sarawak that would be the vast majority of pregnant women – are screened for anaemia and provided with nutritional supplements, if needed. In addition, they are also screened for STDs. In more recent times, women have been screened for breast and cervical cancers, while diabetes screening has also become routine.

The coverage of dental services, however, is patchy, and focused on primary and secondary school children and antenatal mothers. In 2001, it covered 87 per cent of primary school and 23 per cent of secondary school children. Elsewhere, in rural areas, there are hardly any dental services.

Finally, to compensate for the distance and expense of rural persons accessing secondary care services – usually located in urban centres – persons from the interior are given priority.[29] In addition, it is also standard practice for clinics in the remote interior to absorb the costs of sending a person to the nearest public secondary care centre in emergency cases, and for assistance to be provided for transport costs to and from secondary care centres in referral cases.

Most recently, a major public health and preventive care initiative is an on-going anti-smoking campaign. Smoking – using home-grown tobacco – has been part of the culture of indigenous communities in Sarawak for centuries, although in a few communities the practice – together with the consumption of alcohol – was abolished by Christian missionaries. In 2003, the Health Department made a major breakthrough in one rural district, Kapit, when some 200 longhouses[30] agreed, after considerable discussion, to institute non-smoking measures *within* the longhouse, subjecting offenders against the regulation to local customary practices (a fine); smoking is not banned, but permitted only in areas beyond the longhouse.

Traditional medicine

While there were systems of traditional medicine and a traditional pharmacopoeia amongst the indigenous communities of Sarawak, they have largely fallen into disuse – except for the art of massage and simple orthopaedic care – and knowledge of the traditional pharmacopoeia is rapidly disappearing.[31] Current talk of traditional medicine and the traditional pharmacopoeia is partly a result of a growing awareness of the importance being accorded to traditional knowledge of medicinal plants; it is partly non-governmental organization (NGO)-driven, and partly due to recent Malaysian Ministry of Health initiatives, seeking to leverage the global popularity of nutriceuticals. In brief, there is widespread popular faith in contemporary medicine, although people may still resort to traditional medical practices – their own, and that of other communities – should contemporary medical care not produce the desired result.

Health outcomes

The provision of facilities and services and the policies and practices adopted have resulted in outcomes that are amongst the best in the developed and developing world. Indeed, in some areas, Sarawak's outcomes were so good that administrators in the federal capital were suspicious of the reported figures and would routinely adjust them. More recently, however, it is acknowledged that the reported figures do indeed reflect the actual status.[32]

A major contributory factor to these outcomes is the provision of safe water and sanitation. In rural areas, the provision of safe drinking water, usually via gravity-feed systems, and pour-flush latrines has largely fallen upon the Sarawak Health Department. Maintenance can, however, be a problem, although the department does provide training in basic mainten-

Table 11.7 Provision of water and sanitation, Sarawak, 2001

	Per cent of population provided	
	Urban	Rural
Safe drinking water from Public Works Department	94	33
Safe drinking water from Sarawak Health Department	0	64
Safe drinking water	94	97
Sanitary latrines	100	98

Source: Sarawak Health Department.

Table 11.8 Immunization coverage, Sarawak, 2001

Immunization	Coverage (%)
BCG	100
Diphtheria, tetanus & whooping cough	98
Polio	97
Measles	93
Hepatitis B	97

Source: Sarawak Health Department.

ance to the longhouse communities. Nevertheless, the bulk of the provided systems are functional. Table 11.7 summarizes the situation.

Another major contributory factor has been the coverage of the childhood immunization programme, in accordance with the World Health Organization's Expanded Programme for Immunization (EPI). This is, by now, well-nigh universal, as shown in Table 11.8.

Unfortunately, however, near-universal coverage in a context like Sarawak's can still miss out a remotely located ethnic minority, especially if that ethnic minority is also very mobile. This was what happened with the Penan in one corner of Belaga, a remote district in the interior of Sarawak. The Penan in this location, total population of less than 500, were not immunized for measles. Thus, at the end of 2004, when a visitor brought in measles, an outbreak of epidemic proportions occurred, resulting in the death of some 15 children, equivalent to about 15 per cent of under-15s, over a three week period.[33]

Nevertheless, the overall coverage, which includes the rural areas, is a significant achievement, reflective of the extent of antenatal and child care, of the very high proportion of births in a health care facility, and of the practice of the population, urban and rural, to refer to available health care services. This is reflected in the infant mortality rate for Sarawak as a whole, and for the major ethnic categories. Table 11.9 shows the comparative figures for the different states of Malaysia. Evidently, Sarawak has amongst the lowest infant mortality rate (IMR), bettered only by Selangor, the state with

Table 11.9 Infant mortality rate by state and territory, Malaysia, 2000 and 2003

State	Total $(2003)^1$	Male $(2000)^2$	Female $(2000)^2$
Selangor	5.3	6.1	4.4
N. Sembilan	5.5	6.7	4.1
Penang	5.7	5.8	5.7
Sarawak	**5.7**	**6.0**	**5.3**
Johor	6.2	6.5	6.0
Perak	6.4	7.4	5.4
WPKL*	6.5	7.0	6.0
Sabah	6.8	7.2	6.4
Terengganu	6.9	7.7	6.0
Melaka	7.5	8.9	6.1
Kedah	7.6	8.3	7.3
Pahang	8.5	8.4	8.6
Perlis	8.6	11.2	5.9
Kelantan	10.5	12.1	8.9
WP Labuan	20.4	25.1	15.4
MALAYSIA	6.8	7.4	6.0

Sources: [1]Ministry of Health, Malaysia (2003: Appendix 2); [2]Ministry of Health, Malaysia (2004: 42).

Note
* Wilayah Persekutuan Kuala Lumpur, the Federal Territory of Kuala Lumpur.

the highest per capita income and urbanization rate in the country, and by Negeri Sembilan, a west coast state adjoining Selangor.

Moreover, this low IMR is not a recent achievement. Time series data indicates that the IMR has dropped from 11.2 per thousand live births in 1985 to 7.5 in 1995, and 5.7 in 2000.[34] Toddler mortality rates have been less than 1 per thousand since the 1980s and are now around 0.5 per thousand (Department of Statistics, Malaysia, 2001b). Concomittantly, the maternal mortality rate is also a low 0.4 per thousand live births in 2001. The reported equivalent for the 1980s was around 0.1–0.2 per thousand live births.[35] The overall improvement in the IMR has brought about a decrease in the crude birth rate (CBR) from 28.7 in 1985 to 25.3 in 1995 and 23.2 in 2000, and a corresponding decline in the crude rate of natural increase (CNR) from 24.9 in 1985 to 21.3 in 1995 and 18.9 in 2000.[36]

Given a broadly similar ethnic composition, West Kalimantan, which abuts Sarawak, forms a natural comparison. Thus, West Kalimantan's IMR in 2002 was 52 per thousand, while some 78 per cent of the population had no access to clean water and 35 per cent had no access to sanitation (UNDP/BPS/BAPPENAS 2004).

Areas of concern

The achievement in basic and preventive care has brought about a change in disease patterns, even over the last 30 years. Thus, the usual communicable diseases and diseases resulting from unsanitary conditions and the non-availability of safe water supplies have largely disappeared. Instead, lifestyle diseases – heart disease and diseases of pulmonary circulation – accounted for 18 per cent of deaths in public hospitals in 2001, whereas they did not reckon in the top ten causes of death in 1970.[37] Of course this is not just due to the health care system, but also to the general economic development of the state resulting in changes in economic activity and incomes and, correspondingly, lifestyles.

Despite these achievements, there are several areas of concern. At the top of these concerns are the rate of undernutrition amongst under-5 year olds, and the rising levels of malaria, both in absolute number of cases and in incidence. However, these are problems that are intractably related to socio-economic changes and developments impacting on the environment and on the nutritional and disease status of people. Moreover, these concerns arise in the context of a general decline in poverty rates and a rise in incomes, especially monetary incomes.

The first of these can be attributed to uneven progress in the elimination of absolute poverty, as seen by the coincidence of higher rates of undernutrition amongst under-5s and in Iban districts. The Iban, as mentioned above, have the highest poverty rate in the state. But it may also be due to changing eating and feeding patterns arising from changes in work organization and practices amongst farm families, although careful fieldwork would be required to confirm this.

The rate of moderate and severe undernutrition of children under five[38] is still high, averaging around 15 per cent for the period 2001–2003.[39] However, it has seen a secular decline from 29 per cent in 1985 to 26 per cent in 1990, to 19 per cent in 1995 and 17 per cent in 2000, averaging about 20 per cent for the 1995–1999 five-year period.[40]

Districts with more than one-third of their population classified as urban have a combined average moderate and severe malnutrition rate of around 13 per cent, compared to 23 per cent for the rest.[41] The data is available only by district, hence the only proxy for ethnicity is the ethnic proportion in the district. As some of the ethnic groups form a very small proportion of the population and also tend to cluster by district, it is not useful to attempt a least-squares fit for malnutrition rates by ethnicity, using ethnic proportions in a district as the proxy. Nevertheless, statistical analysis shows that the Chinese, with the lowest malnutrition rates, also have the lowest poverty rate in the state, and are the most highly urbanized; in contrast, the Iban, with high rates of malnutrition, have the highest poverty rate in the state and are much less urbanized.[42] Ethnicity, in effect, becomes a proxy for socio-economic inequality.

The second concern is the rising level and incidence of malaria. While there have been no systematic studies of the reasons for this, anecdotal evidence suggests it may be attributable to a number of factors. Amongst them are (i) cocoa cultivation and the haphazard disposal of the pods which become water containers, and (ii) logging, de-forestation and plantation

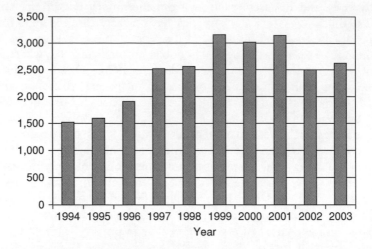

Figure 11.1 Malaria cases 1994–2003, Sarawak
Source: Sarawak Health Department.

development resulting in changes in the ecology. The latter was the experience in Peninsular Malaysia at the end of the nineteenth and the beginning of the twentieth century when large areas of forest were cleared for rubber cultivation.

Figure 11.1 shows the rising numbers of malaria cases, while Table 11.10 shows the incidence rate for 2000 by ethnicity, in this instance, a proxy for the rural–urban divide and for the degree of remoteness, with the Penan being the most remote.[43]

Table 11.10 Malaria incidence by ethnicity, Sarawak, 2000

Ethnic group	Incidence per 100,000
Malay	33
Iban	154
Chinese	35
Bidayuh	408
Melanau	16
Kayan	282
Kenyah	687
Kelabit	80
Penan	2928
Other indigenous	268
Total Sarawak	150
Total Malaysia, 2000*	57

Sources: Sarawak Health Department; *UNDP Human Development Indicators, 2003.

Table 11.11 Incidence of syphilis and gonococcal infections per 100,000 for 1999

Region/State	Syphilis	Gonococcal infections
Peninsular Malaysia	7.03	2.69
Sarawak	23.33	67.83
Sabah	32.18	18.21
Total Malaysia	11.78	10.53

Source: Ministry of Health, Malaysia.

The total incidence for Sarawak, while much higher than for Malaysia as a whole, still places it in the low end for the region, and is comparable with that of Thailand. However, the incidence for Penan is amongst the highest in the region.

A third concern, seemingly relating to lifestyles and sexual mores, is the very high incidence of sexually-transmitted disease, in particular amongst the Penan. While HIV is apparently not yet a serious concern, the high incidence of STDs needs greater monitoring as it suggests that HIV could be devastating for some of Sarawak's indigenous communities should it be introduced amongst them.[44] Table 11.11 shows the incidence per 100,000 for 1999 for syphilis and gonococcal infections.

Issues for the health care system

The foregoing presents the remarkable achievement, at low cost, in basic health care delivery in what, until very recently, were very difficult circumstances. This is despite the high rates of moderate and severe malnutrition for children under 5 amongst the rural population and, specifically, the Iban, the largest of Sarawak's native ethnic groups. A health system can only be expected to cover its brief; it cannot be held responsible for inequality and poverty. Indeed, by that measure, Sarawak's health system may even have compensated for some of that inequality and poverty, as indicated by the infant mortality rates which do not map conveniently onto poverty or under-5 malnutrition rates.[45]

Nevertheless, there remain significant issues – especially to lower income rural end users, people usually categorized as indigenous peoples – of cost, distance and travel time to access the primary health clinics and the referral centres. Allied with this is the fact that rural and poorer people often present late or very late for serious illness, resulting in unnecessary deaths or more severe sequelae than might otherwise have been the case.[46]

But even in rural areas, the spread of education and, generally, a higher standard of living has resulted in challenges to the way the system is staffed. Thus, village clinics are usually staffed by medical assistants; but the population increasingly demands to see a medical officer/doctor, perceiving a medical assistant to be insufficiently qualified, even if they is quite capable of handling a majority of the cases presenting at the village clinic and has been trained to recognize and refer those cases that he cannot manage.

With the growth of the private sector, such demands will be increasingly difficult to meet as doctors are generally reluctant to serve in remote rural areas, and the private sector will not find it profitable to set up clinics and hospitals in those areas.

In this regard, the issue of the growing privatization of health care represents perhaps the single greatest threat to the continued success of Sarawak's health system. Given the demographic distribution of the state, any reasonably good health care system will have to carry a certain burden of inefficiency, in terms of the use of personnel and of facilities (hence of expenditure), in order to be efficient in health care provision.

Thus, for example, data from 1995 shows that the average bed occupancy rate in Sarawak was a low 58 per cent, ranging from 16 per cent to 102 per cent. Moreover, in seven of the 18 hospitals, excluding the two special hospitals, bed occupancy rate was under 40 per cent. There is no reason to believe that the situation has changed substantially. Given such a situation, it is evident that only public provision, with its ability to accept cross-subsidies, can meet the needs; no private system will be prepared to accept such economic inefficiencies.

The growth of the private health care sector has resulted in huge disparities in income, especially at higher levels, between personnel in the public and in the private sector. This has had an inevitable toll upon both the numbers and quality of personnel, not only at the higher, but also at the lower levels. While there have been substantial increases in public sector incomes at the higher levels (although there remains a substantial gap with private sector incomes), incomes at the lower levels have not risen as much.

At the lower levels, this has been exacerbated by the broader change in values. Whereas previously a medical assistant was a respected person at the village level, this is no longer the case, with a corresponding toll upon morale and commitment. Indeed, where previously public health teams comprising lower level staff were well regarded, both for the medical services they rendered and as sources of information and contact with the wider world, today they have suffered a loss in status, again with a corresponding decline in commitment.

There are also problems with notification and information transmission from local health offices and hospitals to the state centre, especially for communicable diseases, resulting in greater severity of outbreaks than might otherwise have been the case. At the same time, Sarawak is well known for its longhouse communities. This results in large 'households' for contact tracing for public health interventions, and therefore in correspondingly higher investigation and immunization costs.

Finally, the demographic transition in Sarawak has occurred rapidly, resulting in a rapidly ageing population, exacerbated locally by significant rural–urban migration of younger people. Thus, in many rural settlements, the elderly population aged 65 and above can comprise 10 per cent or more of the population. Yet, the system was devised to cater especially to child and maternal health. To the credit of the system, it has begun to pay attention to elderly health care under the Family Health Development programme, but this remains very limited, and confined to urban areas where the need is not as pressing as in a significant number of rural areas.

Concluding remarks

Given the broader Malaysian context and the intent of its policy-makers on health care reform to move the system away from tax-financing and public provision, Sarawak's health care system provides an example of a tax-based publicly provided system that has served its people well. The context in which it has had to do so suggests that, even if desirable, privatized health care is not about to enter Sarawak's rural areas, nor be able to provide the care and services that have been provided by the public sector. In thinking about reforms, there is a temptation to think at the macro-level, without cognizance of the particularities of time and place, but this approach is inadequate.

Notes

1 Needless to say, monetary income should not be equated with total income. Nevertheless, the growth of the market economy means that monetary incomes become increasingly crucial for accessing many goods and services.
2 Unfortunately, the last National Health and Morbidity Survey (NHMS 2) conducted in 1996 did not canvass expenditure on accommodation, only on transport.
3 This may be an underestimate of the actual level of urbanization. The official definition of urban would tend to exclude those living in the fringes of towns and cities.
4 This number changes from time to time. There are also differences between the official categories and groups on the ground.
5 They are, in alphabetical order, Bidayuh, Bisaya, Iban, Kadayan, Kajang, Kayan, Kelabit, Kenyah, Lun Bawang/Murut, Malay, Melanau and Penan, and a residual Other *Bumiputera*. Chinese and Indian are further sub-divided into sub-ethicities, but these are not available in the published tabulations.
6 *Bumiputera* is the official Malaysian category for 'indigenous'. Literally, the word means 'sons of the soil'. It broadly covers all those who, by descent, are taken to be native to the Malay archipelago on the eve of European colonial rule. Thus, it excludes ethnic Chinese and Indians who, by descent, are from outside the archipelago on the eve of European colonial rule. Note that this definition of 'indigenous' differs somewhat from the current United Nations/International Labour Organization/World Bank usage; thus, only a subset of '*Bumiputera*' would come under 'indigenous' by such usage, which is clarified in United Nations Development Programme (UNDP) (2001).
7 Indians and 'Others' comprised a tiny 0.4 per cent of Sarawak's population in 2000, considerably smaller than the 3 per cent classified as 'Non-Citizens'.
8 It is a resource rich state. It has petroleum, the bulk of whose revenues accrue to the federal government. It has vast tropical forests, still recorded as covering

some 60 per cent of the state, but which have been extensively and intensively logged over the last 30 years; timber revenue, until recently, provided up to one-half and, even now, still accounts for about a quarter of the state's revenue. It also has coal reserves. Historically, it was also known for its gold reserves, which have been rediscovered recently.

9 *Mid-Term Review of the Eighth Malaysia Plan* (Malaysia 2003: Tables 3.12 and 3.2, respectively). Poverty is defined by a poverty line income (PLI), adjusted for various regions of the country. The PLI for Sarawak for an average household of 4.8 persons was estimated at RM600 in 2002 (Malaysia 2003: Table 3.1).

10 Malaysia (2003: 64, Table 3.3). Median household income in 2002 was about two-thirds of mean household income.

11 Meaning those ethnic groups falling under the category of 'Other *Bumiputera*' in the official statistics, or 'Orang Ulu' in popular discourse. The figures are in Wan Abdul Aziz (2005) but the discrepancy between these figures and those shown in Table 11.2 above suggests there are some problems with the data processing.

12 Much of the data for this section comes from the Sarawak Health Department. Since it is a little behind in issuing its annual reports, much of the most recent data has been sourced from its website, available at <http://www.sarawak.health.gov.my/index2.htm>.

13 Malaysia is a federal state. Thus, individual states within the federation have some services provided by the federal government and some by the state government. Health is a federal function.

14 This structure is based on the administrative organization of the state which currently has 11 divisions and 33 districts.

15 In rural areas, maternity and child health services are covered by health or village clinics or, for the most remote areas, the FDS. Thus, separate MCH clinics are only available in urban areas.

16 The number of mobile clinics has been progressively reduced, partly due to improvements in the communications infrastructure, partly due to budget and personnel constraints.

17 This is a helicopter-based service. A team, usually including a doctor, makes monthly visits, weather permitting. The schedules are announced over the public radio services in the vernacular.

18 The figures in this and the next paragraph are in current prices.

19 Average household size in Sarawak is around 4.8 persons, and falling. The difference in the public per capita expenditure between 1986 and 2002 does represent a real increase.

20 Health clinics are headed by a medical officer.

21 Personal communication from women in rural areas, 1997–1998.

22 The NHMS 2 dataset for Sarawak is flawed for a number of reasons, one of which is that it adopted a federal bias in the final coding of ethnicity. Thus, it coded ethnicity as 'Malay', 'Other *Bumiputera*', 'Chinese', 'Indian' and 'Others' – for a state in which 'Other *Bumiputera*' amounts to almost half the population! Additionally, there were evident errors in coding for district, thus negating any possibility of using district as a proxy for ethnicity.

23 In the NHMS 2, Malay and Chinese together comprised 64 per cent of the sample that was urban, while 'Other *Bumiputera*' comprised 57 per cent of the sample that was rural. In the 2000 Census, Malay and Chinese account for 68 per cent of the urban population, and conversely, other indigenous comprised 67 per cent of the rural population. Thus, an urban/rural tabulation would roughly approximate to Malay/Chinese and other indigenous. Note that in this scheme, 'other indigenous' would come under the category of 'indigenous' in current UN/ILO/World Bank usage.

24 This of course ignores the type of facility. Thus, the public facility usually available to the rural population is a village clinic, without a doctor, whereas that available to the urban population is a health clinic (including polyclinics), with a doctor.

25 Use here is defined as the facility consulted by those who were injured or sick in the two weeks preceding the date of survey and sought treatment. This covered a very small proportion of the surveyed population, hence the various categories have been collapsed into 'public' and 'private'. 'Other' is a residual category referring to facilities such as traditional medical practitioners etc.

26 The NHMS 2 definition is used here, namely bypassing occurs when the nearest facility is not accessed. In the tables above, the column and row extremes together measure the degree of bypassing. Thus, for example, while 67.5 per cent of the urban population list a public facility as the nearest, only 43.7 per cent used it in the relevant survey period.

27 There is an irony in this. As rural incomes increased, some households purchased domestic water filtration systems, thus removing the iodine from the water which had been iodized at source!

28 The Penan numbered about 15,000 according to the 2000 Census. The FDS serves other groups besides the Penan.

29 However, the system is dependent upon the attentiveness and behaviour of reception personnel in secondary care centres. There is anecdotal evidence that they do not always give priority to rural people, who claim that this is one reason why they access a private clinic or hospital (personal communications with rural people 1997–1998).

30 Longhouses were the common settlement form in all of Sarawak's indigenous communities, excepting Malays. Over the past half-century, however, a number of communities have abandoned this settlement and architectural form in favour of individual homesteads, clustered in villages. Nevertheless, many communities continue to favour this form, and it is still the most common form in the interior. Briefly, a longhouse comprises a number of contiguous apartments opening upon a common, covered verandah. Individual apartments are responsible for their portion of the verandah, but the verandah itself is public space where community gatherings, celebrations and meetings are held. The space within individual apartments is private space.

31 Chinese and Malay traditional medicine has shown much greater resilience.

32 One measure of this is the close match between the population projections and the actual census. Thus, for the 1990s, the projected citizen population for 2000 was 2,001.1 thousand, while the actual 2000 census, after adjustment for underenumeration, reported a citizen population of 2,008.8 thousand. Population projections are conducted on the basis of the registered births and deaths, i.e., the crude rate of natural increase. It should be noted that Sarawak experiences net out-migration. The register of births and deaths is the basis for the infant mortality rate, a figure that used to be disputed by administrators and analysts in the federal capital.

33 To be fair, healthy, well-nourished children do not die of measles; poor, undernourished children do. The high fatality rate in this instance, while avoidable if they had been immunized, reflects the socio-economic status of the Penan, poor to begin with, but made worse by socio-economic changes and developments that have, in many instances, undermined their traditional economy and food sources.

34 Department of Statistics, Sarawak, *Yearbook of Statistics*, various years, which is also the source for the maternal mortality rate (MMR) and the CNR. The decline in the IMR is spread across all ethnic communities, albeit unevenly. Thus, the Chinese, with the highest mean household income in the state have the lowest

IMR, However, the Iban, with the highest poverty rate in the state, are not far behind. Indeed, the IMR figures by ethnicity do not map conveniently to poverty rates nor to mean household income by ethnicity.

35 Maternal mortality rates reported in the 1980s are less accurate than more recent ones. For example, official documents have reported the overall Malaysian maternal mortality rate to be 0.2 per 1,000 live births since 1991. In 1991, however, a system of confidential enquiry into maternal deaths was initiated, following which the number of maternal deaths reported increased more than twofold. It was found that previous tabulations were under-enumerated, and the more accurate rates were 44 per 100,000 livebirths in 1991, 48 in 1992 and 46 in 1993 (Chee 2005).

36 The crude death rate has hovered around 4 per 1000 since the 1980s, with some variation among ethnic groups (Department of Statistics 2001b; Department of Statistics, Sarawak Branch, various years).

37 Sarawak Health Department.

38 This is based on weight-for-age measurements, with deviations of between −2 standard deviations to −3 standard deviations of the median being counted as 'moderate' and greater than −3 standard deviations as severe. The rates given here are for the two categories combined. Data are from the Sarawak Health Department.

39 This average is not inordinately high: the average for Malaysia as a whole was 12 per cent, and the average for East Asia and the Pacific was 17 per cent. See UNICEF (2004: Statistical Tables, Table 2).

40 This is an *unweighted* average of the reported incidence by district. A *weighted* average would be lower. Subsequent discussion refers to this five-year unweighted average.

41 This is statistically significant at the 5 per cent level. A simple least-squares fit of the average moderate and severe malnutrition rate to the urbanization rate accounts for about 30 per cent of the variance, with the coefficient of the urban percentage at −0.19, significant at the 5 per cent level.

42 A least-squares fit for malnutrition rates by the percentage of Iban in a district accounts for 16 per cent of the variance in malnutrition rates, with the coefficient of the Iban percentage at 0.10, significant at the 5 per cent level. Conversely, a corresponding exercise for percentage of Chinese in a district accounts for 34 per cent of the variance, with a coefficient of −0.31, significant at the 5 per cent level. Iban make up 30 per cent of the total population, as do Chinese. While it is possible to interpret these results in ethnic terms, it is probably more useful to interpret them in more directly socio-economic terms, namely the level of urbanization and, even more, the income levels.

43 Incidentally, the availability of such figures, even if incomplete, is testimony to the reach and coverage of the health system, particularly its front-line workers in the anti-malaria unit.

44 Most cases of HIV have, apparently, been in urban areas. There have been a few cases in rural areas but, to date, they have been limited to carriers and their immediate families.

45 Basically, seeing that poverty incidence is highest amongst the Iban, then if there were straightforward mapping, the infant mortality rate should also be the highest amongst them; it isn't.

46 The latter happens in cases of Japanese encephalitis (JE), for example. Early presentation generally provides better chances of recovery with minimal cognitive and neurological deficit. This chapter has not reported the incidence of JE because it is believed, on good grounds, that the epidemiological data are deficient. While there are significant pockets of outbreaks, there are no grounds for believing that its incidence has increased.

References

Chee Heng Leng (2005) 'Achieving the MDGs: health and mortality trends in Malaysia', in *Emerging Issues of Health and Mortality in the Asian and Pacific Region*, Asian Population Studies Series, No. 163.

Department of Statistics, Malaysia (2001a) *Population and Housing Census of Malaysia 2000: Population Distribution and Basic Demographic Characteristics*, Kuala Lumpur: Department of Statistics.

—— (2001b) *Vital Statistics Time Series, Malaysia, 1963–1998*, Kuala Lumpur: Department of Statistics.

Department of Statistics, Sarawak Branch, (various years) *Yearbook of Statistics*.

Leete, Richard (2004) 'Eradicating extreme poverty: Sarawak's challenges', paper presented at a seminar organized by the Sarawak Dayak Graduates Association, Kuching, 25 September.

Malaysia (2003) *Mid-Term Review of the Eighth Malaysia Plan 2001–2005*, Kuala Lumpur: Economic Planning Unit, Prime Minister's Department, Malaysia.

Ministry of Health, Malaysia (MOH) (2003) *Malaysia's Health 2003: Technical Report of the Director-General of Health Malaysia*, Kuala Lumpur: Ministry of Health.

—— (2004) *Indicators for Monitoring and Evaluation of Strategy for Health for All*, Kuala Lumpur: Ministry of Health.

Sarawak Health Department (SHD) (various years) *Annual Report*.

Shireen Mardziah Hashim (1998) *Income Inequality and Poverty in Malaysia*, Lanham, MD: Rowman & Littlefield.

UNDP (various years) *Human Development Report*. Online. Available at <http://hdr.undp.org/> (accessed 20 September 2005).

UNDP (2001) 'UNDP and Indigenous Peoples: a policy of engagement'. Online. Available at <http://www.undp.org/cso/resource/policies/IPPolicyEnglish.doc> (accessed 20 September 2005).

UNDP/BPS/BAPPENAS (2004) *Indonesia Human Development Report 2004*. Online. Available at <http://www.undp.or.id/pubs/ihdr2004/index.asp> (accessed 20 September 2005).

Wan Abdul Aziz Wan Abdullah (2005) 'National policy, current status and future challenges in promoting *Bumiputera* minorities' participation in commerce and industry', paper presented at *Bumiputera* Minorities Economic Congress, Kuala Lumpur, 7–8 February.

A note on data sources

The data sources for this paper, aside from the statistical publications of the Sarawak Health Department, the Malaysian Ministry of Health and the Department of Statistics, are the websites of the Sarawak Health Department, available at <http://www.sarawak.health.gov.my/index2.htm> and of the Ministry of Health, available at <http://www.moh.gov.my> unless otherwise stated. The data set for Sarawak from the National Morbidity and Health Survey, 1996 (NHMS 2) is as provided on CD-ROM through the auspices of the Sarawak Health Department.

Epilogue
Civil society and health care policy in Malaysia

Chee Heng Leng and Simon Barraclough

Since the colonial era, non-profit organizations have played significant roles in the provision of various health services in Malaysia. By contrast, the organized political involvement of non-governmental organizations (NGOs) in seeking to influence public policy on health is relatively recent and is primarily a reaction to the state's ideological rejection of a universal welfare model for public health care. Efforts to defend the principles of equitable access to public health care have led to a marked politicization of health policy in Malaysia, with challenges posed to the state's vision of a greater role for the private sector and its claims that a universal welfare model is unaffordable. These challenges question state domination of the policy process while asserting the values of participatory democracy, accountability and transparency.

In exploring how non-governmental bodies have sought to influence health policy we are able to draw upon the growing literature dealing with the wider phenomenon of civil society in Malaysia and make use of a range of theoretical and conceptual insights from these studies.

Several of these writers have pointed out that the current debates on civil society stem from the recent political upheavals in Eastern Europe and burgeoning social movements in many parts of the world that occurred in the 1970s (Verma 2002: 1; Weiss and Saliha 2003: 2; Lee 2004: 1–2). According to Verma, while the term is ambiguous and the boundaries between state and civil society are not always clear 'the idea of civil society represents a spontaneous order, a set of associations and communal bodies that acts as a buffer between state power and its citizens' which 'exist outside the state but possess a legal and institutional structure of their own' (Verma 2002: 2).

In reviewing the literature, Lee (2004: 1–13) discerns two divergent views of civil society: a 'conflict view' that sees civil society as a space that disadvantaged individuals and groups can organize to protect their interests and articulate their positions, thereby acting as a necessary countervailing force to the state, while moving toward a democratization of society; and, in contrast to this, the 'social capital' view of civil society, which sees it as having a complementary relationship with the state. Likewise, Ramasamy (2004: 199) identified two competing positions on civil society: (i) the liberal position which regards it as a buffer against the domination of society by the state, and as contributing to the general welfare of society and strengthening democratic practice; and (ii), the Marx-Gramscian position, which considers civil society as an arena for the contestation of ideas. Following the Marx-Gramscian tradition, this writer defines civil society as a space where hegemonic ideas, values and norms hold sway, and societal consensus may be manufactured, although it is also the space where these ideas may be challenged (Ramasamy 2004: 202–3).

The chapters in this volume have raised some of the crucial issues in the provision and financing of Malaysian health care. The main arguments that run through many of them point to the threat that current trends in privatization and corporatization pose to health care access for broad segments of society. In closing, it is only apt to highlight some of the efforts made in civil society in response to this threat. While taking cognisance of the debates mentioned above, the term 'civil society' will be broadly used here to mean the associational space located between the private and public spheres, and in juxtaposition to the state and the market. Our objective here is not to present an analysis of civil society, but only to give a brief and tentative account of the current contestations in health care policy. Nevertheless, to set the context, we will first briefly review the nature of civil society in Malaysia.

Civil society in Malaysia

Most observers agree on two major features of the Malaysian experience of civil society. First, there is a wide range of NGOs, some of which have increasingly sought to play a political role by seeking to influence policy. Second, that the Malaysian state, while tolerating a legitimate role for civil society organizations, has both the strength and the will to closely control this role and the 'space' in which it takes place. Nor has it been averse to coercive actions when it has felt threatened by the actions of certain groups. In short, Malaysia has not had a history of strong civil society participation in the policy process.

The UMNO-dominated coalition government, which has governed Malaysia since Independence, has historically regarded civil society organizations[1] with suspicion, and at times hostility. To some extent this attitude was carried on from the British colonial administration, which regarded the activities of leftist trade unions and student groups, as well as nationalist organizations, as a threat to its authority and as actual or potential vehicles for subversion, and closely regulated them. In the early 1980s the entry of middle-class activists to the arena was seen as an unwelcomed extension of the political realm and a threat to the regime's management of the political system.

A host of legislation circumscribes civil society activity, among them the Printing Presses and Publications Act 1984, the Official Secrets Act 1972, the Sedition Act 1948 and the Universities and University Colleges Act 1971. In 1984, civil society was further controlled by the Societies (Amendment) Act 1984 which had the ironic effect of creating a coalition of NGOs united across ethnic lines in their opposition to such controls (Barraclough 1984). This prototype coalition and its networks have subsequently been revived to exert pressure on the government on a range of other issues ranging from violence against women and the privatization of water supplies to health financing policy.

The willingness of the state to deal coercively with civil society activists has been demonstrated by its use of the Internal Security Act 1960. At times, individuals have been detained without trial. In 1987 some 106 NGO leaders were detained during Operasi Lalang (Saliha 2002: 205). Not surprisingly, many Malaysians regard the state as ever-ready to stifle those wishing to participate in the political process when such participation is regarded as threatening the legitimacy of the regime.

Nevertheless, a recent policy document seems to suggest that the government, under the new Prime Ministership of Abdullah Badawi, has mollified its antagonistic stance towards politically active elements in civil society. As part of its public thinking about the need to infuse Malaysian society and its institutions with integrity, the government concedes that NGOs serve as partners in its efforts to address a range of social, consumer and environmental problems, and that the 'space for NGOs to operate needs to be expanded' (Malaysia 2004: 42). However, the government classifies NGOs as separate from political parties and, as part of its national integrity policy, wishes to institute a programme to ensure that they remain both non-partisan and 'focussed on their core business, that is, to articulate the interests of the public without prejudice or favour' (Malaysia 2004: 85).

In spite of the efforts of the government to restrict the activities of NGOs, however, they have played a significant role in Malaysian politics. As aptly summarized by one writer:

> Despite the strength and centralization of the Malaysian state, forces from civil society have exercised substantial, if sometimes indirect influence over policy agendas, popular demands, the currency of certain political ideas and the shape of political contests, at least since the 1970s.
>
> (Weiss 2004: 259)

Civil society and the Malaysian health system

Civil society in Malaysia has a long-established functional role in the provision of health and welfare services to the population. As we have seen in an earlier chapter of this book, charitable hospitals have been a feature of the health care system since colonial times and were welcomed by the state as providing assistance for the disadvantaged. Furthermore, a number of organizations – such as the St Nicholas Home for the Blind (now known as the St Nicholas Institute for the Visually Impaired) and the Spastic Children's Association – have long provided support for those with mental and physical disabilities (Ungku Suraiya 2001: 58). More recently, haemodialysis has been made available to poorer patients by several not-for-profit organizations with the assistance of government grants, and other organizations – such as Hospis Malaysia, the Malaysian AIDS Council – have become established. Moreover, as Weiss points out, several necessary health services for marginalized groups, too politically sensitive for government involvement, are provided by NGOs. These include HIV/AIDS-related programmes for gay people, intravenous drug users and transvestites (Weiss 2004: 266; see also Chapter 9 of this volume).

It is difficult for NGOs involved in service provision to avoid a policy dimension to their work. For example, as Ungku Suraiya has argued, even apolitical non-government organizations dealing with advocacy for the mentally disabled must deal with problems such as the lack of financial support for costly surgery and the exclusion of the disabled from insurance schemes. Such issues demand a policy response (Ungku Suraiya 2001: 58).[2]

Nevertheless, there are civil society organizations that consider advocacy, public education and policy input as their primary focus. Among the NGOs which have, for many years, sought to influence wider health care policy and which have adopted a high public profile are the Malaysian Medical Association (MMA) and the Consumers' Association of Penang (CAP). The MMA enjoys a privileged position as a health interest group since it is the principal representative of the medical profession and its members are essential to the health system, both public and private (see Chapter 2 of this volume).[3]

The MMA has commented on various policy issues, including advocating better health care for workers in plantations. At times its leadership has been hostile to moves towards privatization and has urged a continued commitment to equitable care for all (see, for example, *Berita MMA*, June 1995: 19). Perhaps because of its elite status, but also due to a desire to avoid overtly political activity, the MMA has largely chosen to influence policy independently of other interest groups. The MMA is regularly consulted by the Ministry of Health (MOH), although its representatives are restricted from publicly using sensitive information by the operation of the Official Secrets Act.

In contrast, CAP has not shied away from strident criticism of the government on a range of subjects, including health policy. Declining to join the Federation of Malaysian Consumers Associations (FOMCA), it has regularly made submissions on the government's annual budget, and through its newspaper, pamphlets and press releases has argued for an equitable and public health care system. As long ago as 1983, it published a critique on the rising costs of health care (Consumers' Association of Penang 1983).

In recent years, the concern over increasing health care privatization and the consequent dismantling of the public health care services has led to attempts within civil society to influence public health policy. These efforts have primarily sought to preserve the welfare basis of the national health system. A notable development has been the formation of broad-based coalitions seeking to gain greater space for participation in the decision-making process on matters that impinge on the overall health care system.

The Citizens' Health Initiative

In 1997, the Citizens' Health Initiative (CHI) was formed immediately after a large conference on privatization and health care financing that was sponsored by CAP, Universiti Sains Malaysia (USM) and the MMA. It was primarily a response to government policy that has introduced privatization into Malaysia's public health care system and includes plans to corporatize public hospitals, which would substantially reduce the previously welfare-based scheme, available to all for a token payment, to a 'residualist' scheme in which only certain categories of patients would be exempt from payment.

In the following year, the CHI launched the Citizens' Health Manifesto, which was endorsed by a range of organizations, as well as by a list of individuals that included a former Lord President and several former leaders of the Malaysian Medical Association. It was clear from the wide spectrum of endorsers that this was viewed as an issue that would affect the whole population.[4] Two opposition parties, the Democratic Action Party and Parti Rakyat Malaysia, also endorsed the Manifesto.

When the General Elections were announced in 1999, four political parties opposing the government issued a joint manifesto in which they pledged, if they came to power, to abolish health care privatization programmes, to review the cost and quality of private health services and to explore options for a national health insurance system (*Towards a Just Malaysia* 1999).

In the run-up to the elections, the CHI launched a campaign against the corporatization of public hospitals, which received the strong support of the Malaysian Trades Union Congress (MTUC) and several of its affiliate unions, including the Union of FELDA Workers (Kesatuan Pekerja-Pekerja FELDA) (Citizens' Health Initiative 1999).[5] The campaign by the CHI and the politicization of health care by opposition parties clearly had the government worried as it was an issue of concern to all Malaysian voters. In the wake of this campaign and on the eve of the General Elections, the Malaysian government announced that public hospitals and clinics would not be corporatized and that more public funds would be put into the public health care system (*The New Straits Times*, 14 August 1999).

Coalition Against Health Care Privatization

Despite the government's assurances that plans to corporatize public hospitals have been scrapped,[6] other plans and practices such as incremental outsourcing, permitting private practice in public hospitals, and a proposed compulsory insurance scheme which would permit entitlements in private hospitals have once more incited organized opposition from Malaysian civil society.

In 2004 the government announced a range of measures to introduce private practice into public hospitals: pharmacies in public hospitals were to be privatized and private wings introduced (*The New Straits Times*, 4 December 2004; *The Star*, 20 July 2004). In addition, a trial scheme would allow specialists in government service to practise privately after office hours. If successful, the scheme would be extended to all public hospitals. Proposals for the major new initiative in health care financing, the National Health Financing Scheme, included provisions for compulsory contributions being used in either public or private hospitals and the encouragement of private health insurance to supplement such entitlements (*The Straits Times*, 2 April 2005; *The Sunday Star*, 17 April 2005).

In response, the Gabungan Membantah Penswastaan Perhhidmatan Kesihatan (GMPPK) or Coalition Against Health Care Privatization (CAHCP) was formed from a coalition of 81 NGOs, trade unions and political parties, many of which had also endorsed the Citizens' Health Manifesto a few years earlier (Aliran 2006a; Aliran 2006b). The Coalition articulated the basic values it wished to see incorporated in any Malaysian national health financing system: universal and equitable access to comprehensive care regardless of income levels. Among its specific demands for any future financing scheme were that there should be no payment on a fee-for-service basis, and that no further privatization of any component of the health services be permitted. It also demanded that there be local health and/or hospital boards with elected ordinary citizens to oversee the scheme.

The CAHCP has engaged in a range of actions in seeking to influence public policy. Public measures have included the establishment of a website, press releases, distribution of pamphlets and a petition to the Prime Minister, encouraging citizens to lobby their members of parliament, public meetings and even a demonstration outside the offices of the MOH.

The leaders of the Coalition have successfully approached civil servants in the Ministry to hold dialogue sessions, but there have been no meetings with the Minister of Health. Coalition members have emphasized that they wish to act as allies of the Ministry against the demands of the political decision-makers (CAHCP 2005). In March 2006, a Coalition delegation was granted a 60-minute meeting with the Director-General of the Health Ministry (Aliran 2006c).

Reflections on the role of civil society in Malaysian health policy

The ability of groups to organize and promote common interests is vital in any political system. Civil society participation in the policy-making process is necessary to the state, both for the sake of legitimacy and for the practical benefits of the ideas, technical expertise, experience and information provided by interest groups. Moreover, transparency and openness are promoted by the present Prime Minister as desirable in governance. Yet such imperatives contradict a longstanding culture of closed decision-making, reluctance to provide information to the public and selective consultation.[7]

Moreover, the mobilization of civil society to influence national health care policy, while involving a range of organizations, is closely identified with organizations that are critical of government. Both the CHI and the CAHCP are supported by Aliran, a longstanding organization which has opposed the government on various issues. In the case of the CAHCP, the oppositional image is further enhanced by its affiliation with the major opposition political parties, including Parti Islam Se Malaysia, Parti Keadilan Rakyat and the Democratic Action Party, while one of its prime movers is a leader in the Parti Sosialis Malaysia. Not one non-profit hospital, however, is identified with these protest moves, nor is the MMA.

While the involvement of opposition parties might add to the degree of pressure which can be brought to bear upon the government (for example through parliamentary debates), there is also a risk that the civil society coalitions can be accused of being hijacked by oppositionist partisan politics. On the other hand, there is no clear reason to argue that political parties – whether in government or in the opposition – should necessarily stand apart in the civil society arena.

Significantly, health care issues have provided Malaysian civil society with a unifying agenda devoid of ethnic divisions. Unlike such issues as language, culture, education and religion, health is of universal concern and an object of common action. Both the CHI and the CAHCP comprise groups from various ethnic, geographical and religious affiliations, as well as groups that cut across these boundaries.

The policy advocacy of the CHI and the CAHCP has been concerned with both the very process of health policy-making and the nature of wider national public health care policy. Their use of tactics common in participatory democracies, such as petitions and public meetings, although focused upon health issues, also serves to reinforce a broader agenda of civil rights. Their demands for transparency and accountability similarly restate broader democratic aspirations. By appearing to respond to demands for consultation in policy-making, the state gains a degree of legitimacy for its claims to endorse a participatory and democratic role for civil society.

In Malaysia, the CAHCP and the CHI are articulating a counter discourse to that promulgated by the state. They have tapped widespread concerns about the direction of policy that is moving away from an established and effective welfare-based model of public health care delivery to one increasingly characterized by ability to pay and by private provision. Ironically, the demands of these groups are not for radical policy change, but are essentially conservative, aimed at preserving the status quo. The success of the existing health care scheme in terms of low levels of public expenditure, universal access and internationally recognized positive health outcomes are lauded. In mounting a defence of the status quo these groups are also seeking to reaffirm the primacy of the equity principle in Malaysia's health system and to re-socialize policy-makers into values which had remained unchallenged and unpoliticized for several decades after Independence.

The efforts of NGOs to influence policy has posed political challenges for the state, since they demand a degree of power sharing and transparency in the policy process and offer alternative visions of good policy. Moreover, the participation of opposition parties in civil society coalitions adds a keener political edge to attempts to influence health policy. Not surprisingly, as in most areas of Malaysian public policy, the state has adopted a measured response to these efforts.

From a comparative perspective, it should be noted that in western liberal democracies, the institutionalization of wider civil society groups within the health policy-making process, previously dominated by bureaucrats and representatives of the medical profession, is also a comparatively recent phenomenon. In Malaysia, civil society groups have staked their claim to participation in the health policy process and have made it difficult for the state to ignore the issues raised. However, the extent to which they are able to influence and change policy decisions remains to be seen.

Notes

1 Referring to organizations that sought to be involved in the political process, broadly speaking. The government of course views positively the many welfare and service organizations, and the grassroots organizations which are linked to itself or to political parties in the ruling coalition.
2 Another example is that of Marina Mahathir, the then President of the Malaysian Aids Council, taking a stand against the privatization of health care services by endorsing the Citizens' Health Manifesto when it was launched in 1998; prompted no doubt by the threat that privatization will pose to the campaign against HIV/AIDS, and the hardship that it will cause for people with HIV/AIDS.
3 Besides the MMA, other medical professional organizations include the Academies of Medicine, the Federation of Private Medical Practitioners' Associations of Malaysia and the Primary Care Doctors' Organization of Malaysia (PCDOM). There are also organizations such as the Association of Private Hospitals Malaysia and the Association of Managed Care Organizations of Malaysia.
4 They include health-related organizations such as Hospice Butterworth and the Malaysian Mental Health Association, organizations of health-service professionals such as the Malayan Nurses' Union and the Estates Hospital Assistants Association of Malaysia, as well as non-health related organizations such as the Malaysian Trades Union Congress (MTUC), CAP, FOMCA, several branches of the Young Women's Christian Association (YWCA) and the welfare organization for Muslim converts (Pertubuhan Kebajikan Islam Malaysia, PERKIM) (Citizens' Health Initiative 2000).
5 This campaign was initiated by Dr Jeyakumar Devaraj and his colleagues at the Ipoh Hospital, the Perak state hospital. He was later to lead the Coalition Against Healthcare Privitization.
6 In fact, these plans have been fine-tuned rather than scrapped, and given a new name, 'restructuring'.

7 There is sparse mention of wider consultation about policy in MOH annual reports and official publications. When consultations do occur with professional bodies and interest groups they are usually subject to the Official Secrets Act, which provides for mandatory imprisonment for anyone possessing information deemed to be an official secret.

References

Aliran (2006a) Coalition Against Health Care Privatization. Online. Available at <http://www.aliran.com/health/atom.xml> (accessed 21 April 2006).

—— (2006b) Coalition Against Health Care Privatization. Online. Available at <http://www.aliran.com/health/index.html> (accessed 10 May 2006).

—— (2006c) Coalition Against Health Care Privatization. Online. Available at <http://www.aliran.com/health/2006/03/who-is-calling-shots-in-health-care.html> (accessed 10 May 2006).

Barraclough, S. (1984) 'Political participation and its regulation in Malaysia: opposition to the Societies (Amendment) Act 1981', *Pacific Affairs* 57: 450–8.

Citizens' Health Initiative (CHI) (1999) Online. Available at <http://www.prn.usm.my/chi/media4.html> (accessed 10 May 2006).

—— (2000) Online. Available at <http://www.prn.usm.my/chi/endorsers.html> (accessed 10 May 2006).

Coalition Against Health Care Privatization (CAHCP) (2005) Discussion session with KKM officials 27 September 2005 (unpublished document).

Consumers' Association of Penang (1983) *Curing the Sick or the Rich? The Rising Cost of Medical Care in Malaysia*, Penang: Consumers' Association of Penang.

Lee Hock Guan (ed.) (2004) *Civil Society in Southeast Asia*, Singapore: Institute of Southeast Asian Studies.

Lim Hong Hai (2002) 'Public administration: the effects of executive dominance', in Francis Loh Kok Wah and Khoo Boo Teik (eds) *Democracy in Malaysia: Discourses and Practices*, Nordic Institute of Asian Studies Democracy in Asian Series 5, Richmond, Surrey: Curzon Press, pp. 165–97.

Malaysia (2004) *National Integrity Plan*, Putrajaya: Integrity Institute of Malaysia.

The New Straits Times, 14 August 1999, 'Hospitals, clinics won't be corporatised'.

The New Straits Times, 4 December 2004, 'Hospital drugs to cost more'.

Ramasamy, P. (2004) 'Civil society in Malaysia: an arena of contestations?', in Lee Hock Guan (ed.) *Civil Society in Southeast Asia*, Singapore: Institute of Southeast Asian Studies.

Saliha Hassan (2002) 'Political non-government organizations: ideals and realities', in Francis Loh Kok Wah and Khoo Boo Teik (eds) *Democracy in Malaysia: Discourses and Practices*, Nordic Institute of Asian Studies Democracy in Asian Series 5, Richmond, Surrey: Curzon Press.

The Star, 20 July 2004, 'Private wings in hospitals: pilot project likely to start next year'.

The Straits Times, 2 April 2005, 'Free health care coming to an end for Malaysians'.

The Sunday Star, 17 April 2005, 'Patients get to pick medicine'.

Towards a Just Malaysia (1999) Common manifesto issued by Parti Islam Se Malaysia, Parti Keadilan Nasional, Parti Rakyat Malaysia and the Democratic Action Party. Online. Available at <http://www.geocities.com/tatkean/election99/me.pdf> (accessed 10 May 2006).

Ungku Suraiya Omar (2001) 'The development and role of non-governmental organizations (NGOs) serving the intellectually disabled', in Amber Haque (ed.) *Mental Health in Malaysia: Issues and Concerns*, Kuala Lumpur: University of Malaya Press, pp. 35–66.

Verma, Vidhu (2002) *Malaysia: State and Civil Society in Transition*, Boulder, CO.: Lynne Rienner.

Weiss, M.L. (2004) 'Malaysia: construction of counter hegemonic narratives and agenda', in Muthiah Alagappa (ed.) *Civil Society and Political Change in Asia*, Stamford: Stanford University Press, pp. 259–91.

Weiss, M.L. and Saliha Hassan (eds) (2003) *Social Movements in Malaysia: From Moral Communities to NGOs*, London and New York: Routledge Curzon.

Index